The
Spirit of Inquiry

The Spirit of Inquiry

THE GRADUATE LIBRARY SCHOOL AT CHICAGO, 1921–51

John Richardson Jr.

Foreword by Jesse H. Shera
ACRL Publications in Librarianship, No. 42

AMERICAN LIBRARY ASSOCIATION • Chicago 1982

Designed by Ellen Pettengell

Linotype composition by FM Typesetting in
Palatino. Photo display type
composed by Total Typography in
Palatino.

Printed on 50-pound Antique Glatfelter,
a pH-neutral stock, by Malloy
Lithographing, Inc.

Bound in B-grade Holliston cloth by
Zonne Bookbinders

Library of Congress Cataloging in Publication Data

Richardson, John V., 1949–
   The spirit of inquiry.

   (ACRL publications in librarianship ; no. 42)
   Bibliography: p.
   Includes index.
   1. University of Chicago. Graduate Library School—
History. 2. Library education—Illinois—Chicago—
History. I. Title. II. Series.
Z674.A75 no. 42 [Z669.C53] 020′.7′1177311 82-11582
ISBN 0-8389-3273-8

To DK, NBR, and the
memory of GAW

Contents

Tables

Foreword

The founding of the Graduate Library School at the University of Chicago—the "GLS," as it became affectionately known to all who have been affiliated with it—was a watershed in the history of professional education for librarianship. It came upon a library world that had been stultified by the dogmas of the past, but was not yet quite ready for the innovations that the school was to bring. As John Richardson has shown in his account of the arguments that went on before the school was established, there was no certainty about what libraries should be, what librarians should be professionally educated to do, or what problems relating to such professional education should be addressed. There was not even agreement about whether a graduate program in library education, at the levels of the master's degree and the doctorate, was either needed or desirable, much less what the curriculum should contain.

When the school finally became a reality, it floundered in a welter of uncertainty. Its first dean, George A. Works, resigned in dismay, to go to Connecticut as a college president. For several years thereafter, the school's faculty made rather futile attempts to operate the school.

When Louis Round Wilson, after a considerable period of indecision, came to Chicago as its dean, he found a small but highly competent faculty with a diversity of opinions. The school was, indeed, as Robert Maynard Hutchins told Wilson, "off the rails and bouncing along on the cross-ties." Wilson was, as Ralph A. Beals once told the present writer, "Just what the doctor ordered." He knew very well what he wanted to do, and he lost no time in setting about the task of doing it. He gave the school purpose and direction and leadership, from lack of which it had been suffering. He also found a great antagonism toward the school from the profession at large, an antagonism that, in later years, was to solidify its graduates with a fierce and uncompromising loyalty.

Wilson's achievements are narrated in the pages that follow, so there is no need to recapitulate them here. Rather, it is sufficient to say that Wilson raised professional education in librarianship to a true graduate level, and a spirit of intellectual freedom, almost unknown in other library schools, prevailed. Chicago became an exciting place during those ten years between 1932 and 1942, when Wilson was "the Dean," years which were animated by a spirit of free inquiry, of asking questions, of taking nothing for granted, which displayed intense awareness of the importance of research to the future of librarianship. He was able to augment the teaching staff and to attract students, especially at the doctoral level, who were intellectually worthy of the challenge. The subsequent professional record that many of these graduates have written and the impact that they have had upon the profession is eloquent testimony to Wilson's success.

From the Press of the University of Chicago there poured a whole shelf of books sponsored by the school and stimulated by the spirit that characterized the entire university. There was Butler's seminal philosophy of librarianship, Waples' studies in the social effects of reading, Joeckel's work on the government and administration of the American public library, and Randall's treatise on the college library, not to mention Wilson's *Geography of Reading* and his *University Library*. But such activity was not confined to the faculty; the students were publishing, too: studies of the users of the New York Public Library, library service to Negroes in the South, the history of the Chicago Public Library, book selection, microphotography, and many others which, because of the Second World War, were not completed until after Wilson's retirement. Also, one should not forget the published proceedings of the summer institutes which were Wilson's venture in continuing education. These conferences are still being held annually and are the most important examples of their *genre*.

Much of the excitement that so strongly influenced those of us who were fortunate enough to share in it, as well as the *Sturm* and *Drang* that accompanied it, comes through to the reader in Richardson's account. It is most fortunate that, at long last, the narrative is getting into print. John Richardson has written a book that has long been needed. He has presented the necessary detail without being tedious and has communicated the spirit that animated the school with commendable clarity. That the book has been written by one who, through the accident of birth, could not have been privileged to study there during the Wilson years is fortunate. Unlike those of us who were students during those ten eventful years, his vision and his judgments are not beclouded by emotional residues, and his voice is not distorted by "the old school tie."

Jesse H. Shera

Preface

While working on a paper six years ago, I read Jesse Shera's *Foundations of Education for Librarianship* (1972), wherein he called for "a well-documented and evaluative history of the Graduate Library School at Chicago" (p. 245, n. 48). As I wrestled with Chicago's contributions, I became convinced that the GLS had radically altered our profession in several significant ways. Furthermore, in conversations with different individuals it became apparent that they considered the early GLS as a model, a school which set a high standard for research and publication. Clearly, the Carnegie Corporation, by granting Chicago more than a million dollars in 1926, intended that the GLS do for librarianship what Johns Hopkins had done for medicine and Harvard for law.

The importance of Chicago's story demanded that it be told. In doing so, I thought it only fair to evaluate the GLS in light of its own objectives and the degree to which these were met, modified, or made obsolete over time. Specifically, I became interested in the definition or orientation of librarianship and the conception of research as developed by the GLS. Finally, I came to view my work as a contribution to the history of three intersecting ideas: an advanced or *graduate* library school, a *scientific* research posture, and a real library *science*. My perception of the GLS's accomplishments is that they imbued a formerly hollow phrase, "library science," with real meaning, created a *de novo* approach to librarianship by stressing the spirit of inquiry, and emphasized the fundamental unity of our profession, whether it is viewed as an art, science, or craft. In fact, Pierce Butler may have said it best: Each profession has its "triune character, including a science, technology, and a humanistic discipline" (*Library Quarterly* 31: 240).

As the work progressed, I had three years of continuous financial assistance from Indiana University in the form of fellowships and scholarships. There, my dissertation committee was helpful and supportive, consisting of Ellen Altman, Bernard M. Fry, George Whitbeck, David Zaret, and headed by the finest man I know in our profession, David Kaser.

Among the former GLS faculty, their families, and students, I would like to thank Ruth Butler (Mrs. Pierce), William Randall, Eleanor Cary Waples and Dorothy B. Waples, Penelope Wilson, and George Alan Works Jr.; Susan Gray Akers, Ben C. Bowman, J. Periam Danton, Thomas Harding, Richard Logsdon, Robert A. Miller, Julia Sabine, G. Donald Smith, and Edward A. Wight. The assistance of two GLS deans, W. Boyd Rayward and Don Swanson, was also appreciated.

I should acknowledge a host of conscientious librarians and archivists who made my work easier at the following institutions: the Carnegie Corporation, the Graduate Library School and Library Quarterly Papers; the University of Chicago Presidents' Papers and the Graduate Library School Papers; the Chicago Library Club; Columbia University, the C. C. Williamson Papers; the Denver Public Library, its Western History Department, and the University of Denver and its Department of Special Collections; Harvard University, the Walter Lichtenstein Papers; the University of Illinois, Champaign-Urbana, the American Library Association Archives; the State University of Iowa, Iowa City, the Walter Jessup Papers; the University of North Carolina, Chapel Hill, the Southern Historical Collections, the L. R. Wilson Papers; the University of Michigan, its Michigan Historical Collections, in particular the W. W. Bishop and Theodore Koch Papers and the Department of Library Science Archives; State University of New York, the Samuel P. Capen Papers; Northwestern University, its Presidents' Papers; the Ohio State University, the W. W. Charters Papers; the Public Library of the District of Columbia, the G. F. Bowerman Papers; and Yale University, the Andrew Keogh Papers.

During the process of submitting the revised work for publication, G. Edward Evans served as my counselor, ready, willing, and always able.

1

The State of Education for Librarianship
1876–1926

The Graduate Library School at Chicago developed in a new academic environment, but a generation or two earlier that would not have been possible. Between 1876 and 1926, American universities were undergoing a period of intellectual foment. In general, these institutions were experimenting with the German model of higher education. By the time the GLS was established, many universities had worked out a program of graduate education which included seminars and research. In particular, a student wrote a scholarly dissertation and the better students were often encouraged, if not required, to publish. By being set in this new environment, the GLS made a radical departure from the existing professional education of librarians. It is worth a closer examination of the academic milieu into which the GLS was introduced, if only to understand the Carnegie Corporation's eventual selection of the University of Chicago as the appropriate site for an advanced graduate library school.

THE ACADEMIC MILIEU

Many scholars cite the beginning of graduate work as 1876, when the Johns Hopkins University was founded in Baltimore with Daniel Coit Gilman, formerly of Yale, as its first president.[1] This new kind of higher education was based on the German model, which encouraged the "ardent, methodical, independent search after truth in any and all its forms, but wholly irrespective of utilitarian applications."[2] American universities found that the former educational system was

1

not particularly successful in teaching the techniques of original research.

In the American university of the nineteenth century, the predominant method of instruction was the lecture. As a classroom technique, it antedates the nineteenth century; the term was used as early as 1545 and meant literally "to read." The professor read his prepared notes and was not to be interrupted. Obviously, this served to impart information rapidly. If the student did not understand, he was expected to ask his colleagues, consult a textbook, or talk with the professor in the few minutes after class.[3]

Similar dissatisfaction with the educational system existed in Great Britain. Sir William Thompson expressed his opinion that the system of examinations at the universities had the tendency to repress original inquiry and exert a very injurious effect by obstructing the progress of science.[4] Still, the use of a lecturer was quite popular and the British have preserved this concept in its English form at Oxford and Cambridge in the title "Reader." The growing interest in original investigation led J. C. Irvine, vice chancellor of the University of St. Andrews, to observe that "the word 'research' is on every tongue."[5]

To promote the research ideal here and abroad, the seminar style of instruction was adopted. The concept of the seminar had evolved from a medieval form of teaching debate to a scholars' workshop. In the seminar, a small group of students investigated a problem under the close scrutiny of the professor. Studying under such a senior researcher, a student acquired firsthand the craft of his discipline and initiated his own inquiries. The student was expected to adopt a critical mind, challenging statements of his colleagues and the authorities. In addition, each week one or two students were to discuss what they had been reading during the past week, and generally the time was spent getting suggestions and exchanging ideas. Understandably, some referred to the technique as a kind of armchair teaching.

Increasingly, universities began to take on this additional mission: besides imparting "old" knowledge, the discovery of "new" knowledge became the central task. Research was the watchword and touchstone, although there were those who needed convincing that research should become "the vital spirit of teaching in a university."[6]

At Yale, President Arthur Hadley had to point out that there were two groups of professors now, at least in good schools. One group was valued for disseminating "old truth" via the lecture and a second group was valued for discovering "new truth" via the seminar and research.[7] The growing dichotomy gave rise to the popular phrase, attributed to G. Stanley Hall, president of Clark University and professor of psychology and education, that "the professor who knows shall give place to the artist who does, or produces." As Hadley saw it, there was a need to unify teaching and research, which could be accomplished in this manner: "Free the best teachers . . . to make researches of their own. [And] give to our younger men . . . the opportunity for independent investigation and independent management of their classes."[8] At Harvard, William James felt strongly that the Ph.D. had turned into an octopus, even though "graduate schools still are something of a rarity." Regrettably, where the original purpose was to promote scholarship by creating new knowledge, that had been replaced by "the general promotion of a spirit of academic snobbery."[9] There should be no artificial distinction between these two groups of professors: the university's overarching mission was scholarship, whether old or new knowledge was imparted.

By the turn of the century there was considerable confusion over what constituted research. Because "all university men will doubtless agree that there is great abuse of the word research and investigation now,"[10] G. Stanley Hall was compelled to define research in the university sense. Research embodies the sharing of knowledge which is developed through the choice of a problem, a literature review, and a synthesis. The difficulty came in the third and main stage of Hall's steps for problem solving, the synthesis. "That such a synthesis transcended the capacity of the individual scholar became all too clear in the early years of the present century."[11] Hall emphasized that

> a candidate for the doctor's degree must get certain results in a certain time, and, therefore can only very rarely attempt heroic work with large risks and possibilities of indefinite delay. His voyages of discovery must be coasting voyages, and he cannot set out to find new continents.[12]

At the University of Chicago, Albion W. Small, chairman of the Department of Sociology, suggested "in plain English, research at its lowest terms, is merely trying to find out things." Furthermore, he thought research could be fitted into one of six categories. The first five were "naive research (childish curiosity), socratic or dialectical research, partisan research, pedantic research, and pick-wickian or curio-hunting research."[13] The final category was what he termed "practice research," the "first genuine type of research." Practice research was composed of two parts: (a) the problem and (b) the method of solving it. Small advised against asserting that one type of research was better than another; those procedural differences should not allow for any academic snobbery.

The dissertation was still at the heart of the matter. In his address to the eighteenth annual conference of the Association of American Universities, Hall expressed specific concern regarding the value of his students' inquiries. The bottom third had "little value" while the top third had "real, and some of them, permanent worth." Approximately one quarter of all his theses became "the basis of the subsequent life-work of the candidate."[14] Throughout academe there was general dissatisfaction. Reacting to the earlier criticism of the doctoral degree and expressing a similar concern for quality in doctoral work, the report of Committee O on requirements for the Ph.D. degree was delivered to the members of the American Association of University Professors in their January–February 1919 *Bulletin*. As chairman, James R. Angell of the University of Chicago wrote:

> The Committee regards the creation of a genuine appreciation of research work and the providing of satisfactory conditions for its encouragement as of vastly more consequence than any agreement upon technical requirements or administrative details. . . . The committee feels that the doctor's degree should always involve distinct proficiency in research, but are [sic] doubtful whether this can always be distinguished from technical proficiency. A majority of the Committee hold that wherever applied science is implicated in the work for the doctorate, the pure science most nearly related should also be definitely represented, and emphasis should particularly fall upon making a definite contribution to knowledge in the work of the thesis.[15]

Here, the groundwork was laid for applying the tools of more scientific areas, such as sociology or political science, to an applied science such as librarianship. An interdisciplinary approach to problems had gained a fairly wide acceptance.

The other part of research was the diffusion of findings. Like the dissertation, publishing had come under attack. For instance, Frederick Keppel in his history of Columbia University states that as late as 1857 the board of trustees of Columbia College attributed the poor quality of the college to the fact that three professors "wrote books."[16] Nonetheless, the need to communicate findings was recognized, and the university publishing house was the response. Chester Kerr observes in his *Report on American University Presses* (1949) that these presses, "a medium for publication," were dedicated to the extension of the boundaries of knowledge and that these boundaries were to be pushed in all directions.[17] For example, Columbia University Press's 1893 charter provided for the publication of studies in economics, history, literature, philosophy, and other related subjects.

By 1928, a consensual definition of research in academia appeared in a survey undertaken by the American Council of Learned Societies (ACLS). In this report by Frederic A. Ogg, research was defined as

> any investigative effort—in library, laboratory, field or shop—which has for its object an increase of the sum total of human knowledge, either by additions to the stock of actual present knowledge or by the discovery of new bases of knowledge.[18]

Interestingly, the possibility of failure is suggested as an element in the definition, but as long as the objective is new knowledge, the effort should be described as research. If the library is a legitimate place for research, according to the ACLS report, then the GLS at Chicago was preparing to make it a legitimate subject of research.

COMPETITION FOR THE CARNEGIE GRANT

The history of formal education for librarians is older than one might at first suspect,[19] but the real story is the search for an appropriate graduate program.

The first professional training program for librarianship in an academic institution was authorized at Columbia University in 1884, and was moved to Albany as a state institution five years later. Of the four library schools that offered formal instruction in the 1890s, Dewey's library school at Albany was considered the leader;[20] one of its graduates even went so far as to say that "library school" signified only one school—Albany. Thus when Albany is used as the example in the discussion of contemporary instructional methods, it is well to remember that it is the exemplar.

Two seminars, a general seminar and a reading seminar, were offered at Albany in the 1890s. The general seminar was open to senior students and required four hours' recitation per week. Laurel A. Grotzinger has written that

> in order to develop techniques of analysis, synthesis, and public report, seminars were begun which required the students to individually select topics and to present them before the entire class for criticism and discussion.[21]

It is not surprising that Dewey's school employed the seminar technique, as he was current on the teaching methods. During the summer of 1892 he sat in on an enlightening convocation in which the seminar method of advanced instruction was debated, pro and con, by Columbia's Edwin R. A. Seligman, Harvard's Ephraim Emerton, and others.[22]

The successful use of the seminar method in the preparation of students was exemplified in Albany graduate Katharine Lucinda Sharp. Called "the best of the best" by Dewey, she may well be atypical; nevertheless, her record indicates what the Albany Library School could attract and produce. A member of the Class of 1892, she wrote "the best essay on the relations of local libraries to university extension," and received a $100 award. In the report of the award committee, Professor Herbert Baxter Adams of Johns Hopkins noted:

> It is a paper not only of great practical value as showing the ways and means for libraries to cooperate with this great movement called university extension, but it is a paper of very great historical value as showing the progress of the movement in this country. It is accompanied by an elaborate set of statistical tables showing in what centers all over the country university extension courses have been already given and to what extent in those centers libraries have cooperated with lecturers and other educational forces. I have asked Mr. Dewey, as representative of the Library School, the privilege of having it published in a government report which I have the honor of editing for the Bureau of Education in Washington.[23]

Four other students earned honorable mentions from the review committee.

By the turn of the century it had become widely apparent that reading on one's own and even the apprenticeship model were inadequate preparation for learning the profession. As a result, in 1901 the American Library Association appointed Askel G. S. Josephson of the John Crerar Library to chair a round table on professional instruction in bibliography. Although a critic of contemporary library school instructional methods, he credited the existing "library schools [for having] done much to encourage the professional spirit of librarians and to develop the technical side of the work, [but he felt that] something more is needed."[24] He called for a postgraduate school of bibliography which focused on sound bibliographical scholarship. Such a school would recruit two types of students. The first type was students, already in other departments of the university, who were working on their dissertations. An appropriate program could, he felt, aid them in preparing their bibliographies. The second type of students should be interested in being librarians and bibliographers. These students should be allowed to take their minor in the other departments of the university, thereby aiding their studies, "such as literary history, philosophy, American history, mathematics, or the like."[25] Unlike the existing library schools, the postgraduate school's curriculum would consist solely of bibliography.

The profession's definition of research seems limited to bibliographical method. A typical library school student was exposed to the scholarly side of librarianship, especially bibliographical rules (cataloging) and bibliographical systems (classification). The recognition given to bibliographical research is evident in the *honoris causa* M.L.S. degrees awarded by the Albany library school. According to the school's *Register, 1887–1926*:

> The degree M.L.S. was conferred only on graduates of recognized fitness and character who, after having received the degree, bachelor of library science, successively completed not less than five years in professional work and who submitted in print a satisfactory contribution to library science or library history. It was required that this work show independent thought and research, an intelligent grasp of the subject and that it should be satisfactory in literary form.[26]

Of the eleven recipients, all were either library school instructors or holders of elected positions in state or national library associations. Evidently the degree was also given for professional achievement, as well as for research.

One need only look to the professional library literature of the time to find an explanation for why there was not more solid research. "Librarianship was not a top university position"[27] even at such schools as the University of North Carolina or the University of Virginia in the 1910s. At the University of North Carolina, for example, the head librarian could not be ranked higher than associate professor. Not surprisingly, many writers[28] in library literature were encouraging the profession to upgrade itself, particularly in terms of education.

The need for an advanced library school was increasingly recognized in the next few years. Librarians were examining the concept of an advanced library school but as yet they had not truly adopted the methods which existed in the world of scholarship. A consensus was still lacking as to the appropriate model. Before a graduate library school was established, a particular combination of events occurred which quickened its realization.

The Carnegie Corporation

Andrew Carnegie's philanthrophy to public libraries is well known. Despite efforts on the part of Melvil Dewey as early as 1890 to change the emphasis of Carnegie's philanthrophy from library buildings toward library training, the corporation had by 1911 supported only four library schools.[29] For the most part, the training of librarians was ignored by the foundation until Alvin S. Johnson made his report to the corporation in 1916.[30] At the corporation, there was growing concern regarding the broken pledges and other abuses of Carnegie monies, which resulted in Johnson's being hired to investigate these charges. As a result of his investigation, he urged a policy of "philanthropic intervention," proposing "a program wherein the Corporation would shift its emphasis to library service and to the promotion of a broader concept of library training."[31] He specifically attributed the contemporary stress in the library schools to the fact that the entering student had only a high school education and that this, in combination with the library training, did not allow the prospective librarian to advocate effectively the library's importance in the community. Through the Johnson Report, the kernel of an idea, that the foundation should involve itself more substantively in library training, was planted at the Carnegie Corporation. However, detailed attention to the educational requirements of librarians was delayed until the appointment of a new president of the corporation in 1922.

In December of that year, Frederick P. Keppel was elected president of the Carnegie Corporation of New York. His term of office, nineteen years, was to be the most eventful in the history of education for librarianship. In fact, some events had already been set in motion by the corporation's board.

THE WILLIAMSON REPORT

The trustees of the corporation had selected C. C. Williamson, chief of the Economics Division of the New York Public Library, to be director of a study of education for librarianship on 28 March 1919.[32] (Anyone who is curious about his ideas on education should read his views as published in the July 1919 *ALA Bulletin*.)[33] In the course of the next three years, Williamson was able to develop a scheme for grading positions and establishing minimum standards of qualification. His final report, based upon visits at library schools and interviews and correspondence with leading librarians, was presented in 1922. However, the published version was delayed a year while confidential material was deleted.[34]

When his published report appeared, in 1923, the library profession learned that Williamson urged the division of library work into professional and clerical classes.[35] More attention, he argued, should be given to this distinction, and library schools should only train the former. Furthermore, he felt that entrance requirements for those who were entering the professional programs of library schools should include college degrees.

Regarding the teaching staffs and their methods of instruction, Williamson felt the existing schools were highly inadequate. Only 52 percent had graduated from college, 93 percent had no teacher training, and 80 percent had no previous teaching experience. Furthermore, the quality of instruction needed improvement, as he felt there was excessive dependence on the lecture, and there was a lack of suitable textbooks. Field work and class visits to libraries should also be utilized.

In terms of the present study, his most important conclusion was that only a library school that was organized as a professional school, in a recognized university, could increase the prestige of the profession.

Carl M. White has observed that the Williamson Report should not be treated as "the solitary cause of all the changes"[36] in education for librarianship. Rather, the report's importance lies in the fact that it helped focus the Carnegie Corporation's plans and the library profession's attention on education. Another cause of change was the Learned Memorandum, a study begun about the time Williamson's report was completed.

THE LEARNED MEMORANDUM

A plan of attack was needed at the Carnegie Corporation, and William S. Learned, a corporation staff member, was directed to study the matter further and make recommendations in the form of a memorandum. Although it was "written for office use," the trustees considered his findings significant enough to publish (in June 1924) as *The American Public Library and the Diffusion of Knowledge*.[37]

Learned's work, aimed at significantly strengthening the library profession, listed "a series of specific objects that must sooner or later receive attention in any adequate treatment of the problems arising with the development of the modern library movement."[38] Following Williamson's lead, Learned made four recommendations to the Carnegie Corporation which formed the basis of its subsequent Ten-Year Program in Library Service. His third recommendation, that "adequate support [be provided] for the professional preparation of librarians and the training of library staffs," concerns the present study directly. Learned argued strongly that

if a rapid and wholesome development is to take place in the process of adjusting libraries to their users, the most vigorous and drastic changes should be made at this point. . . . Professional curricula for the higher, responsible positions must doubtless be associated with comparable professional curricula in the universities. It is possible, too, that the immediate situation could be greatly relieved by the opportunity for individual selection on a basis of scholarships for experienced library workers of unusual promise.[39]

By the early spring of 1925, Keppel had been able to formulate a plan based on Williamson's and Learned's reports, and he wrote Carl Milam, ALA's secretary, that the corporation's executive committee had

> *Resolved,* that the Carnegie Corporation is interested and does hereby express its interest in the possibility of advancing the librarian's profession:
>
> 1. Through the support over a term of years, under conditions to be hereafter specified, of a system of scholarships and fellowships, and
> 2. In the establishment of a graduate school of librarianship, to be an integral part of an American university
>
> *and Resolved,* That the Corporation express its desire to receive specific suggestions from qualified organizations or individuals as to these two enterprises.[40]

The possibility of an advanced library school was recognized. What was less well known at that time was that the University of Chicago was already considered more favorably by the foundation than Columbia University as the site for such an advanced school of librarianship.

The Board of Education for Librarianship

Seemingly, any school in competition for the Carnegie Corporation's grant would have to be recognized by the American Library Association. The only difficulty was that ALA did not yet have a formal mechanism for accrediting such schools. In April 1923, ALA acted to establish a Temporary Library Training Board which would recommend an appropriate response by ALA to the Williamson Report. Its provisional accrediting scheme reflected many of the same points as Williamson's, but it provided for a graduate library school which would grant master and doctor degrees in library science. At the Carnegie Corporation, Keppel was able to write Williamson and say that he had "started something that won't stop in a hurry."[41]

The ALA Saratoga Springs convention in 1924 was busy, for

several important actions had to be taken. ALA Council "unanimously adopted" the Library Training Board's report and recommendations, which called (among other things) for a new, permanent Board of Education for Librarianship (BEL). In September, many of the original members were reappointed, including Adam Strohm, Harrison W. Craver, Andrew Keogh, and Malcolm G. Wyer; Linda A. Eastman was replaced by Elizabeth M. Smith. In addition to Sarah Bogle, acting as secretary, the board obtained the services of Harriet E. Howe as executive assistant.

Near the end of the convention, the *Christian Science Monitor* interviewed Andrew Keogh, who acted as a spokesman. Keogh told them of his plan, which the board had adopted. Little was left to do, he said, except select a university of "high rank," which would likely be "located near one of the important library centers," and work out "the settlement of a mutual co-operative working plan between it and the association."[42] Little did Keogh know what a problem the latter would turn out to be.

Library schools in competition for the Carnegie grant and ALA accreditation read the BEL's first *Annual Report* (for 1924/25) with great interest. Therein, the board outlined its recommended minimum standards, as follows:

Advanced Graduate Library School:

An integral part of a university which meets the standards for graduate study laid down by the Association of American Universities

Requires for entrance a college degree and the successful completion of an approved one-year professional curriculum

Grants a master's degree for the satisfactory completion of one year of further professional study; and the Ph.D. degree under the university regulations governing the granting of that degree.[43]

These recommendations were based upon input obtained from many sources during open meetings and visits to library schools throughout the country. Its first recommendation dashed the plans of at least one proposed library school (the National School of Library Science in Washington); however, the BEL stated that it

hoped that some of the schools already in existence will adopt these standards and that advanced graduate library schools will be developed as rapidly as may be consistent with the needs of the profession.[44]

It seems apparent that the BEL was aware of a Carnegie Corporation statement that in spite of the fact that there are now in existence a number of library schools of excellent professional standing, some of them connected with universities, there is no school where professors and students can be regarded as forming an integral part of a university of the first class, and as a result, no school which can be said to occupy for the librarian's profession a position analogous to that of the Harvard Law School or the Johns Hopkins Medical School.[45]

When its next *Annual Report* appeared, the BEL could claim

at least *one* new school is the direct result of the educational campaign carried on by this Board—a school that will admit within its door only those whose general education fitness is not speculative but in compliance with definite academic standards and to be further developed under the guidance and scrutiny of educators of eminence in the world of scholarship.[46]

Four years later, however, *no one* seemed interested in claiming credit for this new school (an incident to be covered in chapter 4). In the meantime, however, it will be profitable to examine the schools which were in competition for the Board of Education for Librarianship's approval[47] and an accompanying Carnegie endowment of $1 million which, it had been announced, would go to the school selected.

THE EXISTING LIBRARY SCHOOLS

As the necessity of having a graduate library school connected with a strong university became increasingly apparent and as the sentiment grew against building on an existing library school, the chances decreased of such schools as Washington (Seattle), California, Michigan, Albany, and Illinois being selected to receive Carnegie's favor.

In the fall of 1921, when Williamson was writing his *Training for Library Work*, he received a letter from Sarah Bogle, former director of the Carnegie Library School in Pittsburgh, saying

I have been convinced for some years that the only solution for the problem is to strengthen existing schools worthy of so doing, eliminate unworthy ones and surround the establishment of new schools with such care and conditions as may result in standards worthy of professional schools.[48]

At the time his report was being written, only the Washington, Albany, and Illinois library schools required college graduation for admission, and only two of those schools were associated with universities. After the published version of Williamson's report appeared, in the late summer of 1923, it was obvious to most that any quality library school would have to be associated with a university. In a characteristic letter (containing simplified spellings), Melvil Dewey explained to Carl Milam that the Albany school was out of the running because it was a state institution. Furthermore,

> don't encourage a lot of weak skools to attempt work beyond them. Let us all unite on 1 strong skool preferably in a *strong* university that will offer the master's degree and after a few years more growth a doctor's degree and get librarianship on the full plane of the teachers.[49]

(Albany's ultimate strategy of merging with the Library School of the New York Public Library will be discussed in the following section.)

On the West Coast, the University of Washington never seemed to be a strong possibility, although both W. E. Henry, director of its twelve-year-old library school, and the university library staff were anxious that the strongly local and regional pull of the school be made national. He reported that the dean of the university graduate school was "strongly in favor" of a graduate library school.[50] However, the Carnegie sentiment for creating a school *de novo* blocked Washington's advances.

Henry's colleagues farther south did not fare much better. In Berkeley, Sydney B. Mitchell, chairman of the Department of Librarianship at the University of California, spoke in 1923 for the faculty of his graduate school regarding a graduate library school there:

> Should not expect any enthusiastic welcome . . . but I believe there would ultimately be close cooperation provided support . . . were not chargeable to regular university budget. . . . Cost of really [*sic*] graduate work would be very high. . . . Instruction leading to higher degrees should be given first at one of older universities on Atlantic coast. . . . Should be at university rather than at even such a library center as Washington [D.C.].[51]

Evidently, this diffident welcome did not stop plans for an advanced school at California. On 8 March 1926 its academic senate adopted the Report of the University Council on the Proposed School of Librarianship,[52] and the regents of the university authorized its establishment on 13 April.[53] A day earlier, President W. W. Campbell asked the Carnegie Corporation to match the amount the University of California was providing to the new school.[54] Keppel responded that neither he nor his colleagues on the board could see any "present possibility of favorable consideration [on] additional grants in this field."[55] At this time, coincidentally, Mr. Mitchell received an offer from the University of Michigan to head its Department of Library Science, on terms which California could not meet.

At the University of Michigan, library courses had been offered since 1904; and by 1926 Theodore W. Koch and his successor, W. W. Bishop, had developed the library school into a department of the university. Earlier, Bishop circulated a seven-page "Memorandum on Instruction in Library Methods in the University of Michigan,"[56] followed by a "Tentative Outline of Courses of Instruction for Graduate Students in Library Science and Bibliography."[57] Ironically, these documents were useful to Ernest D. Burton at the University of Chicago. Bishop's role settled into that of adviser, although he was considered at one point for the deanship of the GLS at Chicago—a development that is discussed in the next chapter.

THE PROPOSED LIBRARY SCHOOLS

At this point it was fairly clear to most everyone involved that the competition for the $1 million Carnegie grant was limited to library schools not yet even in existence, and five institutions were in the running.

Yale. The university librarian, Andrew Keogh, was attempting to avoid a potential conflict of interest, yet press the case for his institution. When he was appointed to the ALA Library Training Board in 1919, he was asked to serve as chairman of its special committee on educational qualifications and status of professional librarians in colleges and universities. The charge of his committee was to choose the best location for a graduate library school.

Keogh had already recommended to his administration that it establish a Sterling Professorship of Bibliography and Library Administration. He was convinced that

> there will probably be little difficulty in obtaining a degree for meritorious bibliographic work in a regular M.A. program; . . . the rare bibliographic dissertation that not only incorporates discoveries of importance, but by sound criticism throws light on disputed literary or historical or other problems, might be offered for the degree of doctor of philosophy. The dean of the Yale Graduate School is very willing to give degrees for bibliographic work.[58]

Regrettably, however, his recommendations were closely related to the Yale Corporation's plans for the Sterling Memorial Library. By 1923, when it seemed "likely that the Carnegie Corporation will finance (at least for a term of years) a library school of university grade,"[59] the Yale Corporation had not made much progress; in fact, the library was not built until 1931.

In any event, it would have been difficult for Keogh to conclude that Yale was the best location without people considering him "self-seeking" and questioning his committee's objectivity. It was unlikely, moreover, that a new school of librarianship would be established at Yale since it was an all-male school. The profession was unlikely to want to repeat another fiasco such as Dewey's at Columbia. For these reasons it was rumored in December 1924, via Harriet Howe of the BEL, that Yale was abandoning its aspirations to be the site of the new school.[60]

Andrew Keogh, however, had another role to play in this unfolding drama. One of the leading senior scholars in librarianship, then in his early fifties, he was to become a close adviser in the matter both to Frederick Keppel of the Carnegie Corporation and to the young Robert M. Hutchins, then of Yale.

Washington, D.C. It should not be surprising that the District of Columbia, rich in bibliothecal, cultural, and political resources, was also considered as a site for a graduate library school; indeed, the idea had been raised several times. In 1922, area librarians formed a Committee on Organization of a National School of Library Science, with Emma V. Baldwin as Secretary.[61] At an early meeting of the BEL on 31 December 1924, Herman H. B. Meyer, chief of the Legislative Reference Service at the Library of Congress, and George F. Bowerman, librarian of the District of Columbia Public Library, formally presented a five-point proposal. The proposed national school would attempt:

1. The formulation of facts in relation to library science which can be deduced from years of experimentation within this field, and the organization of this material for the more satisfactory teaching of the science.
2. The encouragement of further research.
3. The creation of a center to which those who have had preliminary training or years of practical experience may turn for further instruction in the larger problems of library administration and bibliographical research.
4. The development of adequate courses of instruction for those who wish to prepare themselves for highly specialized work.
5. The training of those competent to teach library science.[62]

Also in December, four members of the BEL[63] met in Washington with Meyer and President Alfred F. W. Schmidt of George Washington University, where the proposed academic work was to be offered.

Unfortunately, a major objection was raised: George Washington University was not a member of the Association of American Universities or the North Central Association. At a meeting of the District of Columbia Library Association on 29 April 1925, a unanimous resolution was passed asking the Board of Education for Librarianship "to eliminate mention of any association whatever" in its standards.[64] However, it was a futile gesture since support for the school was already waning. While the Washington area may still have been a possible site in the thinking of the Carnegie Corporation as late as mid-April 1925,[65] the BEL by then was favoring either the New York or Chicago area.[66]

Iowa. Superficially, Iowa may seem an unlikely contender, but it definitely influenced the turn of events at the Carnegie Corporation and the University of Chicago. It all started in the fall of 1924, when Tse-Chien Tai, librarian of the Tsing Hua College in Peking, came to the United States on a year's leave of absence. At the invitation of President Walter A. Jessup of the University of Iowa, Mr. Tai went to that institution to study for his doctorate in educational administration. Although he initially proposed writing a dissertation on " 'University Library Administration' (treated not only in detail but in its relation to general university administration),"[67] he shortly thereafter changed his topic to "Current Theories of Professional Education for Librarianship."

The following June, Tai defended his dissertation, now entitled "Professional Education for Librarianship; a Proposal for a Library School at the University of Iowa."[68] His dissertation is often called the first ever written in library science; with little doubt, it is "the first time that library education has been allowed as a minor subject for the doctorate."[69] Tai recommended establishment of a library school which should do three things:

1. Train professional librarians for medium-sized libraries and assistants for large public libraries in its undergraduate department.
2. Train librarians and research scholars in the graduate department for large public libraries, special libraries and university libraries.
3. Train instructors for other library schools.[70]

His recommendation concerning a university library school is both interesting and significant because it varies from the four-level system of grading library programs concurrently developed by the Board of Education for Librarianship. Tai also rejected a program of job analysis as a method of curriculum construction, then being proposed by Professor W. W. Charters,[71] preferring instead the consensual method, which consisted of consulting experts for their opinions.

The day before Tai and his wife left the United States to return to China, Frederick Keppel interviewed him on the state of education for librarianship in the United States. According to his interview memorandum, Keppel confidentially showed him certain documents prepared by the University of Chicago. Tai commented on the similarity of their ideas and his—a point which would be apparent when his book appeared the following September. Tai was "sympathetic" to the idea of building a school *de novo* rather than building on an existing school. Furthermore, Tai observed that, theoretically, New York was "the place for the graduate school, but practically he [saw] the advantages of Chicago."[72] Should Chicago be selected, Tai suggested that the Illinois school be transferred to it.

Newspapers across the country announced that the new graduate library school was going to the University of Chicago, even as the Iowa State Library Commission was meeting in Des Moines on 18 May 1926[73] to pass a resolution, drafted by President Jessup, asking the Carnegie Corporation for a graduate library school.

New York City. How New York finished second, and still secured a major Carnegie grant, is an intriguing story. Geographically speaking, the strongest competition with the city of Chicago for the site of the new school was New York. As a major population center, it was the center of book publishing, with extensive as well as intensive library collections, a wealth of cultural resources, and a great need for highly trained librarians. New York lacked a library school associated with a major university, although the New York Public Library maintained one. The discredited view of education for librarianship as a function of library administration made it difficult to consider seriously the NYPL as a possible site. The major hope for an advanced school of librarianship in New York seemed to rest on a possible merger of the Library School of the New York Public Library and the State Library School at Albany and the relocation of the single school to Columbia University.

The Albany faculty prepared a five-page report in 1923/24 considering the requirements of advanced library training.[74] Unfortunately, faculty and administration sentiment at Columbia University was not favorable to its becoming the locus of the new school, as evidenced by F. J. E. Woodbridge's comment on behalf of the Joint Committee on Graduate Instruction: "Inasmuch as it is now possible for students who have had a four-year college course to go forward to research . . . it seems inadvisable at this time to undertake the establishment of a new school."[75]

Furthermore, there was another matter to be addressed. The minutes of a meeting of the Board of Education for Librarianship, held on

12 March 1925, report a consensus that the university library at either choice (Chicago or New York) must have a professionally trained librarian.[76] This requirement could have been a problem for Columbia, although the informal vote of the BEL at that meeting was still three (Keogh, Smith, and Craver) to one (Strohm) in favor of New York. Concurrently, however, Keppel reported to the executive committee of the Carnegie Corporation that "the President has looked rather closely into this question, and is inclined to believe that arrangements could be made with the University of Chicago for the establishment of such a school."[77]

Three months later, Keppel reported again that the "Columbia Library situation is improving greatly. The present incumbent [William H. Carpenter] has been removed and [Secretary] Fackenthal reports that Columbia will undertake to get a first-class librarian."[78] W. W. Bishop was first choice, but he chose to stay at Michigan after his administration offered to increase his salary substantially and appointed him to the deanship of the new library school at Michigan.

In the following year, on 26 March 1926, things began to happen in New York. The Carnegie Corporation awarded Columbia $25,000 a year for a period of ten years. In April the regents of the University of the State of New York transferred the State Library School to Columbia. And on 1 May, C. C. Williamson became director of the Columbia University Library and director of the university's new School of Library Service.[79]

It is evident that the existing schools were not always associated with a university and tended to emphasize technical matters in their curricula. The proposed schools, such as New York's, separated the professional and clerical tasks of librarians. Furthermore, in their *de novo* response, college graduation was required for admission and a higher level of instruction was provided. At Iowa, especially, attention was paid to the content of the curriculum and research at the proposed National School of Library Science was stated as one of its objectives. Events appeared propitious for the establishment of a truly advanced school for librarianship.

2

The Formative Chicago Period, 1919–27

Roots in the Chicago Area

Several groups were interested in having a library school in the Chicago area; the focus of interest, however, was the Chicago Library Club, which in turn involved both the University of Chicago and Northwestern University. The American Library Association, with its headquarters in Chicago, played an ancillary role in locating the school there. The final sections of this chapter pick up the thread of the University of Chicago's interest and identify critical incidents in its selection as the site for an advanced school for librarians.

THE CHICAGO LIBRARY CLUB

As C. C. Williamson was making his visits to library schools, Chicago-area librarians were beginning to recognize the need for a local source of well-trained librarians. In the summer of 1921 the Chicago Library Club, a group of more than four hundred Chicago-area librarians, passed a resolution to form a three-member committee to investigate the possibilities of a school in the Chicago area.[1]

This committee, responsible for preparing a four-page "Memorandum on the Establishment of a School for Librarians in the City of Chicago,"[2] recommended that a proposal be submitted to the trustees of the Carnegie Corporation, requesting a subvention for "a school for the education of librarians." Before doing so, however, the support of all the major public and university libraries in Chicago should be obtained. Furthermore, it was proposed that the school be under the jurisdiction of "the trustees of one of the universities in Chicago or its immediate vicinity, or under a separate directorate to be created by said trustees."

The purpose of the proposed school was not limited or designed solely as a resource for the local libraries; rather, it was expected to offer "systematic and thorough instruction in two separate though related fields: . . . practical librarianship . . . [and] the cultural, literary, bibliographical and sociological aspects of librarianship as a learned profession built upon ideals." It was suggested that high standards of entrance, equivalent to other professions, be adopted and that the relationship of librarianship to these other professions, particularly education, be realized. The memorandum cited other library schools as local in character or "inadequate to supply the constant demand for trained library personnel in the Middle West." None of these schools emphasized the broad cultural and theoretical principles in their curricula, but placed the emphasis on "purely technical processes."

During March 1923 the memorandum was circulated among club members, so that by the time of the CLC meeting on 12 April (in the Ryerson Library of the Art Institute), the proposal had received the support of the directors of the major public and academic libraries in Chicago. The fifty members in attendance heard an address by Chicago's President Ernest D. Burton on the "idea of a school for librarianship in Chicago."[3] Burton discussed the need for scholarly librarians and the difficulty of obtaining them; he concluded his speech by endorsing the "school for higher librarianship in Chicago and promised to coöperate in every way possible if such an idea should take permanent shape."[4]

The communication that was sent to the trustees of the Carnegie Corporation on 20 April embodied the entirety of the memorandum prepared by the CLC Committee on the Library School. Minor changes were made to it, primarily in the division of some of the longer paragraphs. Then a section was added concerning the need for a "highly competent and experienced Director and a staff of thoroughly trained and expert instructors."[5] The communication concluded with a budget estimate of not less than $20,000 to $25,000 a year. That sum could be provided by the Carnegie Corporation as an annual sum or in an endowment over a period of years, after a "full survey, investigation and discussion of all aspects of the proposition hereby."[6]

Within a week of its receipt, William S. Learned (of the corporation) was in Chicago to discuss the proposal with Carl Roden of the

Chicago Public Library and Carl H. Milam, secretary of the American Library Association. Learned pointed out that there was to be a change in management at the corporation and that it would be some time before the new president, Frederick P. Keppel, could orient himself.[7]

THE NORTHWESTERN UNIVERSITY PROPOSAL

Walter Lichtenstein, librarian of Northwestern University, had not only raised the issue of a graduate library school in 1918 but had suggested a possible organization for it along the lines of "departments of knowledge." Fortunately, his successor, Theodore Koch, was no less interested in the idea of a library school. Koch "fully endorsed and supported"[8] the Chicago Library Club's proposal of a library school for the Chicago area. Furthermore, his interest had the support of the university administration, in particular President Walter Dill Scott.

In a 1923 meeting with Carl Milam, Scott indicated he was receptive to a library school at Northwestern only "if the School of Librarianship can really 'advance the boundaries of science' in this field, if it can make a real contribution nationally."[9] Scott's plans took substantial form following a meeting of the university council on 15 December. At its Saturday meeting,

> The Council requested that a Committee of three be appointed to draw up resolutions of approval for a proposal to establish a School for Librarians as outlined by the President.[10]

Three weeks later, President Scott reported to his board of trustees on his negotiations with the Carnegie Corporation. At this meeting it was apparent that Northwestern was prepared to provide space on its McKinlock Memorial Campus if the corporation would provide the building and endowment for the School of Librarianship. The board instructed Scott "to proceed with negotiations . . . and to report to the Trustees after his visit to New York City."[11] In preparation for his visit with President Keppel, Scott consulted Carl Milam regarding the likely number of students in such a school and the cost of such a venture. Milam suggested that Northwestern plan for one hundred students a year, increasing this number to five hundred by the end of the fifth year. Approximately $60,000 should be provided for the first hundred students and $40,000 for each additional hundred.

The meeting of the university council on 16 February heard the Committee of Three's memorandum. Unfortunately, the memorandum in its entirety evidently no longer exists, although an extract prepared five months later for the Board of Education for Librarianship does. The extract reviewed the Chicago Library Club proposal and emphasized that the proposed school at Northwestern University would offer instruction along the two lines previously suggested in the CLC proposal. In fact, much of the extract is a verbatim copy of the club's proposal.[12]

Everything went smoothly, with the council's "hearty approval of the plan as outlined."[13] Following its approval, the memorandum was sent to Keppel at the Carnegie Corporation, where William S. Learned also examined it. Comparing it to the "Tentative Plan for a Library School in Connection with University College of the University of Chicago," which was received at the end of January, Learned concluded that the University of Chicago proposed a better plan; however, this fact was not revealed to either group.[14]

The next action on the part of Northwestern University was to submit the extract (mentioned above) to the Board of Education for Librarianship on 8 July, thus informing the BEL of Northwestern's intent. Later that fall, however, Chicago's representative, Edward A. Henry, of the University Library, talked to President Scott about the possibility of Northwestern's dropping its plans for a library school.[15] In a similar vein, George Utley of the Newberry wanted the two proposed schools to merge, a view reflected in the extract from the Northwestern University statement, which recommended admitting students "to courses in several departments of one or both of the universities."[16] Northwestern's interest seemed to have waned visibly when President Scott appeared at the BEL meeting on 30 December 1924, where he stated that "Northwestern would be interested in a library school, but not as a favorite child. It would, however, care for it if it came."[17]

Perhaps Henry's conversation had been persuasive, or perhaps President Scott had become convinced that the Carnegie Corporation was not going to award the endowment to Northwestern University anyway. Whatever the reason, Northwestern's plans for a library school seem to have been abandoned by 14 March 1925, when the CLC Committee on the Library School voted unanimously to support the University of Chicago's proposal.

THE AMERICAN LIBRARY ASSOCIATION

The role of the ALA in the selection of the University of Chicago involves several persons, most notably the ALA secretary, Carl H. Milam; his assistant and "right-hand man," Sarah C. N. Bogle; and their educational adviser, Professor Werrett W. Charters.[18]

Bogle had long been interested in library schools and in the Williamson Report in particular. She had discussed Williamson's ideas at a meeting of the Association of American Library Schools (AALS) in March 1919 and had been consulted by him in her sometime capacity as director of the Carnegie Library School in Pittsburgh. She had also written him candidly in 1921, expressing her opinion concerning the Drexel Library School. In July 1922, however, she wrote of the Chicago situation:

> I am giving the matter of a prospective library school in Chicago very careful thought. There is no question as to what the establishment of such a school would mean to the Middle West and even the South, as well as to the West itself.[19]

After becoming the assistant secretary of ALA, she was able to promote the idea of an advanced library school when she and Milam were asked to examine the Williamson Report before it appeared in its final version.[20] In their notes, dictated by Carl Milam, the following comment is found:

> Yes, there may be enough accommodations to take care of all the people. But are they properly distributed geographically? We think there is a need for an advanced library school in Chicago.[21]

There were only four schools in the Middle West: Illinois, Western Reserve, Wisconsin, and St. Louis. Thus Bogle had a solid basis for her aforementioned support of a Chicago-area library school when she was president of the Chicago Library Club.

The next major escalation of ALA interest in education for librarianship occurred just before submission of the final report of the Temporary Library Training Board. On behalf of the ALA, Carl Milam invited Werrett W. Charters, professor of education at the Carnegie Institute of Technology in Pittsburgh and author of *Curriculum Construction*, to "serve as advisor to authors and committee in preparation of textbooks for library schools."[22] In this action, ALA was responding to a criticism of existing texts in the library field that had been raised in Williamson's report.

Apparently, the newly formed BEL had to be convinced of the need for an advanced graduate library school before it began to examine the minimum requirements for it. Charters played a role in defining the function of an advanced school of librarianship when on 16 December he met with Milam, Howe, Luther L. Dickerson, executive assistant for the Commission on the Library and Adult Education of ALA, and John Dale Russell, a University of Chicago education professor.[23] In February 1925 Miss Howe again asked Charters' opinion of their "Tentative Notes on Principles Underlying the Plans for a New Type of an Advanced School of Librarianship."[24] ALA also had the opportunity to hear Charters' reactions in his address on 16 April in Chicago on "formulating curricula standards for library schools."[25]

Interestingly, Charters was asked, about this time, to join the School of Education at the University of Chicago, an invitation which he accepted. When Charters moved there during the summer, he wrote an old friend, Gordon Laing, chairman of the University Committee on the Library School, on his ideas concerning the proposed library school.[26] It is not clear, however, what Charters' official role was concerning Laing's committee. Charters prepared several memoranda for the future director of the library school and was present at a meeting in August 1926, when potential directors of the proposed library school were discussed. It is conceivable that he was simply sitting in for the absent Professor Judd of the Education Department, a regular member of the committee. But Charters' name was also mentioned, at least once, as a candidate for the directorship in 1927. Also, Laing later acknowledged Charters' contribution to his final report for the president on 7 January 1926, a development that will be discussed in the following section.

THE UNIVERSITY OF CHICAGO LIBRARY

At exactly the same time that Williamson made his first widely available statement on librarian training to the profession, an assistant professor of German literature at the University of Chicago presented his own views on university libraries in *School and Society*.[27] It is significant that while Williamson was stating what librarianship *was*, Adolf Carl von Noé[28] was stating what librarianship *should be*.

In his article, Professor Noé noted the fact that "immediate service is the keynote of every American library administration," but he lamented the fact that "today a university librarian has rarely more time for research than the registrar of the same institution." Pointing out that the gap between faculty members and librarians is "now very pronounced," he conceded that this was due in part to the great growth of the American university, but more importantly, he felt, it resulted from the

> one-sided development of library technique and organization which is not sufficiently balanced by an equal growth of scholarly opportunities for librarians. . . . In other words, everybody on the staff has

to give his best efforts to keeping the library system efficient and practically no time or energy is left for intensive studies, not to mention research. . . . [Because] university men are accustomed to rate the production of knowledge much higher than its mere acquisition and practical application . . . the question arises, how could our university libraries encourage productive scholarship among their staff members.[29]

Noé concluded with several possibilities and again called attention to this matter which is "of paramount importance . . . something should be done to counterbalance the departmental efficiency movement in our university libraries."

In a July 1920 letter to Williamson, Ernest DeWitt Burton, then librarian of the University of Chicago, referred to Noé's paper, agreeing that there was

a very real problem. There is a constant and grave danger that the entire library staff shall be so burdened with technical duties in connection with purchase, cataloging and delivery of books that they shall be out of touch with the teaching and research of the institution with which they are associated.

[Whether library schools] can give the kind of training that is needful to produce such men as I have been speaking of, or rather perhaps I should say that by far the major part of that training would be obtained in an ordinary University course rather than in a Library School. To such University training it might be desirable to add a brief period in library technique, but I am inclined to think that for such service as we are now speaking of, that training need not be at all extended.[30]

Apparently, Burton's letter was part of Williamson's "preliminary inquiries" and was useful in preparing an outline of topics to be covered in his investigation.[31]

After J. C. M. Hanson, Burton's associate director of libraries, was appointed to the Chicago Library Club's Committee on the Library School, Burton wrote his president, Harry P. Judson, in order to assess the University of Chicago's interest in a library school: "I should like to raise with you the question . . . if the means for its maintenance were furnished by the Carnegie Corporation."[32] Burton also mentioned that the school could go to Northwestern University, which should be no surprise since one of the CLC's committee members was Theodore Koch.

President Judson answered Burton the following week:

I have never been very enthusiastic about that kind of organization. I can readily see how Northwestern might be anxious to get it. If one could be provided so that the present budget should incur no responsibility I should be interested in considering the matter.[33]

Judson, at times described as "just, unselfish; and a very kindful man," could also be described as an "irritable septuagenarian"; however, his last sentence was probably reasonable, considering the general economic depression in 1921. With that small encouragement, Burton, with J. C. M. Hanson, began to work on tentative plans for the school.

The University of Chicago Administration

UNDER PRESIDENT ERNEST D. BURTON

The biggest advance, in some people's minds, for the University of Chicago's chances to get the advanced library school was the appointment of Burton to the position of acting president upon Judson's retirement in February 1923. Mary E. Ahern, editor of *Public Libraries* and a two-term CLC president, succinctly compares his appointment to the elevation of Pope Pius XI: one year "a librarian is made head of a great religious organization; the next year, a librarian is made head of a truly great university."[34] Following his appointment to the presidency on a regular basis in July 1923, Burton appeared to be in an even better position to keep his promise to "coöperate in every way possible"[35] should a library school come about as a result of the Chicago Library Club proposal of 12 April. Regrettably, however, he lived only twenty months after his appointment.

Evidently Burton had the opportunity to express his views as president personally to a staff member of the Carnegie Corporation, for there is a memorandum on his views in the corporation archives, dated 26 November 1923:

> Burton says that Chicago, while not seeking new schools, would like to be kept informed of the possibility of library development in Chicago. Would gladly back Northwestern scheme if that proves most promising. U of C will probably have downtown building before long, which might house both school and A.L.A.[36]

During 1924 the increased demands of administration caused President Burton to rely more upon his library staff—first on J. C. M. Hanson, his associate director, and later upon Edward A. Henry, the head of the Readers' Department. Since Burton was preparing to meet with Frederick Keppel in the early months of 1923, he assigned Hanson some responsibility in putting together a tentative outline. Hanson, replying that "my familiarity with library schools is, as you know, very limited,"[37] mentioned ten points to be considered, and he enclosed "A Tentative Plan for an Evening School of Library Science in Chicago" which had been prepared several years earlier.[38] Armed with these old plans and new ideas, Burton wrote Keppel from a fashionable resort area in North Carolina: "I have been wondering what progress you have made in your thought about a Library School in Chicago"; and he asked to meet with Keppel in New York the following week.

Keppel also received a five-page "Tentative Plan for a Library School in Connection with University College of the University of Chicago."[39] The proposal included a general plan and listed facilities which the University of Chicago could furnish. In particular, Burton thought "a purely graduate school would be very desirable. It is doubtful, however, whether it will be possible to begin on that basis." Consequently, he proposed an undergraduate department.[40] Keppel's memorandum of their meeting indicated that

> Chicago is much interested in the establishment of such a school. . . . President Burton pointed out that the proposed site was inside the loop whereas the Northwestern site was 15 minutes away from the big public libraries. The University of Chicago campus is only 30 minutes away.[41]

The potential site was downtown, and not on campus, primarily because of the state of campus construction.

Meanwhile, William S. Learned, who had also looked at the Chicago proposal, concluded:

> It seems to me from this memorandum that Chicago University can offer practically everything that could be expected of Northwestern, together with much more extensive facilities for practice. Of course, all of the existing independent library facilities of Chicago would be quite as available in one case as in another, and the location in either situation would, I understand, be downtown. It looks to me as though Chicago University had the best of the argument.[42]

Not only was the University of Chicago on record as desiring the school, but the Carnegie Corporation's investigator of the library profession had concluded, although unbeknownst to the university, that the University of Chicago was gaining preference.

Back home on the Chicago campus, matters still were not settled. Apparently Burton was not satisfied, after talking with Keppel, that the selection of the Chicago area was a foregone conclusion. Based on his interview with Keppel and the additional input from his library staff,[43] Burton had another five-page proposal prepared, this time entitled "A Library School in Chicago."[44] Claiming that "Chicago is the natural center" in the Middle West, he pointed out that while the school at the University of Illinois is a most excellent one, it is limited both by the lack of library facilities other than those of the University itself, and also by the fact that it is a state school which finds it necessary to publish in its circulars regarding special students and the six weeks summer course that they are, "Primarily for the benefit of Illinois librarians." There is room and need for a school of the highest standards which will receive all students on an [equal?] basis.[45]

Strategically, Burton was aware that Andrew Keogh of Yale was due to report on the advanced school of librarianship at the Saratoga Springs convention and that the Temporary Library Training Board was also due to make its report. Thus he considered it politically astute to have the executive board of the American Library Association hear of the University of Chicago's plans. On 20 June, ten days before the convention, Henry wrote of his university's plan to both Carl Milam and Sarah Bogle, and he also kept Carl Roden and others informed. Specifically, Burton had requested Henry to ask Bogle to write to Keppel

> 1) commending the idea of a School of high graduate professional type, and 2) if you are convinced in the matter, recommending that such a School should be established in connection with the University of Chicago.[46]

He concluded with the expectation of "realization by October 1, 1925."

The first statement should have been no problem since she had already made such statements on several occasions and, as the former Chicago Library Club president, would likely want to continue the project. Carl Milam, however, answered for them, stating that it would be inappropriate for them to comment on the enclosed proposal because the Temporary Library Training Board and the proposed Board of Education for Librarianship had jurisdiction in this matter.

In mid-July Clement W. Andrews, librarian of the John Crerar Library, wrote to President Keppel that both Albany and Illinois were "handicapped" by being associated with state institutions and local needs.[47] As president of the American Library Institute, he intended to bring the matter up at its Lake Placid meeting on 22–25 September. He concluded with a discussion of the proposal, but he did not want to choose between the University of Chicago and Northwestern University.

By September, another draft of "A Library School in Chicago" had been prepared, consisting of fourteen pages. Henry summarized the status of the proposal in a letter to Burton,[48] pointing out that the executive board of ALA had considered it at Saratoga Springs at the urging of Milam. However, Roden, as a member of the executive board, did not want to take sides with either of the two Chicago universities. Henry quoted Phineas Windsor of the University of Illinois, who said: "We will meet the competition or get off the map, but I am sure there is ample room for two schools in Illinois," especially if Chicago were to be a national school. As far as the New York State Library School was concerned, it was a professional school, but it was not graduate in character; so it should not matter either. The proposal left the reasons for establishing such a school largely unchanged; however, the type and course level of the proposed school responded directly to the concerns expressed at the Saratoga Springs convention. Such a school would be a *de novo* reaction to the recommendations of both the Williamson Report and the Temporary Library Training Board.

Edward Henry's growing responsibility for designing the library school was due in part to Hanson's hospitalization during the previous winter and in part to Hanson's responsibilities in directing the library. In another letter, Henry outlined his method of constructing "the School of Librarianship at the University of Chicago."[49] It was based partly upon a study of catalogs of all the existing library schools and partly upon his own experience, or what he termed "the example of the Divinity School."

More importantly, Henry defined the content of library science as he perceived it and the Ph.D. degree was suggested for the first time. For the former, he stated:

> It conceives of library science as the science of the care and the use of books both for the control of knowledge already in existence and for the discovery of new knowledge through researches in books themselves or with books in connection with other sources of information.

With regard to the latter, the doctorate was not awarded

> on the basis of the completion of a certain amount of time spent upon a specified program, but as the recognition and mark of high attainments and ability in the candidate's chosen province, shown, first by the production of a dissertation evincing the power of independent investigation and forming an actual contribution to existing knowledge; and, secondly, by the passing of examinations covering the general field of the candidate's subjects.[50]

Now, for the first time, librarianship was addressing a university model of education for librarianship, although only insofar as degree requirements for the doctorate were concerned (rather than its implications for research).

On 27 October 1924, Burton received his answer from President Keppel.[51] Essentially, Keppel asked him to wait until the next fiscal year, when the Carnegie Corporation's financial position would be better and the amount to be available would be clearer. Henry, however, read between the lines: Keppel was hoping that the University of Chicago "would answer the demand of the library world for a University Library School."[52]

In the remaining two months of 1924, Burton talked as well as corresponded with Hanson, Henry, and Harriet Howe of the BEL. The result was an appointment for President Burton before a closed session of the BEL on 30 December 1924 at 2:30 p.m. Strohm, Keogh, Wyer, Smith, and Howe were present at the board meeting. Accompanied by Hanson and Henry, Burton talked for approximately forty-five minutes on the "acute need of assistants in his library, . . . the Chicago Library Club recommendation, . . . Dr. Keppel's initiative," and the Ph.D. and graduate students. Also present were Koch, and Roden, Andrew, and Utley as representatives of the Chicago Library Club. In particular, Andrews reported that there was no opposition from the American Library Institute, which had met in September. Other sentiments included desires for location of the library school in downtown Chicago and that faculty members be taken from existing library schools.

BEL members received a four-page "Memorandum in Regard to a Possible Library School in Chicago,"[53] which was intended to elicit a favorable response. This time the proposed school would not only respond to the Williamson Report and the Temporary Library Training Board, but also the BEL. In the curriculum, "vocation work," as practiced in the Divinity School, would also be required. Among the advantages for locating such a school at the University of Chicago was its "long experience in the gathering of material of instruction in new fields" and "a School of Education of high rank," a consideration that would be castigated three years later. Curiously, the "summary of capital grants needed for the permanent establishment of the school" was reduced to $1,025,000.

President Keppel met with Burton in Chicago on 9 January 1925, and in Keppel's report to the corporation he stated that "the more I think of it, the more favorably I am inclined toward Chicago, as the locus for the school."[54] Interestingly, Burton's memo on their meeting indicates that his meeting with the BEL confirmed that the school should be located at the University of Chicago. This judicious overstatement was news to Keppel, but it was all right with him, even though Keppel wanted to be sure that, somehow, ALA obtained permanent headquarters as part of the negotiations.[55]

During the month of March, three propitious events occurred. At the BEL, when the members discussed the location and academic status of the proposed school, they could only "unanimously agree that it must be either Chicago or New York." However, the BEL also agreed that the University of Chicago's statement was "in accord with the best judgment of [the] Board."[56]

The second propitious event was a Friday-the-thirteenth meeting of the Chicago Library Club. By unanimous vote,

> the Committee of the Chicago Library Club on a Library School in Chicago has examined with care and interest the plan drawn up at the University of Chicago.
>
> The Committee believes that this plan in its general outlines embodies satisfactorily a way of meeting the needs of the library profession, and hopes that such a school may be established in Chicago.[57]

But Keppel's news of 23 March was the most momentous. At the morning meeting on that date, Keppel recommended an action based on the Williamson Report and the more recent Learned Memorandum which was intended to strengthen and advance the librarian's profession. In short, he stated that

> Chicago is the natural center of the American library world. Its own public and private libraries offer extraordinary laboratory facilities, and in Dr. Burton, the University of Chicago has a President who was himself for many years Director of the University Libraries and is peculiarly well qualified to direct the organization of such an enterprise.[58]

In an early-April consultation with Burton, however, Keppel was more circumspect.[59] He mentioned several "possible loci"—New York and Washington besides Chicago. Secondly, a grant of $1.25 million would be the maximum amount awarded; the capital sum would not be available until 1927 because the recent $5 million grant to the Carnegie Institution in Washington was a considerable drain on corporation resources.

On 1 April, Henry wrote to Burton that it was no joke: Milam was convinced that the University of Chicago had it, "though of course no definite word was spoken by Dr. Keppel."[60] Finally, the fifteen long months of work at the University of Chicago, led by Burton and assisted by Hanson, Henry, and administrative assistant Emery T. Filbey, were beginning to pay off. But in May Burton died—a tragic death to the CLC supporters and a near fatal blow to Chicago's plans.[61]

UNDER PRESIDENT CHARLES MAX MASON

The school's future was not secure. In June, when Keppel and Morse Cartwright, a corporation staff member, got together to discuss the library school situation, "the question [arose] as to whether or not the death of President Burton of Chicago and the New York situation should be given more careful consideration than it was thought advisable at first."[62] Obviously, Keppel's thoughts ranged back to his meeting of 23 March with the corporation's executive committee, when he informed it that

> an alternative which has been suggested would be to combine the Albany Library School with that of the New York Public Library, and put the combined school under the direction of Columbia University, possibly in Teachers College.[63]

The BEL had earlier favored the New York area. The situation regarding the library directorship at Columbia was improving as a search was initiated. At the conclusion of their meeting, Keppel asked Cartwright to assess ALA sentiment.

During June and July, Henry tried to advise Vice President Tufts in the matter. Primarily, it was a question of what to do with the documents, and Tufts asked the chairman of the board, Harold H. Swift, for his opinion on the matter. To ascertain any unwritten understandings with the Carnegie Corporation, Swift recommended that Tufts tell Keppel that the present proposal had not had the benefit of revisions suggested in the April meeting between Keppel and Burton.[64] By early August, Tufts was able to send Keppel a six-page letter and a revised fourteen-page "Library School at the University of Chicago: Suggestion [*sic*] and Recommendations." [65]

Late that summer, Max Mason began a three-year tenure as the fourth president of the University of Chicago; and although nearly as brief as Burton's, his presidency saw the opportunity to recapture the pioneering spirit of the university's first president, William Rainey Harper. From Detroit Harbor, a resort area favored by many Chicago people, Mason wrote candidly to Keppel that he was not aware of the graduate library school plans; nevertheless, "I have taken steps to get in touch with the project, pending my return to Chicago in about ten days."[66] Advising the new president, Tufts commented on the early history of the library school, with its origins in "2 or 3 separate roots."[67] Eventually, Milam was told that there was "no progress to report"[68] but that Mason was interested and would see Keppel.

Mason went to New York on 24 October. Sarah Bogle, on behalf of the BEL, wrote Keppel just as Mason left for New York that there was an urgent need for an advanced graduate library school and that the Carnegie Corporation should consider an "early grant to the University of Chicago for such a school."[69] The meeting between Mason and Keppel seems to have been mostly exploratory. Keppel observed that Mason questioned whether Chicago ought to take on the Library School at all unless the best men in the University really saw an opportunity in it, and is anxious to have us work on that basis. FPK got impression that he thought million dollars was plenty. Glad to hear that we are not interested in large numbers. He personally is interested in Adult Education in the whole newer way of looking at things.[70]

They discussed personalities in the library field—individuals, apparently, who might advise Mason on the proposed school.

Back home on the Midway, Mason resolved that the solution to his problems with the proposed library school was a committee, for only in this way could he ascertain if "the best men in the University really saw an opportunity in it."

THE LAING COMMITTEE ON THE LIBRARY SCHOOL

To chair the committee, Mason settled upon Gordon J. Laing, dean of the Graduate School of Arts and Literature, where the proposed school was to reside. Assembling the committee in early December,[71] Mason charged it "to consider first whether such a school would be a desirable addition to our university work, and second what, in general, would be the ideals and the organization of the school."[72] It was to report as soon as possible. Thus armed, in mid-December the eight-member committee consulted a number of Chicago-area librarians, the individual members of the BEL, and two "outsiders" concerning the potential curriculum. When Laing's committee met on Monday, 21 December, it had received letters from W. W. Bishop, Carl B. Roden, George B. Utley, Edward A. Henry, J. C. M. Hanson, and William W. Rockwell.

The first "outsider," Bishop, wrote that he was particularly concerned about the organization of the school. At this point he felt there was not enough content in library science for a Ph.D.:

Personally, I have very grave doubts whether there is justification at present for admitting persons as candidates for the Doctor's degree with Library Science as a major subject. Intensive work in certain subjects allied to Librarianship may serve as the basis for the doctorate, and without question certain types of bibliographical work carefully and faithfully performed should show evidence of ability to carry on research work fully equal to the preparation of the average thesis for the doctorate.[73]

Consequently, he argued that the school should be organized as a department wherein individuals could pursue library science as a minor on the way toward a doctorate in another subject.[74]

Roden's letter was more philosophical:

> My own conception of the kind of instruction that should be given in a Graduate Library School may be summed up in the proposition that more attention should be given to theory, by which I mean the objects, motives, possibilities and historical, literary, and sociological implications underlying the administration of libraries.[75]

He urged that stress be placed on "principles (as against 'rules')." Using the analogy of nursing, Roden pointed out that the shift away from practical nursing meant that nurses now "know not only *what* they are doing but *why*."

Utley, librarian of the Newberry, divided the curriculum into library science and "the more important part of the curriculum, [which] would devote itself to cultural courses and to research work in connection with them."[76] Less than half the time should be spent on technical courses and the larger portion of time, dealing with cultural courses, should recognize the students' interests in "side lines," such as library work with children or library work in high schools and normal schools.

Henry's letter also reenforced the idea of library work in a particular subject or area. As one of the few who had offered a definition of librarianship, Henry stated that

> librarianship, which may be defined from one point of view as the classification and proper correlation of all recorded knowledge and the art of making that knowledge available quickly and conveniently to anyone needing any portion of it has its deep fundamental principles. We must think of it as library work in English or History or Medicine.[77]

He concluded with an aside (mentioned to him by Adam Strohm of the BEL) to the effect that no one was "so well prepared by experience to work out a plan for advanced research in the fundamental principles of cataloging and classification as our own Mr. Hanson."[78] Indeed, the committee members received from Hanson a detailed "Outline of Curriculum for the Graduate School of Library Science."[79]

The other "outsider" was William W. Rockwell, librarian of Union Theological Seminary in New York, who may have been consulted at Shailer Mathew's suggestion.[80] A Göttingen Ph.D., Rockwell's comments were based on a discussion with his chief cataloger, Julia Pettee, an 1895 graduate of Pratt Institute. They agreed with the Association of American Universities' statement[81] regarding degrees in library science and suggested six points in a master's degree program.[82] As for the doctorate, "Ph.D. training should be combined with library training." Courses might include "study of the psychology and of the metaphysics of classification . . . training at foreign universities, and foreign apprenticeship or 'journeyman' years." Obviously, the suggestions for doctoral work reflect much of Rockwell's experiences, although he had no objection to a major in library science at the doctoral level.

The major conclusion to be drawn from these divergent ideas of education for librarianship is that no consensual ideal existed at this time. Indeed, a graduate library school may have been needed simply to focus attention on this area.

In a letter to Andrew Keogh, John Manly revealed the results of the Laing committee meeting:

> The committee had no difficulty in reaching the conclusion that a real graduate school of librarianship was very desirable in itself and would be a desirable addition to the University. . . . But we found it difficult to determine what specific new lines of work should be provided for in such a school and what might well be provided by proper coordination with departments already existing in the graduate school. [The committee] did not formulate a curriculum—for we did not regard that as lying within our province but as being matter to be determined after careful study by the officers of the school, if such a one should be established—we did nevertheless form some conception of the general problems of such a school and the personnel requirements.[83]

While the committee had difficulty defining the new school's work, it was able to state what it should *not* do. In particular, the committee thought "undue stress" was placed on "such subjects as children's libraries, storytelling, and the organization and development of special libraries for commercial and industrial firms."[84] The neglect of the latter area may in part account for the later rise of a new intellectual discipline, "information science."

In the meantime, President Mason was meeting with President Keppel, and a memorandum of that meeting indicates that the two primary topics of discussion were the amount of money to be appropriated and the school's objective.[85] Under Burton's proposal, the University of Chicago had asked for slightly more than $2 million; now Mason said that $1 million was the upper limit. Furthermore, "Mason has the idea that the school should be pointed largely toward research in bibliography. He is not going to force it on his faculty and will only move when they consider it to be the thing that they want."[86] The following day, Keppel met with Carl Milam, who expressed "his fear that [Mason] lacks understanding of importance of research and administration organization. F. P. K. said that man to be appointed for new school would undoubtedly clear this situation."[87] Milam had never been convinced that the administration of the University of Chicago knew what it should be doing. Several years earlier, Milam had expressed to Keppel similar doubts about Burton.[88] Evidently, however, President Keppel was able to placate him both times. President Keppel's confidence in Chicago would be clearly apparent two weeks later.

On 24 December 1925 the corporation resolved

> that the University of Chicago be invited to submit to the Executive Committee through the President a program for the organization and maintenance of a graduate library school, and that if the Executive Committee, acting on behalf of the Corporation, approve such program, the Committee shall be authorized to obligate the Corporation to the University of Chicago for an amount not to exceed the total set aside in the proposed program for the establishment and endowment of a graduate library school, namely $1,385,000, payable in accordance with the schedule set forth in the aforementioned program.[89]

Thus the Board of Education for Librarianship's extensive discussion on Thursday afternoon, December 31, would appear to matter little.[90]

When President Mason returned to his office following the Christmas–New Year break, he found a package from the Carnegie Corporation. Keppel had sent him a copy of Tse-Chien Tai's *Professional Education for Librarianship* (New York: H. W. Wilson, 1925) and a note calling it "a bully book [which] has lots of good sense in it."[91] Furthermore, Keppel enclosed a copy of "the famous Williamson Report, since, when it was written, I take it you weren't particularly excited by education for librarianship." Besides this gentle chiding, Keppel concluded by mentioning C. C. Williamson "for a professional position." Perhaps Keppel foresaw that the Laing Committee was going to return a favorable report the very same week!

In fact, on Thursday, 7 January 1926, Laing wrote President Mason concerning his committee's report on the proposed graduate library school.[92] The report was based on the revision of the previous year, with little change of the proposed objectives for the school, except that it "shall be open only to those who have a bachelor's degree from an approved institution, including or supplemented by a year's training in library science."[93] Research in library problems continued to be emphasized. The most important modification was in "suggested Organization and Faculty Membership." First, "the Library School should be *organized as a Graduate School* of the University and the members of its staff should be members of the Graduate Faculty" (emphasis added).[94]

Significantly, a research institute was also recommended, and provided with a $5,000 budget. In the curriculum section, the committee made recommendations in spite of Manly's earlier statement to Keogh. The curriculum was divided among professional technical courses, professional cultural courses, and general cultural courses. The offerings reflected the input from the committee's correspondence, especially Hanson's outline. Finally, the committee stated "that the School should not provide the preliminary year of library training since a year of such training is one of the requirements of admission."[95]

Mason informed Keppel that he had received the committee's report and that it was "unanimously in favor of the desirability of forming a Graduate Library School."[96] The following week, Laing wrote to Carl Milam, informing the American Library Association of his committee's enthusiasm for such a school.[97]

On 20 February at 11 a.m., the university senate heard the "proposal to organize a graduate library school at the University of Chicago" as the fourth item on its agenda.[98] As the senate agreed with the committee that the proposed school should be strictly graduate in character and "with the exception of the cost of providing space, it shall be financed from some outside source," it recommended the proposal to the board of trustees.[99] Mason was now assured that the interest in the library school was solidly based.

In writing to Keppel on 26 February, Mason forwarded copies of the Laing Committee's proposal, but he indicated that the curriculum and budget were "put forward as suggestive only."[100] He further stated:

> I am certain that there is very real interest in furthering the work of the School on the part of the members of the Faculty, and that thorough cooperation will result if such a School be instituted at the University of Chicago. Personally, I have high hopes that matters of deep importance may be the result of the research work of members of the staff of such a School and the students as well, and feel that the whole project is a most important one in the field of general education. The Faculty and Trustees of the University of Chicago will be most happy in cooperating with the Carnegie Corporation to further this work.[101]

Contrary to other writers' statements,[102] and as should be obvious from the above passages, the University of Chicago's selection was not yet assured.

First of all, the Carnegie Corporation had not approved the ten-year program in library service or appropriated the monies necessary for the graduate library school. And second, the university's proposal was stated in the future rather than in the present tense.

On 19 March, however, the Carnegie Corporation resolved to request from the University of Chicago a proposal for the "organization and maintenance" of a graduate library school as part of its ten-year program in library service.[103] The following day, Charles F. D. Belden, president of the American Library Association, received a letter from the Carnegie Corporation detailing the annual appropriations and capital grants for the graduate library school,[104] and the University of Chicago received a similar telegram. Mason responded that he was glad to hear of the action and he reported that the university's board of trustees had voted authority for him to proceed.[105] Essentially, Mason wanted to know if the proposal he sent on 26 February was satisfactory to the executive committee. Cartwright, in a memorandum to Keppel, stated that he thought it constituted a "satisfactory program, although it is stated in the form of what the University *should* do rather than what it *will* do."[106] Thus the next day Keppel responded to Mason that it looked fine, though it ought to say what *would* be done. To satisfy this request, Mason wrote a two-page, eight-point letter on 20 April, stating what the university would do should the funds be made available from the Carnegie Corporation.

Keppel's 5 May 1926 letter informed Mason that the corporation's executive committee "unanimously approved grant to the University of Chicago on basis of your letter April 20th and accompanying memorandum.[107] Keppel indicated that the corporation was willing to commit $1,385,000, but that the university should look to other sources of funding in the future. All that was left was the approval of the University of Chicago's board of trustees.[108] On 3 June the secretary of the board wrote to President Keppel that the board accepted the Carnegie Corporation grant.[109] The graduate library school now had a home at the University of Chicago.

The Dean, Librarian or Scholar?

With the library school project fairly well secured, Mason proceeded to the matter of personnel. In attacking this task, he continued to rely upon the Laing Committee. Several experts were brought in to discuss the matter with the committee, and a volume of correspondence was created.

W. W. Bishop and Louis R. Wilson of the University of North Carolina, a recently appointed member of the BEL to take Keogh's place, were brought in for on-site visits. Unfortunately, there does not seem to be a memorandum of Bishop's comments on the situation at

Louis R. Wilson

Chicago, although Laing acknowledged that his visit had been profitable.[110] Prior to Wilson's visit with Laing on 20 May, the Carolinian had written Milam that he wanted to talk with him and Howe before seeing Laing. As it turned out, he met with Milam and Strohm in New York the weekend before he went to Chicago.[111] In his letter to Strohm, Wilson mentioned that Laing wanted to talk to him about the curriculum and personnel.[112] Wilson confessed he knew a little about curricula but nothing about graduate library schools. After all,

Wilson said, he had only been to one American Library Association meeting and that was in 1920, which was only a slight exaggeration. In point of fact, although Wilson was an ALA member (no. 3626), he had only attended four annual conferences between 1901 and 1925: 1906, 1907, 1921, and 1922. Wilson continued by asking Strohm's opinion about possible instructional staff and ended: "Please come to my assistance, as I am going to find the situation a pretty difficult one on account of my limitations."[113] Wilson was well aware that following Keogh on the BEL was going to be difficult.

On the train back to Chapel Hill,[114] Wilson studied in more detail the Laing Committee's proposal and wrote his four-page "Memorandum Concerning [the] Advanced Graduate Library School."[115] Regarding the "nature of the school," Wilson agreed with the committee that it should be "conducted in accord with the best standards of American graduate instruction."[116] The curriculum proposed by the committee was also satisfactory in the tripartite division of courses; but, Wilson said, "it would seem to me . . . that a fourth division should be added in which the handling of statistics and methods of research and investigation would receive specific consideration.[117] To further distinguish Chicago from Illinois and Columbia, Wilson encouraged specialization "rather than adding more of the same kind of subject material."[118] Less innovatively, he repeated an earlier BEL statement about the types of positions for which the school should prepare students.

More interestingly, Wilson suggested subjects for investigation and theses by appending a two-page listing of "possible special field of theses subjects" which had been prepared by ALA Headquarters on 11 January 1926 by Harriet E. Howe.[119] Under "plan of organization," Wilson clearly stated his preference for a separate directorship of the school. In the last section on personnel, Wilson recommended (most likely in order of his preference) the directorship of the school: W. W. Bishop, James I. Wyer, Sydney B. Mitchell, Adam Strohm, and Ernest J. Reece; the librarian: Adam Strohm, Harry M. Lydenberg, M. Llewelyn Raney, and George B. Utley; and the professorships: Ernest J. Reece, Henry Van Hoesen, James C. Cleavinger, Margaret Mann, Dorothy Curtis, and Charles B. Shaw.

Undoubtedly there was much curiosity, within and outside the profession, about who would be dean of this new type of library school. Wilson had recommended five men, but winnowing had to await the University of Chicago's board of trustees' action on 3 June, approving acceptance of the Carnegie Corporation grant. The search for personnel began in earnest when, on 22 July, Henry wrote to Laing about one of Wilson's suggestions for a professorship, Henry Van Hoesen. Overall, Van Hoesen was an "unusually scholarly type of librarian"[120] and Henry thought the fact should be made known. Two days later, however, Laing telegrammed Wilson that "the committee of the Library School has reached a decision which has been approved by the President"[121]—would he come for an interview? After several exchanges of telegrams, a conference was arranged for 2 August.

From the outset, Wilson seemed disinclined to go, particularly if things improved at home. He wrote his president, Harry W. Chase, on 31 July that when Columbia wanted Bishop, Michigan's president raised Bishop's salary, gave him a decent budget to start a library school at Michigan, *and* paid him extra for teaching summer library courses. "Similar action on your part *might* interest me!" Wilson told Chase.[122] Upon his return home, Wilson consulted several individuals about the proper course of action. He wrote M. Llewelyn Raney of Johns Hopkins, who was being considered for the post of librarian at Chicago;[123] Edgar W. Knight,[124] visiting professor of education at Columbia University; and his brother. To buy more time, Wilson wrote President Mason and inquired about retirement benefits and housing assistance.

In the meantime, Wilson heard from his correspondents,[125] but his mind seemed to be on personal concerns. On 18 August Wilson wrote to Laing, mentioning the health of one of his young daughters, who fought tuberculosis constantly. Yet Mason persisted, sending him more information on the retirement plans. Wilson finally turned down the deanship and (in a letter to Mason on 21 August) stated three reasons for the decision: his family's health, the University of North Carolina's top administration was resigning, and he was planning a new library building at Chapel Hill.[126]

Into October, Mason was still wrestling with the difficult job of selecting a director for the school, although, according to Sarah Bogle, "Dr. Keppel wrote Dr. Mason that he need not feel hurried in making this appointment so far as the Corporation is concerned."[127] Near the end of November, the University of Chicago felt it was necessary to invite the Board of Education for Librarianship to the Chicago campus to discuss the situation. In a letter to BEL members, Sarah Bogle commented:

> It is well known to all of us that Dr. Raney's ideas in regard to education for librarianship are absolutely at variance with those of the Board and this may be a question which has to be faced, especially as his advice has been sought by the Committee in regard to the Library School. We understand that Dr. Raney believes in the appointment

of a non-librarian and a man quite unknown to the profession as Dean of the School.[128]

Some "reflections" by Carl Milam, three months earlier, give yet another perspective on the ALA reaction to Raney's ideas and the University of Chicago's plans. Milam considered Raney a "danger" because Raney thought the ALA was a failure.[129] Similarly, Milam was not impressed with the University of Chicago's president, primarily because he knew very little about libraries, although Milam granted that Mason was committed to having the "*best* school and library in the world."[130] Milam was aware that they wanted a dean trained in research who was also a *leader*. It would not be surprising if Milam coveted the position for himself.

Perhaps, after a year and a half, President Keppel was beginning to become impatient with the Chicago administration. Thus in January 1927 Keppel began to nudge Dean Laing. As Keppel saw it,

> there are two courses open to the University of Chicago. One is to get a man who is primarily academic but has the confidence of the library profession, and the other is to get a man who is primarily a librarian but who can be counted on to fit in in an academic family, and to see that his faculty includes scholars as well as administrators.[131]

In the first case, Learned was "almost certainly your man"; "on the second choice, I think Milam is your man."[132]

Learned's name had already been mentioned in an August brainstorming session at the university; however, Chicago was still pursuing Keppel's earlier advice. Dean Laing had invited Charles E. Rush of the Indianapolis Public Library to meet with the committee, but before he went, Rush received a letter from Milam in which Milam discussed his own ideas about a graduate library school.[133] Rush gave the committee two pages of notes on the purpose of the school, then waited for its response.[134] No memorandum of their meeting is extant, although the committee must have accepted Keppel's suggestion of seeing William S. Learned.

Following Learned's visit in February, Laing on 27 March offered him the position. President Mason also wrote him with an offer of $10,000 per annum, stating that the committee thought he was better than all of the library specialists.[135] Additionally, Mason wanted Learned to adopt an adult education interpretation as the school's purpose. Like Rush before him, Learned drafted a proposal. He recommended establishment of a research school with high standards of admission, staffed with a "few first-class specialists in different aspects of the field."[136] He suspected that it would be like Columbia. Learned, however, rejected the traditional form of education for librarianship, stating that Chicago's purpose should be "to train leaders and conduct research."[137] He also highly recommended fellowships of $1,500 each. In fact, when Keppel read Learned's memo, he was convinced of the importance of the fellowships, and feeling obligated because he had recommended Learned in the first place, Keppel assured the University of Chicago that there would be $30,000 for five years from the Carnegie Corporation for fellowships.[138] With the assurance of fellowship monies, Mason wrote Keppel that he was confident Learned would now accept the deanship.[139]

Learned, however, replied that he wanted to stay with Carnegie trustee, Henry S. Pritchett, especially since "general education . . . is in a ferment of change,"[140] and he suggested "W. W. Charters, who understands research of this nature and stands well with the library leaders."[141] President Keppel felt compelled to explain Learned's action:

> I'm afraid our friend Learned doesn't know a first-class thing when he sees it, but I suppose he's earned the right to be wrong if he wishes to exercise it.[142]

President Mason suspected that Learned was not excited about the administrative duties of the deanship, for on 9 May he wrote Learned, trying to minimize them, and further stating that he wanted him for his "temper of mind."[143] Learned, not convinced, replied: "My position here is quite exceptional."[144]

In the meantime, the Laing Committee met again to consider candidates. Rejecting both Harrison W. Craver, director of the Engineering Societies Library in New York, and Franklin F. Hopper, head of the circulation department at the New York Public Library, the committee stated that the latter did not even realize "the possibilities of a research library school."[145] Laing, not exactly discouraged, reflected that

> the more I talk to Milam and Miss Bogle, the more I am convinced that the kind of School that we ought to have here is one on a different plan from anything they have ever thought of.[146]

Consequently, Laing informed his president that he should not be concerned about the American Library Association's lack of "enthusiastic approval."[147]

This time, happily, the university offered the deanship to a scholar who accepted it, George Alan Works,[148] chairman of the Division of Education at Cornell University and author of a forthcoming work entitled *College and University Library Problems* (Chicago: ALA, 1927). Who Works was, how he shaped the graduate library school, and how he responded to internal concerns as well as external criticisms is the subject of the next chapter.

3

The Works Era, 1927–29

George Alan Works, who was chosen for and accepted the position of dean of the new graduate library school at the University of Chicago, had been trained at the University of Wisconsin, where he received a Ph.B. in 1904 and an M.S. in 1912; he was awarded an Ed.D. from Harvard in 1925.[1] In 1914, Works joined Cornell University as "professor of Rural Education and head of the Department. When in 1926 the Departments of Education in the Colleges of Agriculture and Arts & Sciences were combined in a Division of Education, he became its first chairman."[2] He received his official appointment at Chicago in the summer of 1927, to become effective in the autumn quarter.

Although George Works was not trained as a librarian, he was not unfamiliar to librarians, especially to the members of the advisory committee on his survey of academic libraries, which was published in 1927 under the title *College and University Library Problems*. The members were W. W. Bishop, Andrew Keogh, Sydney B. Mitchell, Azariah S. Root, and Frank K. Walter.[3] (The study, incidentally, was financed by a grant from the Carnegie Corporation.) Besides meeting with this group on at least four occasions since 1926, Works had studied the libraries of eighteen major institutions, including the University of North Carolina, the University of Illinois, and the State University of Iowa; therefore, he knew many of the leading librarians.

Nevertheless, Works's first actions following his appointment at Chicago were orientation. In particular, he wanted to attend the ALA meeting in Toronto in 1927 and to observe the Institute for Instructors of Library Science which was held in Chicago during that summer. At the ALA meeting it is quite likely that Works had an opportunity to hear C. C. Williamson and sit in on the establishment of a committee for research within the Association of American Library Schools.[4] Likewise in Chicago at the second institute, which was held from 28 August to 2 September, Works would have had the opportunity to observe classes and to talk with W. W. Charters and Professor Frank Freeman, an educational psychologist whose research interests in-

George Works

cluded handwriting and typewriting. (These institutes are discussed in more detail in the following sections.)

Already, however, there were reactions from individuals in the library profession to the appointment of a nonlibrarian to such a post. In a candid letter to Sarah Bogle, Bishop said:

> I have the very greatest possible liking for Professor Works, but I cannot see him filling the office of Dean of an "Advanced Graduate Library School." In fact, I am very pessimistic about this whole enterprise, as you perhaps know; I hope unduly so, I feel sure I can say this to you without having any suspicion that I am influenced in this feeling by personal or institutional considerations. What I want to see is a real *training school of an advanced type.* Somehow I feel that both Keogh and myself, in our anxiety for the best possible conditions for the success of such an institution, may have been foolishly self denying in our insistence that it should go to a large city. If the school is started at the University of Chicago under the combined influence of Dr. Raney and Dr. Charters, I for one shall watch its growth with more interest than hope [emphasis added].[5]

It is tempting to assert that this statement is the beginning of the conflict between those who desire a professional training program and those who want a strictly graduate research program for library science. Later, Dean Works himself would express some of his ideas about the character of graduate education in library science and the conception of research in librarianship.

Harold F. Brigham, a staff assistant on Charters' ALA Curriculum Study, recorded in his diary on 28 June 1927, under "Technical Problems," that the

> reaction to appointment of Dr. Works as director of Graduate School is reported as probably a disappointment generally because he is not a librarian, but that spirit of those spoken to is friendly, hopeful, and cooperative. This applies to [Charles H.?] Compton, [Edith M.] Coulter, [Margaret] Mann, and [James I.] Wyer. Mr. Roden expressed himself as quite sympathetic to Dr. C[harters]'s view, i. e. *to have a research man as director with a strong staff of librarians* [emphasis added].[6]

Again, the last sentence emphasizes the conflict between those who want a professional training program and those who want a research program. In terms of the history of an idea, the librarian's conception of bibliography as research was to be challenged and found inadequate in the GLS at Chicago, where it would be displaced in favor of the university sense of research, meaning "extension of the boundaries of knowledge."

Internal Concerns

During the academic year 1927/28, Works's concerns at Chicago were directed toward the development of objectives, the selection of faculty, the selection of students, and arrangements for instructional work. These four matters will be discussed here *seriatim*.

OBJECTIVES

Objectives are logically derived from the mission or purpose of an organization, and the Graduate Library School was no exception. By June 1928, Works could state succinctly that the

> primary purpose of the School is to organize and conduct investigations of problems confronting society in general or in particular fields of scholarship when such problems fall within the field of librarianship.[7]

Before this statement, however, the dean had expressed on several occasions his ideas concerning several objectives for the new school. The most significant earlier vehicle for this was in response to an invitation from Charles H. Brown—or James McMillan—to address the College and Reference Section of ALA on 31 December 1927, during the ALA midwinter meeting. His main argument in that address was for a cooperative endeavor in research. First of all, he pointed out,

> the number of schools is small enough so that some of the difficulties that are usually attendant on such proposals are greatly minimized. It would seem practicable for the schools to block out at least roughly a program of research toward which concerted action might be directed.[8]

The benefits to be derived from such a cooperative effort would include a minimum of duplicated effort and a maximum of accomplishment. Of course, other schools would not be restricted from pursuing similar topics, nor would participating schools be

> restricting the research interests of any individual or group of individuals. Instead it is simply an expression of a belief in the value of concerted effort on the part of institutions that should have as one of their primary objectives—research.[9]

Thus it was clear from the start that, in Works's view, research was to be one of the primary objectives at the GLS.

An allied objective was to conduct service studies for the profession. Works was aware that the school alone could not accomplish the task of research in library science and that it must also come from the field. As he put it,

The graduate schools should help in the development of research by assisting members of the profession who are in the field. Faculty members should gladly counsel with members of the profession who are interested in making studies. The workers in turn should not hesitate to call freely upon these institutions regardless of whether or not they have studied at them. They should have no hesitation in asking for such assistance. It is not a personal favor they are requesting but a professional service. This phase is an important consideration in the development of research. The productive work of students and staffs of the graduate schools will not result in an adequate development of research. Members of the profession must be constantly adding to the knowledge of their chosen fields. The profession should have many workers who are making contributions in connection with their daily work. The goal will not be in sight until every professional worker carries the scientific attitude into his daily work. This is characteristic to a degree at the present but it should be much more evident if the highest ideals of scholarship are to characterize the profession.[10]

Importantly, Works recognized the value of faculty members "prosecuting studies of their own." If the profession is to consult the faculty, then the faculty must be on the research front. Works also addressed some of the difficulties which might be encountered:

At the University of Chicago school definite provision is to be made so that staff members will have the necessary freedom for research. They will not only have the freedom but they will also face the fact that they are expected to be productive. This is no more unreasonable than the expectation that any other responsibility should be discharged.

The lack of time is the common explanation of failure to do research. In this respect, there is no valid reason why the faculty of a graduate library school should not be given the same opportunities for research as obtained for faculty members of other schools and colleges in the university of which the school is a part. But this phase aside, it is surprising the amount of the world's research that has been done by individuals who were at the same time carrying heavy responsibilities independently of their research.[11]

Another significant objective was publication of the results of the investigation of problems. Works felt that

it may not be amiss to indicate [that] the opportunity for publication is a stimulus to research. If provision is not made for publication thru some other channels the graduate library schools might well address themselves to the possibility of providing opportunity for the publication of the work of students, staff members, and of researches from the field.[12]

Thus Works had articulated his threefold objectives for the new Graduate Library School at the University of Chicago: cooperative research endeavor; research on the part of faculty, students, and the profession; and publication of the results of investigations. A fourth objective will be mentioned in the next section.

FACULTY

Following the Laing Committee's report on the library school, which based its recommendations in part on the BEL standards concerning staff, Works projected an instructional staff which was "relatively small—four or five full-time members—but supplemented by visiting lecturers."[13] The actual choice of faculty members stemmed in part from Works's conception of "the opportunities for research in the field of librarianship."[14] From his discussions with library leaders and his own study, Works presented a few of the potential areas in his program of research:

> The rapid growth of interest in adult education has brought a new crop of problems. The plans of the Committee [of ALA and AAAE] to study the development of habits of reading is illustrative of one type of study in this field. . . . The revival of interests in libraries that has resulted from changed methods of school instruction has brought to the surface much evidence that we are but illy equipped to deal with many of the questions in a fundamental manner. Problems of method, and questions relating to the adaptability of library materials need much more critical evaluations than they have received. Much remains to be done in the determination of the principles of classification and cataloging of such special materials as manuscripts, music, prints, and maps. The increase during recent years in this type of material in libraries emphasizes the urgency of work on this phase. The historical side offers large opportunity for researches in the development of printing and in the growth and influence of libraries. The administrative and financial problems of the public library appear in a variety of forms. Their consideration carries the student into municipal administration, taxation, and statistics.[15]

Works set out to bring together a group of scholars prepared by interest, experience, and methodological skill to investigate actively in these several research areas. Undoubtedly, a major source of suggestions for faculty members was the contacts he had developed during visits to institutions for his *College and University Library Problems.*

Perhaps at W. W. Bishop's suggestion, Works approached William M. Randall[16] of the Hartford (Conn.) Theological Seminary on 30 November 1927, offering him an associate professorship of bibliography, classification, and cataloging, specializing in Orientalia,[17] though J. C. M. Hanson would be the full professor in this area. Randall had worked with W. W. Bishop, first as a part-time student assistant in 1919 and then as a senior classifier from 1923 to 1925 in the University of Michigan's General Library. Although lacking formal library

William Randall

school training, Randall was extraordinarily gifted in languages. In fact, Bishop considered him one of his most brilliant students.

In 1925 Randall had joined the Kennedy School of Missions in Hartford as an instructor in linguistics;[18] and in 1927 he had the opportunity to work on the Garrett collection of manuscripts in the Foundation Library, developing a classification scheme. While there, he became interested in Malay and Turkish. He was already fluent in French and Russian; his knowledge of Italian, however, very nearly kept Randall from joining the GLS at Chicago. W. W. Bishop, as head of the American commission of librarians, charged with cataloging the Vatican Library under the sponsorship of the Carnegie Endowment for International Peace, wanted Randall to assist in cataloging, classifying, and arranging "an infinite amount of material" there during 1928/29.[19] Randall accepted and, consequently, did not join the GLS until the autumn quarter of 1929.

Gilbert H. Doane, then of the University of Nebraska, questioned Randall's qualifications, pointing out his lack of library school training and observing that he was "a bit difficult to get along with until one understands the peculiarities of his temperament."[20] Fortunately, Works asked Bishop's opinion of Doane's allegation and Bishop replied that he "would not pay any attention whatever to it."[21] Works followed Bishop's advice and thus was able to obtain the services of a young but brilliant individual in the field of classification to complement Hanson's competencies.

Evidently, Dean Works had already turned to J. C. M. Hanson,[22] associate director of the University of Chicago Library, to solve the urgent problems of cataloging. Hanson's status as "Dean of American cataloging" (commented on elsewhere)[23] was undoubtedly due to his role in the preparation of the Anglo-American Cataloging Rules of 1908, developed during his stint at the Library of Congress as chief of cataloging. Conveniently, Hanson's appointment allowed the incoming librarian, M. L. Raney of Johns Hopkins, to appoint his own associate director.

Another area in need of research, according to Works, was adult education and the reading habits of American adults. He did not have to look far to discover several excellent individuals in that area—the College of Education was just across the way. When W. W. Charters had moved from Pittsburgh to the University of Chicago's College of Education in 1925, he had brought with him a young scholar, Douglas Waples, to "teach some courses" and to assist in their studies.[24] Dean W. S. Gray, who agreed to the arrangement, found Waples "some courses" to teach.[25]

Douglas Waples

Waples[26] had grown up in Radnor, Pennsylvania, and attended nearby Haverford College. Finishing "about second in the class" of 1914 was good enough for Phi Beta Kappa, and he has said of this period that he had "won some literary prizes, [and] did about as well in sports as I had in school. I won the all-around in inter-collegiate gymnastics and a bid to the 1914 Olympics which were never held."[27] Shortly thereafter he had earned an M.A. from Haverford, on the basis of a paper about Ruskin and Arnold, and in September 1917 he was also awarded an M.A. from Harvard. Following service abroad, he entered the University of Pennsylvania to study for a Ph.D., which he received in June 1920.[28] Before joining W. W. Charters at the University of Pittsburgh, Waples had served as an assistant professor in the Education Department of Tufts College (now Tufts University), near Boston. He supplemented his income by teaching during the summers at the University of North Carolina and at Chautauqua, New York. His time at Pittsburgh was no less busy, for he tried "to run three jobs at once: Assistant Dean of the Graduate School, Assistant Professor of Secondary Education and extension lecturer in the surrounding steel mill towns; and assistant to W. W. Charters."[29]

On 9 February 1928, as a consequence of working with W. W. Charters and on the basis of Works' knowledge of Waples' researches,[30] the board of trustees transferred Waples "from the College of Education and promoted [him] to a professorship of Educational Method in the Graduate Library School, from October 1, 1928, at a salary of $5,000 per year."[31] To some people, Waples' appointment to the GLS also reflected the power of Charles Judd, then dean of the College of Education. Reminiscing fifty years later, Raney's associate director of the university library, A. F. Kuhlman, imputed Judd's motives as "here's an opportunity for me to put one of my men on the faculty of the University of Chicago [GLS] whose compensation will not come out of my budget—just like that."[32]

To work in another area for research in librarianship, Works chose Pierce Butler[33] of the Newberry Library for the position of part-time lecturer in the GLS. Of course, Works had in mind "the large opportunity for researches in the development of printing and in the growth and influence of libraries."[34] Butler was already active in that field, having published a *Check List of Books Published in the Fifteenth Century* (rev. ed.; Chicago: Newberry Library, 1924). Butler, who had been left quite deaf by a childhood bout with scarlet fever, lacked formal library school training, but he was trained as a scholar and bookman. Having received an A.B. and A.M. from Dickinson College in 1906 and 1910 respectively, Butler taught mathematics for a year and then entered Hartford Theological Seminary, where he received a B.D. and Ph.D.[35] in 1910 and 1912 respectively.[36] Butler worked with the Burlington Railroad as an office assistant for a few years before, in a chance conversation, William N. C. Carlton[37] asked him to join the Newberry Library. He progressed rapidly from a reference assistant to head of the order department, and also served as a bibliographer, heading the library's John M. Wing Foundation of Typography until his appointment in the Chicago GLS was made full time in 1931. A lesser known aspect of Butler's life is the fact that he had been a deacon for more than a half-dozen years in the Protestant Episcopal Church, so that Works's "spirit of inquiry" would have fallen on sympathetic ears if Butler recalled St. John's admonition: "Do not trust any and every spirit, my friends; test the spirits, to see whether they are from God, for among those who have gone out into the world

Pierce Butler

there are many prophets falsely inspired."[38] Butler would test students' "spirit of inquiry" in the GLS for the next thirty years.

One of the most interesting appointments was Harriet E. Howe[39] as associate professor. As the only "professional" librarian, her appointment was viewed by more than one individual as a "peace offering to the ALA."[40] Her appointment, however, reflected one of the unarticulated objectives of Dean Works, or more properly one of

Harriet E. Howe

the givens of the GLS mission: to train students to be instructors in library science. When Works approached her, she was the executive assistant to the Board of Education for Librarianship; and she had been responsible for preparing the list of theses which Louis R. Wilson had submitted to the University of Chicago in 1926. Even prior to her experience with the BEL, she had had extensive involvement with library education. Most distinctively, she was the only faculty member with a library school degree, having taken a BLS from the University of Illinois in 1902. At Illinois,

> she immediately came under the influence of Katharine Lucinda Sharp [discussed in chapter 1] who did much to encourage and develop the characteristics that mark Harriet Howe's personality and leadership qualities. Her biographical sketch of Katherine Sharp, published in Emily Danton's *Pioneering Leaders in Librarianship*, cites Sharp's professional knowledge, forcefulness, critical facilities, and management aptitude—these are also key facets of Harriet Howe's successful career.[41]

She had taught at Illinois from 1904 to 1906 as an instructor. She was at the University of Wisconsin during the summers of 1905 and 1906, and at the State University of Iowa Summer School for Library Training in 1907, 1908, and 1909. After working in a public library, she returned to library education at Western Reserve University as an assistant professor from 1913 to 1917. Before joining the BEL, she had served as an associate professor at Simmons College in Boston. At the BEL, Harriet Howe was undoubtedly overshadowed by another woman, Sarah Bogle; nevertheless, Howe frequently ran the day-to-day operations of the board when Bogle was out of town in the discharge of her duties as the board's secretary.

Following the establishment of the Board of Education for Librarianship, the BEL recommended that a summer institute be established which would offer "opportunities for study under the direction of educational authorities and for research in the subjects of major interest to the individual student."[42] The Carnegie Corporation underwrote the cost, and the first institute was held at the University of Chicago in 1926 under the direction of Sydney B. Mitchell. Officers of instruction included W. W. Charters, William F. Russell, and Giles Ruch. The following summer, Ernest J. Reece of Columbia University was the director, and Works had the opportunity of meeting him and discussing library education. This time the three courses were offered with credit by the School of Education's Special Methods Department. Reece taught 301A, "Problems in Education for Librarianship"; Freeman taught 302A, "Principles for Educational Psychology Applied to

Education for Librarianship"; and Charters taught 303A, "Problems in Teaching Library Science."[43]

A third institute was held during the summer of 1928 and this time Works directed the institute, supported by Charters; Freeman; Evangeline Colburn, a Laboratory School grade teacher; Hanna Logasa, librarian of the University of Chicago High School; and Harriet Howe. After that, the new Graduate Library School conducted the institutes with the presence of Miss Howe, who by then had earned her M.Ed. from Harvard, perhaps upon the encouragement of her new dean.

Besides these regular officers of instruction, Works intended to have a supplemental group of visiting lecturers. Perhaps Works anticipated critics' charges that the faculty was pursuing too esoteric concerns to be of use in the so-called real world. To strengthen the program, therefore, Works planned to bring

> to the school for periods of from six to twelve weeks several leaders from different types of library service. These persons, who will have to their credit records of marked accomplishments in their fields of endeavor, will hold conferences with students and staff. This device will be a means of keeping both staff and student body in intimate touch with developments in the library world.[44]

Representing the different types of libraries were J. Christian Bay, librarian of the John Crerar Library; Theodore Koch, director of the Northwestern University Library; Carl B. Roden, director of the Chicago Public Library; George B. Utley, head of the Newberry Library; and Carl H. Milam, ALA's executive secretary. These librarians were joined by Chicago Education Department faculty members W. W. Charters and Frank M. Freeman. In these conferences, one might have heard Bay hold forth on medical bibliography or local history, or pursue his ideas on the role of science in the training of librarians.[45] Koch might have been consulted on his scholarly interests in Romance languages, especially Dante's works, or his ideas of university library administration, or trends in the foreign book trade. Perhaps the lecturer who followed the development of the Chicago GLS with the greatest interest was Roden, who had been instrumental in its establishment through his work with the Chicago Library Club. He might have been approached by students about his recent term as ALA president. Utley, who like the others had been involved in many significant professional activities, might have been conferred with on his role as ALA's executive secretary (before Milam). Finally, Milam could have been consulted about relationships with philanthropic organizations, ALA's reading courses, or the necessity of county library service.

There is little doubt that Dean Works had a choice opportunity at Chicago: to hand-pick the first faculty, thus making a *de novo* response to the problems in education for librarianship, as he perceived them.

STUDENTS

Early in November 1927, Dean Works informed "library and university executives" that

> the student body at the new graduate school will be carefully selected . . . there may be no more than fifteen students in the school at the end of five years. It is possible that in the early years at least all the student body will be persons on fellowships who have been selected because they can make some contribution to the program of work that the school has laid out.[46]

The program, or opportunities for research, had already been addressed; selecting the student body was another concern. One of the major purposes of the GLS was to meet the profession's need for a significant number of individuals who had not only library work experience but "breadth of scholarship." Thus Works was faced with his second major problem, "the selection of a student body."[47] In a letter to Keppel, dated 23 December 1927, Works asked for $12,000 to $15,000 over eight years for fellowships. Works reasoned:

> The school will have students but under present conditions it will have to make its choice from such candidates as present themselves. Experience shows that whenever a new enterprise, like this School, is established, many who seek to participate are those who have not entirely succeeded with what they are doing. For this reason it would be a distinct advantage to the School if during the first five to ten years of its existence it had eight or ten fellowships of $1500 each.[48]

In this way, GLS could approach individuals in the profession on a selective basis and offer them the chance to study at the new school. Ideally, these individuals would already have demonstrated scholarly promise and qualities which would reward the profession if they continued their studies in library science. This selection would benefit not only the school but the profession as well, since these individuals would return to the field upon completion of their studies and further stimulate their colleagues, if "wise selections were made."[49]

President Mason discussed the scholarships with Keppel at the corporation on 28 February 1928. Mason wanted to use a portion of the interest on the endowment for these scholarships, which was satisfactory with President Keppel. Mason also informed Keppel at this meeting that "he [Mason] wouldn't be a college president much longer. Said he thought the conditions at Chicago were ideal, but that he'd broken down too often."[50]

Clearly, Works did not envision admitting elementary students. "The admission requirements have been provisionally stated as college graduation with a minimum of one year of library school training and one year of experience."[51] The object of requiring one year of experience was to ensure that the students had "reached decisions regarding the particular phase of librarianship in which they desire to specialize."[52]

> As previously stated, the standards are also provisional. Provisional in the sense that the failure to possess all of them will not be a bar to entrance if there is ample evidence that the applicant is qualified to make a scientific contribution to the profession. I hope that the school may go even further and search the profession for promising individuals regardless of whether or not they have the specific requirements suggested. There is greater need of finding, conserving, and stimulating research interests and abilities than there is for securing a high degree of conformity to formal requirements.[53]

Unfortunately, the reality of the situation did not meet Works's expectations. In the early summer of 1928, before the opening of the school in October, Bogle wrote to Milam that

> Dr. Works is disappointed in the number and quality of the applicants for admission to his school. Miss Susan Akers and Miss Winslow are the leaders accepted thus far. The paucity of men also disturbs Dr. Works.[54]

Susan G. Akers was "discovered," so to speak, on Chicago's doorstep. She had been in Charters' class during the summer of 1927, coming down from the University of Wisconsin, where she was an assistant professor in the library school. She had studied library science in the same school in 1913. Her early library experience had been in the New York Public Library during the summer of 1917, and she had been a cataloger in the University of North Dakota Library from 1920 to 1922. Akers had already begun contributing to the literature of the profession by publishing *Simple Library Cataloging* (Chicago: ALA, 1927).

Another student, Amy Winslow, would have been made known to the GLS through a book she had coauthored with Charles E. Rush, *Modern Aladdins and Their Magic: The Science of Things Around Us* (Boston: Little, Brown, 1926). Before she became head of the technical department at the Indianapolis Public Library (where she had been since 1919), she had worked in a branch of the Carnegie Library in

Pittsburgh, and earlier she had served at Iowa State College as a reference librarian. She had taken her BLS in 1916 from the New York State Library School.

Joining these women was Eleanor Upton, a Sterling Research Fellow at Yale. Upton had earned her A.B. degree from Smith in 1909 and an A.M. degree from Brown in 1910. Having worked as a social worker and a private tutor, she became a secretary and cataloger in 1916 at the John Carter Brown Library in Providence. In 1921, Upton joined the Yale University Library as its senior cataloger. For her work at Chicago, Upton was to be awarded the first doctorate in library science in 1930.

Also among the students in 1928/29 was Margaret Crompton Taylor. She obtained her B.S.L.S. degree from the University of Washington, where she had been influenced by the school's director, William E. Henry. Before entering GLS, Taylor had had four years of professional experience as the head of circulation at the Vancouver (B.C.) Public Library; her last year there, she was the assistant librarian.

Apparently no male students attended the GLS during the academic year beginning in 1928, but Sarah Bogle had an explanation for Works's disappointment in this matter. First, she thought "not enough [information] has been released about the School";[55] indeed, only a two-page memorandum, "The Graduate Library School of the University of Chicago," had been circulated to library leaders in March.[56] Otherwise, interested individuals had to rely upon the professional literature or word of mouth; the official *Announcements* did not appear until 20 June 1928.[57] Bogle's second explanation was that "the faculty as far as known does not 'pull.' "[58] Objectively, she was probably right on this count; each member of the faculty was a specialist in a rather narrow area. Butler, Howe, and Hanson were from the Chicago area, and were respected by knowledgeable individuals, but she offered no explanation for the paucity of men.

CURRICULUM

Works had alluded to a major problem facing him when he wrote President Keppel in December 1927 about the importance of fellowships: "the organization of the instructional work."[59] Apparently Works had nearly solved it during the Christmas break, for in January he informed his colleagues at the university that

> the instructional duties of both these groups [full-time and special lecturers] will be concerned primarily with helping students in problems they are investigating. There will be few if any courses offered in the school. At least that is the present plan.[60]

Instead of formal course work, the GLS planned to build the curriculum around the student's "previous experience and preparation and the phase of librarianship toward which he is looking."[61] Furthermore, "the opportunities of the students will not be limited to the offerings of the Graduate Library School."[62] Works envisioned a strongly interdisciplinary program, for, as he saw it, "the materials and methods necessary for the solution of problems in the field of librarianship refuse to be confined by the artificial boundaries of schools and colleges."[63] One of the primary advantages of being associated with a university was exactly this kind of access to those materials and methods. The GLS was assured of complete autonomy as a graduate school, but Works expected close coordination with other departments.

When the school opened in October 1928, there were only three courses. Students could select Douglas Waples' 310, "Methods of Investigation"; Pierce Butler's 330, "Origin and Development of the Printed Book"; or Harriet Howe's 350, "Organization and Methods of Teaching Library Science."[64] One other course, 410, offered "individual research" in eleven areas: administration, typographic history, bibliography and bibliographic method, cataloging, classification, children's literature, use of the library, social community, adult education, types of educational service, and education for librarianship.[65] It cannot be overemphasized that the school did not intend to duplicate the typical curriculum of other library schools. For example, Dean Works, writing to Bishop, stated

> I do not believe this school of ours should put a person on the staff primarily for the purpose of teaching what is now generally accepted in cataloging and classification. We expect our students to have this equipment before they come. This school [it] seems to me should devote its energies to those phases in which there are opportunities for research.[66]

Works was well aware that such a program was not without difficulties for students. He said:

> In most departments of graduate work when the time comes for selecting a dissertation subject, a considerable proportion of the students have not decided on the specific problem they wish to follow thru. In general, decisions they have made do not carry them beyond the determination of the general aspects of the subject.[67]

As a matter of fact, that was one reason why Works suggested the program of cooperative research (mentioned in the section on objectives); it provided a framework within which the student could work. On the other hand, Works wanted to avoid too much emphasis on the dissertation. He granted that one of the school's objectives was to extend the boundaries of knowledge in the field of librarianship, [but] it should not be expected that all the studies would serve this end, [although] certainly a fair proportion of them should.[68]

He then quoted G. Stanley Hall's comment about the proportion of dissertations he had supervised which had little value and the other quarter, which became the basis for the "subsequent life work of the candidates"[69] (see chapter 1).

The discussion thus far, Works felt, should *not* be interpreted to mean that

> the value of the dissertation is to be measured alone, or even primarily, by the contribution made to the advancement of knowledge. It should be evidence that the writer has caught the spirit of inquiry and has learned how to search for truth in some department of knowledge. It should be testimony to the effect that he has learned the meaning of research and that he gives promise of continuing to add to knowledge in his chosen field of endeavor. . . .
>
> If our graduate library schools can turn more or less of their attention to the development of students who have this attitude toward the profession there can be but little doubt that over a period of 25 years there will be a large development of research in this field.[70]

Unfortunately, this vision of the future was to be overcast by a shadow of doubt.

External Criticisms

After twenty-one months as Dean of the Graduate Library School, George Works was offered the presidency of Connecticut Agricultural College, to begin July 1929. In early April, Gordon Laing met with Works, and although Laing determined that Works was likely to go, he thought there was a chance to hold him with an increase of $1,000 per annum. Writing to Frederick Woodward, acting president of the university, he mentioned that Works's "family doesn't like the city and his flat rent is very high."[71] Two days later, Woodward scheduled an appointment with Dean Works to discuss these matters. That evening, Dean Works gave a presentation, "The Graduate Library School of the University of Chicago," to the Chicago Library Club,[72] but no mention was made of his impending resignation. The *Detroit Free Press*, however, had already carried an AP wire datelined "Hartford, April 10 "about his appointment.[73]

Milam and Bogle had been critical of the Graduate Library School since the school opened in the autumn quarter of 1928. Both of them wrote Harrison Craver, chairman of the BEL, in December 1929 that

the school was a "failure"; that it was not functioning "as we expected
it to do when the Board voted on the University of Chicago as the appropriate recipient of the Carnegie grant."[74] They argued that something had to be done because all that money was not being used properly. They further stressed that "part of the student body is definitely
mediocre."[75] This echoed George Works's dissatisfaction with the
first group of students.

In his talk to the library club, Works pointed out that far too little
time had elapsed for any genuine assessment of the GLS program.
Even

> when there is a wealth of material to be drawn upon as a result of
> the experience of institutions doing a similar work, several years are
> commonly regarded as necessary for a school to establish itself. What
> shall we say when there are no similar institutions that have accumu-
> lated a body of knowledge to guide the new enterprise? Manifestly,
> under these conditions, the time that has to elapse is much greater.[76]

He ventured that only "things hoped for" could be presented that
evening, then alluded to one of the reasons for his resignation:

> It is desirable for the profession to suspend judgment as to the value
> of the school. You can not have an adequate basis for final conclu-
> sions short of ten years and perhaps even that may prove too brief a
> period.[77]

Indeed, he had earlier stated that if the advanced schools turned their
attention to students who possessed the spirit of inquiry "*over a period
of 25 years* there will be a large development of research in this field"[78]
(emphasis added).

Part of the difficulty centered around the concept of graduate work
and, consequently, the concept of research. As Works pointed out,

> The character of the school was defined, in a measure at least, when
> it was made a graduate school of the University of Chicago. The Board
> of Education for Librarianship has applied the term "graduate school"
> to any library school requiring college graduation on the part of those
> seeking admission. From a certain viewpoint, this is undoubtedly a
> legitimate use of the term. *It is, however, a connotation different from
> that which the word commonly has in university circles.* Graduate
> work means research, and research means the extension of the boun-
> daries of knowledge [emphasis added].[79]

He pointed out that the BEL conceived a graduate school as "primarily concerned with passing on to their students a body of principles
and practices that have been found useful in the conduct of libraries."[80]
Although Works did not say it, this policy was a continuation of the

raw empiricism or utilitarianism of Melvil Dewey's time. Chicago authorities "were not interested in the establishment of a school of that type." Their objective was a research school, dedicated to extension of the boundaries of knowledge in librarianship. Thus the Chicago GLS was undertaking a pioneering effort which Works felt was little appreciated by the profession. Also appearing with him were four students who read papers on cataloging, adult education, and the history of typography, which were intended to extend the boundaries of knowledge in these areas.

Another part of the problem lay with the American Library Association's general headquarters staff. As discussed earlier, the ALA played an ancillary role in determining the location of the graduate library school; however, ALA's headquarters perceived itself as playing a much larger role and, thus, assumed a proprietary interest in what was happening. Basically, it seems the ALA wanted immediate practical results, as evidenced in students' theses. Works tried to make it clear that short-term satisfaction of that desire was unlikely. Undoubtedly, the first two M.A. theses were a disappointment; the first was "A Study of Data Pertinent to the Advising of Adult Readers" and the other, two months later, was "A Technique of Describing the Reading Interests of Adults."[81] Obviously, these topics were not in the mainstream tradition of librarianship (as discussed in chapter 1).

Works tried to counter this point in his speech before the CLC by discussing the service studies, but he did not characterize them as "research in its restricted meaning."[82] He mentioned a new study, being mounted in the GLS, of library standards for the North Central Association of Colleges and Secondary Schools and how it would open the way for further studies "in different types of institutions as to the appropriateness of the preliminary lists for different student bodies."[83] Again, Works stressed the lack of prescribed courses for the student.

Quoting the opinion of C. E. Seashore of the University of Iowa, that "there is no justifiable demand for fixed curriculum or the building of high fences about intensive professional interests,"[84] Works was envisioning a highly interdisciplinary course of study. He chose Eleanor Upton (although he did not name her) as an example. Here was an incoming student who had "a master's degree with a major in social science, and has done some graduate work in history." She had worked in cataloging and classification, and her career goal was to work in a library with a large number of research workers.[85] Thus her course work

> should be made from the offerings in the field of history on the side of historiography and historical criticism. As time passes, she decides

to take as the subject of her dissertation: "A Guide to Seventeenth Century Materials in the Reports of the Historical Manuscripts Commission of Great Britain to date." At once this indicates some special consideration should be given the period of English history involved in the study. On the side of library science, her work has been largely in the field of classification.[86]

To generalize this statement, the related subjects may be chosen according to the following criteria:

1) Will they contribute to the professional equipment of the student for the phase of librarianship in which he has decided to specialize? As a corollary to this criterion, the student has a more specific guide in the selection of work as soon as the specific problem for investigation has been determined.
2) The previous preparation of the student both on the side of study and experience.[87]

Yet Works persisted in his idea of research. His closing remark was a quotation from C. C. Nutting which he had first used in his address to the College and Reference Section in 1927:

The true research worker is of the calibre of the pioneer, and he feels the same lure, the same fascination, that impels him to advance the frontier of knowledge in any direction which may be open to him on earth, in the heavens, or in the depths of the sea. He is seeking neither fame nor fortune, but his aim is always to penetrate a little farther into the unknown than have his forebears or companions; to advance the frontiers of knowledge, if ever so little.[88]

In the dean's mind, the unrealistic expectations of ALA, perhaps desiring only a high-level training school and not a research school, left him little choice. The most poignant observation on the dean's resignation came from Gordon Laing; as he put it, "The officials of the A.L.A. objected to Works and made things rather disagreeable for him because he was not a member of the craft."[89]

The New Search

Douglas Waples tried to persuade Works that he should stay on, using arguments supplied by W. W. Charters, who was by that time at Ohio State University. In a letter to Charters, Waples repeated Works's personal reasons for leaving and stated that "his going is a real grief."[90] James Westfall Thompson, an original member of the U.C. Committee on the Library School, lamented Works's resignation, if only because of the "long search for a director, [and] the school is yet in an experimental stage." However, he too observed that "the open and concealed opposition of the American Library Association is a factor constantly requiring tact and alertness."[91] He recommended that Walter Lichtenstein, "the finest Jew" he knew, be considered. Lichtenstein was then the executive secretary of the First National Bank of Chicago, having been forced to resign from Northwestern University, where he had served as librarian. Charters wrote to Works and asked if he had thought about Waples for the deanship; after all, Waples was a "good researcher" with a "fine personality," if "somewhat immature."[92] More importantly, Charters said, "I know Milam likes him."[93] In fact, Works was "strong for Waples," and Acting President Woodward had sought Works's counsel on his successor.[94]

Waples continued to consult W. W. Charters. In late April, when Waples concluded that the faculty could not persuade Works to stay, he wrote to Charters, asking him to use his influence at Chicago:

> I hope that you will do whatever seems appropriate to prevent the administration from replacing him by a person who does not share his convictions regarding the scope and character of the work this School should undertake. There is no innuendo here. He has talked to me about taking the job a lot. I think I could handle it quite easily *inside* and would naturally rather do so than have some one else come in who couldn't. But I'm perfectly happy at what I'm doing now and would far rather have another Works who would have more weight *outside.* However there's practically no chance that the job will be offered me from present indications. You may be interested to know that Gray is Judd's candidate.[95]

Charters thanked him for the letter, stating that "Gray might do well at that," besides being satisfactory to librarians.[96] He concluded that Waples probably was not "sufficiently well-known and probably in the long run would be better off if [he] had all [his] time for research."[97] However, Waples disagreed on Charters' evaluation of Gray, and "no more does Works."[98] Essentially, Waples thought Gray would be detrimental to the research program of the school. Clearly, Waples wanted the job, rather "than be the victim of the administration we'd be likely to get from any A.L.A. nominee. I hope we get [Samuel P.] Capen,"[99] chancellor of the University of Buffalo. Before anyone could press their case for their favorite candidate, the University of Chicago announced the appointment of the new president, Robert Maynard Hutchins, dean of the Yale Law School and barely thirty years old. Works had already expressed his doubts about the effect of the new president on the selection of his successor; so the ALA took a different tack.

Sarah Bogle wrote to Keppel. She wanted Hutchins to appoint a faculty committee who would not insist that the next dean have a doctorate, because the "best men in library work do not have doctors' degrees."[100] She and Milam named Learned, Ferguson, Compton, Strohm, Brigham, Wheeler, and Joeckel for consideration or reconsideration. In her opinion, Joeckel was an "excellent possibility."[101] Also, as part of their campaign, Carl Milam wrote Hutchins, congratulating him on the presidency but informing him that ALA had a "very special interest" in the Chicago GLS, and he assured him it would help find a "successor to Dean Works."[102] In the meantime, Charters was pressing his case for Waples with Acting President Frederick Woodward.

In a meeting on 14 May, Keppel and Hutchins talked about the Chicago GLS. Keppel advised Hutchins to "go slow about Waples."[103] As a matter of fact, Keppel's "first choice would be Learned, second, Milam, third, Ferguson and fourth, Compton."[104] As far as Joeckel was concerned, Keppel did not know him, although he thought he was "promising."[105] Wyer and Hicks were also mentioned by Keppel and Hutchins respectively. On Chicago's campus, names continued to fly: Works suggested Joeckel and G. R. Lomer of McGill.[106] Waples reacted to the ALA's nominees by saying they were "so crazy that I believe the chances are about even for a complete collapse of our prospects for constructive work along the lines we have got under way."[107] He affirmed Works's suggestion of Lomer at McGill as "the best bet of any whom the public library group might be willing to approve."[108] Laing, writing to Stevens in the president's office, commented on Thompson's suggestion of Lichtenstein, on Van Hoesen, and on Lomer, but, as he said, "the essential thing is to get some one with ideas of research and yet who will be at the same time *persona grata* to the A.L.A."[109]

To assuage the ALA, Hutchins met with Milam and Bogle on 27 May. Milam and Bogle "agreed that there was no one outstanding librarian—that probably Dr. Learned was the best person outside the library field, and Mr. Ferguson inside the library field."[110] They attempted to persuade Hutchins that the "most able librarians didn't have degrees,"[111] and they left the meeting with the impression that Hutchins favored Learned and Ferguson. The next day Hutchins asked Keppel's opinion of Samuel P. Capen, evidently having talked with Dean Works and Douglas Waples. Telegramming Bogle, Keppel wanted to know her opinion of him,[112] and she responded:

> Milam and I think Capen knows even less than Works about libraries and does not seem to understand our objectives in education for librar-

ianship. Believe profession would feel same way and that he would
have one awful time making good.[113]

Keppel then turned to Hutchins, writing that he had sent Bogle a
telegram concerning Capen. Evidently, Keppel was concerned that
Hutchins was moving too quickly; "she and Milam may be wrong,
but I think it might be well before you come to a decision to sound
out some of the other leaders in the library profession."[114] Hutchins
underlined the portion of Keppel's letter which stated, "I don't know
whether you will forgive me for having done so, but . . . ," and wrote
"I won't."[115] Then, at the top of the letter, he wrote: "This guy Keppel
certainly *takes the cake*. I vote we pay no attention."[116] So, on 31
May, Woodward telegrammed Capen that Chicago wanted him for the
library school and the School of Education.[117] Keppel wrote Hutchins
thanking him for his letter of 31 May and stated: "Of course I fully
agree with you that the responsibility for the new appointment must
lie with the University and not with the A.L.A., who, I am sure, will
cooperate loyally in any decision which the University reaches."[118]
The same day, Capen declined.[119] On 1 July, Works took up his new
duties at Storrs, Connecticut. J. C. M. Hanson was appointed acting
dean.

The question of why George Works resigned remained unanswered
for the majority of the library profession; so Mary E. Ahern, editor of
Libraries, pursued the question for her readers. Following the "shock
of surprise," her reflection on Works's "public addresses and personal
conversation with him" led her to the conclusion that it was incon-
sistent.[120] Thus she put the question to him directly in a letter of 11
June, and this letter and his response were published in the July issue
of *Libraries*.[121] Works began by discussing the conditions surrounding the school, its students, the fortuitous location of the school at
the university, and the administrative and instructional staff. All of

these conditions augur well for the future of the School. There are,
however, some factors outside the University not so favorable in character that should be borne in mind by those who are interested in the
contribution that the School may make to the profession. There was
evidence of impatience for results on the part of some even before the
first year's work was completed. Large returns should not be expected
at once. More important, however, is the fact that the School should
not be dominated by any particular library interest as the historical,
administrative, etc. A perspective should be maintained in its program
of work. Its scope should be as broad as the profession. Even a greater
danger is that the School should come to be regarded as an adjunct of
an association or organization. For any such interests to dictate the

policies of the School would be disastrous. The School can stand only for truth as fully and freely reached as is practicable with the resources at its command. It had been placed at the University of Chicago and that institution should be free to develop it in accord with its ideals of research and the needs of the profession as a whole. Those who believe in the future of librarianship as a scholarly profession should adhere to the position that it is not to be regarded as an adjunct to any group in the profession or to any organization of the profession. Under these conditions and these only can the School render the largest possible service to the profession and to the world of scholarship and service.[122]

This extensive statement makes it quite clear that George Works considered the American Library Association, especially its staff, to be meddling in something which was not their business.

4

The Interregnum, 1929–32

In the next three years following Dean Works's resignation, four different individuals served on eight occasions as acting dean (see Appendix D). Nevertheless, the school continued on the course set by its first dean. Speaking on behalf of George Works at the 51st Annual Conference of ALA, held in Washington, D.C., in mid-May 1929, Douglas Waples discussed "the projects reported by four members of the staff as representing the character of the work undertaken by their students."[1] He grouped the first year's activities into seven areas: methods of research, bibliography, library patronage, school libraries, book selection, administration, and library school teaching. Most significantly, his reports continued to view the field of librarianship as interdisciplinary. For example, under "methods of research" Waples indicated that an attempt had been made "to define various implications of "library science" in terms of data and methods of investigation found in quantitative studies in other fields of problems corresponding to problems of librarianship."[2] The school was self-consciously attempting to apply a scientific method in its approach to solving library problems.

The Revolving Deanship

OBJECTIVES AND FACULTY

Waples returned to this self-conscious statement about a "library science" in more detail when he was invited to address a conference of the Association of American Library Schools in December 1929.[3]

71

His address evinced the influence of John Dewey's *The Sources of a Science of Education* (New York: Liveright, 1929), as he paraphrased it extensively in the section "What Is a Library Science?" This section was of premier importance since it helped, in Waples' opinion, to establish the school's "developing concept of its task."[4] Waples confessed that the section was "colored no doubt by the writer's individual views . . . [but it] is believed to approximate a consensus of faculty opinion" nevertheless.[5] He began by stating that, in the faculty's judgment, librarianship was a human science, "primarily a social enterprise," which therefore subordinated library administration to the fulfillment of "human needs."[6] Yet the success of library science resided

> in the minds of those engaged in directing the work and policies of libraries. Results may be scientific whether they are actively present in the observation, judgment, and planning of librarians or not. But unless they are so present, they are not library science. They are bibliography, psychology, sociology, statistics, or something else.[7]

Waples continued by distinguishing the sources and the content of a library science:

> We are in constant danger of confusing the two; we tend to suppose that certain results, because they are scientific, are already library science. But a genuine library science can be developed only as we remember that such results are sources to be used through the medium of the minds of librarians, to make library functions more intelligent.[8]

Further paraphrasing Dewey's book, Waples demonstrated that he subscribed to the pragmatism of William James, which stated that the truth of a proposition is equivalent to what "works" or what is "useful." Consequently, the usefulness of the Graduate Library School's investigations should be measured by the degree to which they are used by the profession. Earlier, George Works had argued that twenty-five years might pass before one could say whether or not the scientific method as utilized in the GLS, or a library science, was secure. (Whether, in fact, the profession was interested in "scientific" librarianship is discussed in the next-to-last section of this chapter.) Waples concluded his address with four "cautions," which he elaborated upon:

1) do not discourage the collection of evidence on the ground that it handicaps the intuitive good sense of leaders in the profession,
2) beware of recipes,
3) do not be impatient for a science of librarianship, and

4) take careful note of the scope and limitation of each particular academic field which is expected to contribute to a library science.[9]

Joining the faculty in June of 1929 was William Randall, who was twenty-nine years old. Upon his return from Rome but prior to his arrival at Chicago, he successfully defended his Ph.D. dissertation in Muslim theology, philosophy, and Oriental paleography, graduating *summa cum laude;* he had studied under Duncan Black MacDonald.[10] At that time, Randall had thought he might undertake a revision of Brockelmann's *Geschichte der Arabischen Literatur,* although he had also proposed to Works that he might engage in studies of

1) bibliographical and biographical material of Northern Europe and Scandinavia for a biographical dictionary,
2) cataloging and classification of Near Eastern material, and
3) cataloging and classification of chemical material.[11]

Randall was satisfied with most of the details concerning his appointment at Chicago:

The work here is very interesting; but the lack of a Dean makes it difficult to know just where one stands. I have been here all too short a time to be able to judge as to whether it is the place for me or not. Mr. Hanson continues to take all the classes, leaving me no real duties and no responsibilities. And since he is more or less at variance with the rest of the faculty and with the late Dean as to just what is the academic policy of the school, it is very difficult to know just how far to follow him, and how far to follow the others.[12]

Writing fifty years later about his arrival at Chicago and his first meeting with Hanson, whom he had not seen since Rome, Randall related the following:

"Bill," he said, "I don't know why you came here to do research in cataloging and classification. There is not any to be done. The present systems are complete and perfect." That, of course, was the attitude of (almost) the entire library profession, who could see no possible need for the type of research organization Chicago was trying to establish.[13]

As it turned out, Randall was primarily involved in "detailed classification and cataloging of *special subjects*" (emphasis added).[14] In December 1929 he reported that he was undertaking or supervising research in twelve areas, but most of this work was in the area of cataloging and classification.[15]

One of these ongoing studies was Randall's work for the Carnegie Corporation's Advisory Group on College Libraries, surveying American academic libraries. Such consulting was encouraged by the university as "it advertised the University and enhanced its reputation."[16] Randall continued in this work from 1929 to 1931, during which time he visited more than two hundred liberal arts colleges, gaining firsthand information on the status and administration of these libraries.[17] The report of his study was published as *The College Library: A Descriptive Study of the Libraries in Four-Year Liberal Arts Colleges in the United States* (Chicago: ALA and University of Chicago Press, 1932). This study contributed to a decision by the Carnegie Corporation to grant more than $1 million to eighty-three institutions for undergraduate reading materials.[18] Randall also served as an acting dean of the GLS during the second summer term, 1930 (see Appendix D), and he was promoted to professor in 1931.

Howe's interests led her to teach at the American Library School in Paris during the summer of 1929. Back at the GLS, she supervised the research of such students as Susan Akers, Margie Helm, and Marion Helms, who were studying various aspects of training for librarianship. Her own research projects included the development of courses in young people's reading, school librarianship, and cataloging; definition of the professional needs of prospective students, with an end of defining problems and methods of investigation; and analysis of a trend, evident at that time, toward a functional division of the library as it related to library school courses. In 1931, however, Malcolm G. Wyer offered Howe the opportunity of organizing the University of Denver's School of Librarianship. As "she felt no sympathy with the purposes of GLS and was most unhappy there,"[19] she accepted, being appointed its director and a professor in the school. Her research in curriculum, nevertheless, led her to make "a complete break with the traditional arrangement of courses in other library schools by organizing what had been offered in various individual courses into three large units, i.e. Book Arts, Library Administration, and Cataloging and Classification."[20]

J. C. M. Hanson had also been in Rome during the winter of 1928, working with Randall on the recataloging of the Vatican Library. When he returned, Hanson, as chairman of the ALA Committee on International Catalogue Rules, recommended that the work already done be extended "by the preparation of a 'synoptic table to show variations between the Anglo-American and the Prussian rules, perhaps also other codes . . . possibly in connection with research under way at the Graduate Library School, University of Chicago.' "[21] This item also appeared in the list of eight research pieces Hanson mentioned in December 1929.[22] Edith Scott, Hanson's biographer, has pointed out that

J. C. M. Hanson

this research was being done in Hanson's seminar in advanced cataloging by Margrethe Brandt [a Carnegie Fellow], the daughter of one of his colleagues at Luther College [Iowa]. When Miss Brandt was prevented by her poor health from pursuing her original research topic, Hanson had assigned as a substitute a comparison of cataloging rules.[23]

Hanson was said to have "thoroughly enjoyed" his teaching at Chicago. Since he was "naturally of didactic inclinations, he found pleasure voicing his well-considered categories, checking their acceptance with the younger generation, and watching new developments."[24] However, Hanson was close to retirement age when he joined the GLS faculty in 1927/28, and on 13 March 1929 he was seventy years old. He had planned to retire as professor emeritus at the end of the 1930 academic year, but he stayed through the 1931 spring quarter teaching one course, advising on students' individual research, and assisting on the proposed *Journal of Library Science*.[25] After 1930, Hanson also served for a time as lecturer in the University of California's School of Librarianship at Berkeley, as well as the University of Michigan's Library School during the summers. He acted as a consultant to the Library of Congress in 1931.

The faculty member who served as acting dean for the longest period of time, a year and a half, was Douglas Waples. In several ways, he was the scientific researcher *par excellence*. He was particularly active in statistical studies of adult reading and school and college libraries, consulting or carrying out funded research with D. C. Heath, the YMCA, the Congressional Teacher Training Survey, and the American Association for Adult Education.[26] In addition, he supervised the largest number of students in the GLS, a group that included Leon Carnovsky, Mildred Harrington, Odella Nation, Martha Pritchard, Agatha L. Shea, Lucile R. Stebbing, Miriam D. Tompkins, John T. Windle, and Ruth Worden. During 1929 and 1930, Waples was too busy with research to serve as acting dean except during the summer terms. When Hanson retired, however, Waples decided it was better to be the dean himself than to have someone at the helm who was not interested in administration. Thus from fall 1930 until September 1931 (when he went abroad for research), he served again as acting dean.[27] (Waples' interest in being appointed the permanent dean is discussed in the last section of this chapter.) Perhaps Waples' most significant research publication during this period was *What People Want to Read About*, coauthored with Ralph W. Tyler and published in 1931 in cooperation with the American Library Association and the University of Chicago.[28]

The other member of the faculty during this period (to be discussed here) is Pierce Butler. His personal research was totally in the area of bibliography and history. Since October 1929, he had been preparing two bibliographies, one identifying sources relating to early American libraries and the other listing rarities in the Berlin Collection of the University of Chicago Library.[29] In 1930 he added the geography of early printing in New England to his ongoing research projects.[30] His students' research included Lester D. Condit's development of a technique to identify Roman types in early printed books, a study intended to supplement Konrad Haebler's work; Chih-pai Kuei's study of the variations of Chinese books from European bibliographical norms; and Eugene V. Prostov's early printing in Slavic countries. All of these projects resulted in doctoral dissertations. Most significantly, the GLS recognized the value of Butler's work by promoting him from lecturer to full professor in 1931.[31] That fall, Butler began serving as acting dean, a responsibility he held until March 1932, when Waples returned from abroad.

During the academic year 1929/30, two new faculty members joined the GLS as lecturers on a part-time basis. The first was James Westfall Thompson, a specialist in medieval history, who was lent to the GLS by the History Department. Thompson was one of the original members of the Laing Committee on the Library School and, consequently, had followed the GLS with considerable interest. Thompson and Butler shared a common idea, which Stanley Pargellis expressed as "the gospel of scholarship for librarians."[32] During his first year Thompson taught a four-course sequence of formal classes, 336 to 339, on Roman, early Christian, and medieval libraries, as well as great libraries and book collectors from 1300 to 1750. During the academic year 1930/31, he taught one course a quarter, again on great libraries and book collectors. The following year the sequence was collapsed into a single quarter's course, covering the sixteenth through the eighteenth century (see table 1).

The other new member of the faculty was Henry B. Van Hoesen, the associate librarian of Brown University in Providence, Rhode Island. In 1926, Louis R. Wilson had recommended him for a professorship, and the university had considered him for the deanship of the new school. His presence at the GLS may have been a period of observation by the university administration; his name was raised again for the deanship in 1931, and is discussed in the section on the next dean. Van Hoesen, a classics scholar, received his Ph.D. from Princeton in 1912;[33] his education was furthered by study at the American School of Classical Studies in Rome and the University of Munich. His major published works included *Roman Cursive Writing* (Princeton: Princeton University Press, 1915) and, with F. K. Walter, *Bibliography: Practical, Enumerative, and Historical* (New York: Scribner, 1928). The latter was undoubtedly the basis for his course, 335, on "Bibliography." Van Hoesen taught at the GLS for three years, returning to become the head librarian at Brown in 1930.

One additional faculty member was listed during the academic year 1931/32: James I. Wyer, who taught a course entitled "American

TABLE 1
Course Offerings, 1928/29–1932/33

Academic Year Beginning	Course Offerings													
	301	306	310	311	312	313	314	330	331	333	335	336	337	338
1928/29		W						B						
1929/30		W	W	W				B			V	T	T	T
1930/31		W	W	W	W	W		B			V		T	T
1931/32	B	W		W	W			B	B	JW	V			
1932/33	B	W		W	W	W		B	B					

LEGEND:
  W = Waples   B = Butler   HH = Howe   JH = Hanson   R = Randall

Course Offerings for Academic Years 1928/29 to 1932/33

301. Librarianship as a Field of Research
306. Problems of Adult Learning
310. Methods of Investigation
311. The Library and Education of Adults
312. School Library
313. Studies in Adult Reading
314. Methods of Book Distribution in Foreign Countries
330. Origin and Development of the Printed Book
     Introduction to Bibliographical History
331. Principles of Bibliography
333. Subject Bibliography
335. Bibliography
336. Roman, Early Christian, and Medieval Libraries
337. The Medieval Scriptorium & the Care of Books
     (500–1450 A.D.)
338. Great Libraries & Book Collectors of the Renaissance (1300–1550)
339. Great Libraries & Book Collectors of the Age of Erudition
     (1550–1750)
     Great Libraries & Book Collectors of the 16–18th Century
340. The History of Scholarship
342. The History of the Care of Books
350. Organization and Methods of Teaching Library Science
360. Classification
360-62. Classification
360-61. Classification
365-67. Cataloging and Preparation of Bibliographic Records
369. Special Problems in Cataloging Manuscript Material

Course Offerings

339	340	342	350	360	361	362	365	366	367	369	370	378	379	380	381	382
		HH														
T			HH	JH R	JH R	JH R	JH R	JH R	JH R							
T			HH	JH R	JH R		JH R	JH R	JH R							
T	B		HH								JW			R		
	B	T	W	JH							R		R	R	R	J LW

T = Thompson   V = Van Hoesen   JW = Wyer   LW = Wilson
J = Joeckel

370. American Government Documents
378-80. College Libraries
380. College Libraries
381. Government and Administration of Public Libraries
382. College and University Libraries

Course Offerings in 410, "Individual Research," for Academic Years 1928/29 to 1932/33

   a) Administration
   b) Typographic History
   c) Bibliography & Bibliographic Method
   d) Cataloging
   e) Classification
   f) Children's Literature
      Adult Education from 1929/30 on
   g) Use of the Library
      School Libraries & Children's Departments in Public Libraries 1929/30
      Content, Organization & Function of Children's Libraries from 1930/31 on
   h) Social Community
      Education for Librarianship from 1929/30 on
   i) Adult Education
      School Libraries from 1930/31 on
   j) Types of Educational Service
      Adult Reading from 1930/31 on
   k) Education for Librarianship

Government Documents." Like Van Hoesen, he too had been considered for the deanship in 1926. Having been director of the New York State Library School at Albany before its transfer to Columbia University, he had stayed in Albany as the director of the State Library, a position he had held since 1908. Perhaps one of the factors in his being chosen to lecture was his recently published *Reference Work* (Chicago: ALA, 1930); the text for his course, on the other hand, was most likely his own *U.S. Government Documents* (Chicago: ALA, 1922).

As William Randall pointed out fifty years later, there were only "three real jobs as a faculty: the acceptance of students, the dispensing of fellowships, and the recommendations for the conferring of degrees. We used to get together very informally and talk things over and come to (usually) unanimous decisions."[34] The rotation of the deanship, he added, "came about because none of us wanted the job permanently."[35]

A JOURNAL OF DISCUSSION

On the other hand, Randall *did* get another job permanently, although the events surrounding that appointment began before the establishment of the GLS. During the fiftieth anniversary conference of ALA in 1926, M. L. Raney, then of Johns Hopkins, proposed the following resolution:

> *Resolved,* That the A.L.A. *Bulletin* should be expanded into a complete journal of discussion, adequate under competent editorial direction to accommodate the major contributions from the profession and give its committee studies regular presentation.[36]

Raney argued that, as the American Library Association had recently begun to consider itself one of the scholarly or learned societies, it might profitably examine, and perhaps attempt to emulate, the publishing activities of such organizations.

Choosing fifteen related fields, Raney compared ALA publishing unfavorably with that of the National Education Association, the American Economic Association, the American Historical Association, the American Chemical Society, and the Archaeological Institute of America—among others. "On the other hand it is only the American Philological Association, the Association of Urban Universities, and the Geological Society that issue proceedings like ours."[37] His argument was compelling; the motion was supported by W. W. Bishop, and H. H. B. Meyer seconded it.[38] The resolution was passed with an amendment directing the executive board to act upon it.

The matter was referred to the editorial committee, headed by George B. Utley. Studying these learned societies' practices more closely, C. C. Williamson, on behalf of the committee, reported in 1928 that nearly all of them distinguished between news publications and scholarly journals. He further suggested that five hundred subscribers at $5 a year could be found for the proposed quarterly journal. Thus the committee rejected expansion of the *Bulletin*, recommending instead the appointment of an editorial board, selection of an editor, and commencement of publication as soon as possible.[39]

In February 1929, Williamson turned down the chairmanship of the editorial board for the journal;[40] in his place, J. C. M. Hanson of the Chicago GLS was appointed. Directing a meeting of the board in late December 1929, Hanson, along with Williamson, Phineas Windsor of Illinois, and Carleton Joeckel of Michigan, concurred that the faculty of the GLS would publish the journal on a quarterly basis.[41] Each issue would consist of ninety-six pages, or approximately 384 to 390 pages a year. At the Los Angeles conference of 1930, they reported that the "journal of investigation and discussion in the field of library science," entitled *The Library Quarterly*, would appear in January 1931.[42]

Hanson sought W. W. Bishop's opinion of William Randall as the editor or assistant editor. Bishop replied that Randall had enough experience to be the assistant editor, but hesitated "to place him in complete editorial charge at the beginning."[43]

With an eye toward financing such a journal, Acting President Woodward wrote President Keppel at the Carnegie Corporation that one thousand copies of sixty-nine (*sic*) pages would cost $7,150; which minus $2,500 income from subscriptions, left a deficit of $4,650.[44] Therefore, he queried, could the corporation provide $5,000 a year, beginning January 1931, and let Chicago know before the ALA Editorial Board meeting of 14 April? Checking with William S. Learned on behalf of Keppel, Robert M. Lester found him quite satisfied with the proposal, as it was "highly important." Furthermore,

> The library profession has long needed such a journal and, if kept on the level of a strictly scientific quarterly, it could serve a great purpose in strengthening the profession at many points. The probable outcome seems to me to be well worth the suggested appropriation.[45]

Keppel still wanted to interview Hanson personally concerning the journal; so on 31 March, they met. Hanson was "very strongly in favor of the library magazine,"[46] but he did not believe it could take on the English-language bibliographical record function which had been talked about earlier. He was certain "there would be no shortage in important material."[47] After the interview, Hanson provided Keppel with a six-point statement of the proposed journal's purpose:

1) To serve as an outlet for publications of the Graduate Library School in Chicago and, in part, also for more extended studies emanating from other library schools; so also contributors by librarians and bibliographers too extensive to be printed in Library Journal or Libraries.

2) To furnish a bond between the Graduate Library School at Chicago and the other library schools of the country, incidentally also the Library Association and other bibliographical organizations.

3) To afford the School a means of recruiting students and make known its plans and projects.

4) To present reviews of current publications in the fields of bibliography and library science.

5) To prepare and publish an annual bibliography of monographs and articles on bibliography and library science, and to make the same cumulative for five or ten year periods, perhaps in cooperation with some other agency, e.g. Library of Congress or H. W. Wilson Company.

6) To publish such studies as the "Annual Survey of Reference Books" by Miss Mudge, which the Library Journal is forced to discontinue because of the extent of the contribution.[48]

In the same letter, Hanson summarized circumstances—as he saw them—surrounding such matters as subscriptions, an advisory editorial board, and prospects for the editor in chief. Finally, he requested a subvention of $4,000 to $5,000 a year for the first three years. Keppel expressed his primary concern that Richard Bowker, the editor of *Library Journal*, be "given an opportunity to get on the bandwagon."[49] Hanson wrote Bowker of these plans, indicating that the new journal would attempt to avoid conflicts with existing journals, particularly by leaving "the public and popular library fields largely to existing periodicals"[50] and by turning its attention to foreign fields. Shortly thereafter, Woodward was informed that the Carnegie Corporation, under Resolution B753 of 23 April, had appropriated $25,000 "for support of a Journal of Library Science,"[51] payable at the rate of $5,000 annually for five years, beginning 1929/30.

William Randall was appointed the managing editor, the duties of which excused him from one class per quarter (see table 2 for impact). By June, Randall was writing to library leaders and requesting material; not surprisingly, he asked Keppel to write an article about the Graduate Library School.[52] The first issue carried that article, as well as C. C. Williamson's "The Place of Research in Library Service" and Douglas Waples' "The Graduate Library School at Chicago." It went to press in late October and was received by subscribers in January. Richard Bowker of *LJ* was openly critical:

The new *Library Quarterly* is to be congratulated on the fact that it has secured more than 800 subscriptions in advance of the publication of its initial issue. It must be said however that the first number, despite its creditable and inviting appearance, is rather disappointing, not in quality but in scope. The plans and announcements contemplated "A scholarly journal" of research which by reason of its endowment might give place to elaborate articles and research studies as well as book reviews for which the existing periodicals could not afford space. Most of the articles are such as would be welcome in any of the existing periodicals, the happy exceptions being the contributions by Ernest J. Reece on the service loads of library-school faculties and William M. Randall concerning what foreigners find to read in the public library, both research articles and generously interspersed with charts and tables. . . . With the new *Quarterly*, a scholarly periodical in appearance rather than in content, it becomes not a distinct contribution to professional literature, but practically just another library periodical of the common, ordinary or garden sort for many years in the field. It is hoped that later numbers will better fulfill the prepublication plans.[53]

Not all of Bowker's comments could be dismissed as sour grapes, but, unfortunately, the record is sparse concerning Hanson's, and Randall's ideas on the lack of "important material." Randall had other difficulties as well; besides working on the scope or character of the articles, he was developing a policy on book reviews and replies. Williamson had advised him to publish only critical reviews, challenging the underlying assumptions of books, answered at the same time the reviews appears, followed by one more round after that.[54] He enclosed with his letter a copy of *The Classical Weekly* of 21 December 1907, in which its editor, Gonzalez Lodge of Columbia University, stated that in his judgment "publication [the criticism and rejoinder] is a sign of life, and often a sign of healthy life."[55] Randall placed the matter on the agenda of the next editorial board meeting, which was held at the 1932 ALA convention.

This time the matter of book reviews was addressed by Louis R. Wilson. He thought there were "too many reviews by the same people" and "too many incompetent reviews."[56] His long experience of editing at the University of North Carolina, where he had directed the university press, was useful; his recommendation was to widen the field. The suggestion that critical reviews be answered by the author was adopted. In another matter, Williamson and Donald Bean, of the University of Chicago Press, thought that the new journal was placing too much emphasis on scientific method. Although not directed toward Waples in particular, a suggestion was made that *Library Quarterly* might stress the "practical applications of findings"[57] rather than method. Finally, more philosophical articles were said by some to be desirable, especially from library leaders, as well as articles dealing with the effects of the Depression on libraries and "methods of meeting conditions of reduced budgets."[58] The "stress at all times" was to be on

1) the social significance of the library rather than its internal mechanism
2) exploratory rather than descriptive articles.[59]

Interested librarians who attended the 1932 New Orleans convention received as a promotional item "The *LQ* Convention Notebook," which contained a "classified index of articles already published" by *Library Quarterly* through April of that year.[60] Of the thirty-three articles listed, more than half dealt with only three subjects: education for librarianship (24%); university, college and reference libraries (18%); and the history of libraries (12%). Readers were informed that "the LQ is the Only Research Journal in the Profession."

(Chapter 5, below, contains a more detailed analysis of types of articles published in *LQ*, as well as of their authors and the occupations of those authors, in light of the above decisions.)

STUDENTS AND CURRICULUM

Student life at the University of Chicago in the 1930s in many ways seems quite like student life today. For example, discussions of 4 percent beer abounded, cars were found in the mornings on Foster's steps, the value of football was debated, and *au courant* women were wearing the Betty Bob hairstyle. In a more serious vein, the 13 May riot of 1930 was memorialized for several years after it occurred.[61] GLS students seemed to be involved in many of these events. Yet the most important event to the life of the university was Robert M. Hutchins' inauguration in 1930. Susan Akers, perhaps because she was a member of the Graduate Council, representing graduate students to the dean and faculties, represented the Library School and "participated in the ceremonies"[62] of his taking office. Leon Carnovsky, another student who was active in campus concerns, worked hard for repeal of a ruling which required deposit with the university library of one hundred copies of all doctoral dissertations completed at the

University of Chicago.[63] His success led to the recommendation that these copies be purchased instead, and an action of such purchase was adopted by the faculty, passed, and noticed in the 1930 handbook. A tragic event during the interregnum period was the death of Margrethe Brandt, due to heart trouble, on 13 August 1931[64] (her work under J. C. M. Hanson has already been mentioned).

Carnegie Fellows who attended the GLS during this period included Susan G. Akers, Eleanor S. Upton, Miriam D. Tompkins, Margrethe Brandt, Helen Martin, and Errett W. McDiarmid. By August 1932, twelve degrees had been awarded: six masters and six doctorates. Of the Ph.D. graduates, Upton returned to her post as senior cataloger at Yale, Lester D. Condit became an assistant in the handling of incunabula at the Henry E. Huntington Library, Chih-pai Kuei apparently returned to China, Akers accepted an associate professorship in the University of North Carolina's School of Library Science, Carnovsky became an instructor in the GLS at Chicago, and Edwin Willoughby was appointed a professor of library science at the College of William and Mary.

As was mentioned earlier, the GLS had opened with three faculty members teaching three formal courses during 1928/29; Dean Works apparently spent his full time administering the program, and J. C. M. Hanson, when he was not in Rome, spent his time supervising research. The size of the faculty jumped significantly, to seven persons teaching sixteen courses in the following year. A slight reduction occurred in 1931/32, when thirteen courses were offered by eight faculty members (see table 2).

The teaching loads of individual faculty members are revealing. Waples began by offering "Methods of Investigation"; in the following year he added "Adult Learning" and "The Library and Education of Adults." His heaviest teaching load, however, was in 1930/31, when he offered five different courses. The results of his six-month trip to Europe during 1931/32 were formally shared the next year with his students in course 314, "Methods of Book Distribution in Foreign Countries."

Another faculty member whose research strongly influenced his teaching was Pierce Butler. Since 1929 Butler had been studying "the transformation and extension of specific bibliographic discriminants which have been worked out for incunabula, to the books of later periods."[65] His findings resulted in course 331, "Principles of Bibliography," beginning in the 1931/32 academic year. Similarly, his wide-ranging knowledge made him a logical choice to offer course 301,

TABLE 2
Reactions of Carnegie Fellows to the Graduate Library School at Chicago,
1929–32

	1929–30	1930–31	1931–32
	Carnovsky	Brandt	Carter
A	Very great	Very great	Valuable
B	4, 3, 1, 2	1, 4, 2, 3	4, 2, 1, 3
C	Great value	Great value	Great value
	Tompkins	Carnovsky	McDiarmid
A	Very great	Very great	Very great
B	4, 3, 2, 1	4, 3, 1, 2	1, 2, 4, 3
C	Great value	Great value	Great value
			Martin
A			Very great
B			1, 4, 3, 2
C			Great value

A = "The value of the work."
B = "Relative value of 1) courses in library science, 2) courses in other
    subjects, 3) thesis work, 4) contacts with other students or with pro-
    fessors outside of class."
C = "Guidance received during fellowship work."

Source: Report of the Carnegie Corp. Advisory Group on Library Fellow-
    ship Grants, 1929/32 (confidential).

"Librarianship as a Field of Research," the same year. The increase
in his teaching load the fourth year, though, is explained by his regu-
larized appointment as a professor at that time.

The second and third years, Hanson and Randall offered formal
courses in classification and cataloging of bibliographic records. These
were dropped in 1931/32 because of Hanson's retirement and Randall's duties as managing editor of *Library Quarterly*. Furthermore,
Randall's interests, following his involvement in 1929 with the Carnegie study, seemed to lie more with college libraries. He offered a
single course, 380, on that subject during the 1931/32 academic year.

Harriet Howe's formal teaching seems to have been limited to
course 350, "Organization and Methods of Teaching Library Science."
Apparently she was quite influential upon her students, since three of
the six doctoral students took teaching posts immediately upon graduation. Upon her acceptance of the directorship at Denver, Waples took
over her course.

Several students' evaluations of the program during the period between 1929 and 1932 have been preserved (see table 2). The majority felt that both the value of the work and the guidance received during their fellowship work had been very great. There was less agreement concerning the value of courses in library science and other subjects, the thesis work, and contacts with students and professors outside the classroom. However, most put the contact with colleagues and professors nearest the top, followed by the courses in library science. The thesis and courses in other subjects were nearly equal in value, both being near the bottom.

Faculty concern about the program seemed directed to two areas: elimination of the master's degree and accreditation of the school. The issue of accreditation by the Board of Education for Librarianship had apparently been raised several times before the fall of 1929. In November 1929 David Stevens, in the president's office, told Hanson, the acting dean, to defer seeking accreditation until after the first of the year.[66] Of course, technically, the GLS could not be accredited until its second year of operation at the earliest, for two visits in two different years were to precede accreditation, according to the *Third Annual Report of the BEL.*[67] There were other complications, however, as Douglas Waples explained to Karl Brown, the compiler of the *American Library Directory:*

> The reason why our school does not appear on the lists put out by the American Library Association is because the University regulations prevent any school of the University from soliciting accreditation by any outside agency.[68]

The question of accreditation would not be answered until after the appointment of Louis R. Wilson, in the fall of 1932.

In January 1931 the *Library Quarterly* published the speech given by Waples at the 1929 meeting of the AALS. In the first section of the speech, in a discussion of major policies, Waples stated the opinion of the GLS faculty that

> the school should concentrate its efforts upon adding to the profession each year a few students who are thoroughly imbued with the spirit of investigation. Hence, the student body should probably never exceed five students to each staff member and *should be confined as soon as possible to students who are candidates for the Doctor's degree or who are conducting studies that meet the accepted standards of the Doctor's thesis in respect to the methods of investigation employed* [emphasis added].[69]

The first sentence reflects the original emphasis given to the GLS program by George Works; however, the second statement indicates a new departure. Apparently the school had been under pressure by the university administration to limit the number of M.A. students. When the GLS announcement was due to be revised in January 1931, Acting President Woodward asked Waples about the possibility of limiting the number of these students. Waples, responding on behalf of the faculty, thought that a statement about no M.A. degrees being awarded would be unwise, since the school wanted to attract capable students. Instead, Waples recommended that the catalogue read:

> All students are expected to meet the standards applied to the selection of prospective Doctors of Philosophy. Librarians or other persons capable of meeting such standards are encouraged to attend whether or not they wish to become candidates for degrees.[70]

The administration agreed to this statement. In 1932 the GLS awarded only one master's degree, but the next year the number was back to two, as it had been before the matter was brought up.

RESULTS AND PROSPECTS

Little effort had been expended in looking backward during the first two academic years of the GLS. The closest document to an annual report to come out of the school during that period was a list of "problems under investigation at the Graduate Library School," which Waples compiled for his presentation to the AALS; and several of those "problems" were only projected. A year later, in December 1930, Waples, as the acting dean, put together another document, "Current Activities," which was sent to the Carnegie Corporation. Again it was a list, this time of forty-seven projects of students and faculty, but it was supplemented by a statement relating to the accomplishment of the school's objectives.[71]

Waples counted nine "results" obtained during the first two years of the school's operation. First, he felt that the school had

> defined problems representing most of the important phases of librarianship which can be studied objectively or which can be studied in terms of evidence sufficiently precise to claim the respect of students in established fields of scholarship.[72]

Commenting on that result, Waples argued that it had been "a necessary first step toward the development of research that shall meet the standards of graduate study in the University as a whole."[73]

Second, he reported that the school had established "contacts with other university departments—notably history, sociology, psychology, and education,"[74] the purpose of which was twofold. Collaborative research could result, and the GLS would be able to recruit qualified students from these fields. Waples believed that such students would be "more productive . . . than experienced librarians."[75]

Third, the school was experimenting with methods to select students. He did not elaborate on what these were, but in his *LQ* article Waples had indicated that student selection in the GLS was based on minimum qualifications; then correspondence, personal interviews of prospective students, and, most importantly, letters of recommendation.[76] Answering the earlier criticisms by Milam and Bogle regarding the "paucity" of men, Waples reported that "the percentage of men enrolled in the school had increased from zero to twenty-five per cent, from 1928 to 1930."[77] He attributed the increase, however, to "changes within the profession itself" rather than to any changes in the school's admissions policy.[78] In the *LQ* article, Waples then stated that several hundred inquiries had been received; 131 persons had applied to the school, of whom ninety-five met the minimum requirements. "Of those admitted," he reported, "fifty-eight have actually been in residence."[79] In 1930, at least seven of those admitted were instructors from other library schools.

Of the graduates, Waples was satisfied that there were "four librarians, who can be relied upon to approach library problems from the basis of trustworthy evidence."[80] For the future, he expected the school to graduate six students a year. His final points in the article concerned the Carnegie grant for *LQ*, "the sources for future investigations," the faculty, and the "large amount of consulting service" undertaken.

If Waples were to have his way, the school should show progress during the next few years toward the following goals:

1. To establish librarianship as a legitimate field for graduate research in the opinion of competent scholars in related and contributory fields as well as in the opinion of the graduate faculty as a whole.
2. To clarify in the mind of the library profession at large the distinction between valid evidence and conventional assumptions regarding the present values and methods of library administration.
3. To identify or to train experienced librarians who are able to direct studies in the field of public library administration.
4. To increase the competence of instructors in library schools by developing candidates for such positions who are qualified to increase the professional content of the training courses as opposed to present content which is largely clerical in character.

5. To identify and organize the source material pertinent to library problems that now exists in various graduate departments, thus economizing and directing the efforts of future students in the field.

6. To produce, select, and publish significant investigations.[81]

At the Carnegie Corporation, a policy adviser, Robert M. Lester, agreed with the goals outlined by Waples. Lester considered most of the projects "highly technical and of remote value to the profession,"[82] although he felt that they were most likely useful training devices. One question that remained in his mind after reading the Waples memorandum was:

Since the library profession is admittedly a new one and confronted with already existing large physical, administrative, and servicing problems, is it advisable, in order to gain professional recognition, (a) to try to build up through research a historical background as in other professions, (b) to devote major effort on educational techniques, measurements, and other pedagogical (and psychological) paraphernalia?[83]

Lester was concerned that the

emphasis on derival and application of formulae to groups (children, adolescents, college, adult, blind, foreign language, hospital, etc.) may result in dehumanizing the librarian as being a mathematically minded pseudo-educator in place of a man of books to aid those in research of reading material—with and without a purpose.[84]

Lester succinctly summarized the conflict between humanist and scientist that was about to occur.

Librarianship, Art or Science?

The view of a dehumanized librarian, expressed in private by Lester at the corporation, was expressed openly by C. Seymour Thompson, assistant librarian at the University of Pennsylvania, at the American Library Institute on 23 June 1931. More than two hundred people were in attendance. According to one member of the audience, "attention stiffened as soon as the speaker began to talk"[85] on "Do We Want a Library Science?"[86] In part, Thompson was reacting to the conception of a scientific librarianship as expressed or implied in a number of places: in Carl B. Roden's 1928 ALA presidential address,[87] in Dewey's 1929 *Sources of a Science of Education,* in Williamson's 1930 founder's day address at Western Reserve University; but mostly he was responding to Douglas Waples' question, "What Is a Library

Science?" raised in his paper "The Graduate Library School at Chicago," which was published in the first issue of *Library Quarterly* in 1931.

Thompson rejected Waples' conception that librarianship was "primarily a social enterprise."[88] In fact, he said, it was an educational rather than a sociological enterprise. He felt that librarianship required cultural bookmen who possessed "a knowledge of good books."[89] In particular, Thompson lamented a recently proposed service slogan calling for librarians to be of "practical value to practical people,"[90] and he despised the new "cult" of efficiency which was appearing. This business orientation, he felt, was creating in librarians "the fear of being called academic."[91] Thompson called for a resurrection of the "*bibliothecal* spirit," as opposed to Works's "spirit of inquiry" or Williamson's "spirit of research and methods."[92] Rather, he admonished his audience,

> let us be content to be librarians—as business-like and efficient as possible, an active influence in community life, but, above everything else, librarians.[93]

Thompson then singled out five pieces of research from Waples' list of "problems under investigation at the Graduate Library School" which he felt were pseudo scientific at best and downright dangerous at worst. Three of these were Waples' own and two were Randall's. As though he had read Lester's mind, Thompson stated his fear for the future of librarianship should studies

> be written in the same keenly analytic style; bloodless and utterly depersonalized; as cold and unsympathetic as the case records of a hospital; appreciative of nothing but minute facts, or supposed facts, their analysis and presentation under the guise of science. This is a conception of science and of librarianship which, if unrestrained, will stifle all true appreciation of books and of people, the two things which make library work a joy and an opportunity, and will develop a generation of librarians who will perceive not the opportunity and cannot know the joy.[94]

With this nearly mystico-religious view, he contrasted Williamson's view of a future in which a reader's adviser would

> "when requested administer scientific intelligence tests, aptitude tests, comprehension tests, etc., and on the basis of scientific findings prescribe a program of reading"; when "for many adult patrons the public library will have on file psychological and other personal data as complete and as scientifically prepared as any to be found in the records of hospitals or social service clinics.[95]

The paragraph sounds like modern-day scientific bibliotherapy. "The attempt to make librarianship a science of this sort," he predicted, "is wrong in purpose and will be almost totally unproductive of good."[96] Playing on the then current adult education slogan, Thompson rejected "Every Library Worker a Scientist" as representing, for him, "a false ideal."[97] Predicting a dim future for it, Thompson concluded: "We can develop only a body of dabblers in imitation science."[98] To the question "Do we want a library science?" Thompson responded:

> Yes, if our conception of science conforms in general with that which I tried to define at the beginning of this paper. But if we can have a science only by adopting the psycho-sociological laboratory methods that are being urged upon us my answer is, No, we do not want librarianship to be a science. Let it be an art; a Fine Art,—untouched by science.[99]

One member of the audience reported that, upon completion of Thompson's indictment, "the audience gave thunderous applause."[100] Three individuals, however—Louis R. Wilson, Pierce Butler, and C. C. Williamson—spoke in rebuttal.[101] Wilson mentioned the need for and utility of service projects and basic research; Butler, the applicability of scientific bibliography to historical studies; and Williamson reaffirmed his belief "that science does not destroy appreciation if real scientific technique is used."[102]

After the American Library Institute meeting, M. L. Raney went to Ely, Vermont, for a vacation. Thompson's speech, however, moved him to write a heated and "a bit outspoken"[103] letter to Vice President Frederick Woodward back at Chicago. Like Bogle and Milam, Raney did not "regard it [the school] as a success from any point of view."[104] There was no library *science*, only *service* for Raney. "The librarian," he thought, "may be an artist at best, but that is a matter of personality."[105] According to Raney, every indictment of Thompson's "was proven."

> I must tell you that the University of Chicago cannot too soon reduce Mr. Waples to the insignificant place he may be able to fill in adult education and put the direction of the School in the hands of somebody like Mr. J. I. Wyer who will at least not make us ridiculous. Mr. Wyer cannot make a science out of a sow's ear, any more than anybody else can, but what he would do would at least be useful.[106]

He further stated that his was no "new opinion." When he had come to Chicago, almost five years earlier, he had foreseen, he now wrote, the rise under Mr. Charters' influence of a weak appendix to the School of Education . . . I wish the University had not touched it. . . . In my judgment, Flexner's[107] criticism of the Columbia and Chicago Schools of Education and their Library School progeny is as sound as a dollar.[108]

Although the weather and letter were hot, he concluded: "I am cool as I write[,] don't forget."[109]

Douglas Waples attempted to counter Thompson's argument in print in the 15 September issue of *Library Journal*; the university administration, however, had seen his reply in late August.[110] Waples organized his response around Thompson's definition of science, Thompson's selection of certain studies as representing "the character and scope" of the GLS, and his ridicule of those studies which were declared "harmful to the profession."[111] Although Waples agreed with him on some points ("that librarianship has won an honorable place for itself without particular attention to research" and the necessity of "a revival of the 'bibliothecal spirit' "),[112] he thought "it would be a catastrophe leading to chaos if all librarians were to become investigators,"[113] Thompson being a case in point.

In the first place, he felt that Thompson's conception of science was based on "a positive dread of modern science and its methods."[114] Waples did not believe that examining mankind in mass "belittles their human dignity," nor did distinguishing "a group with certain traits in common . . . deny the worth of personality."[115] In the second place, Waples wrote, Thompson had misrepresented, ridiculed, and burlesqued studies and explicitly denied findings which represented "positions which he himself does not accept; . . . yet for all this he has been the first to express an irritation at fundamental studies that many members of the library profession have doubtless felt."[116]

Waples explained that many of the studies being made in the GLS were narrow; however, "the more definitely a piece of research is restricted, other things being equal, the better it is."[117] Waples then turned to what he perceived as the personal nature of Thompson's attack: "While he imputes what he dislikes about science to the School as a whole, my particular field of adult reading is the only one he specifically attacks."[118] Waples expressed the University of Chicago's "freedom of investigation" but concluded that "it is obviously silly to call the whole region sterile just because some seed falls on stony ground."[119] Furthermore, he thought Thompson was playing the part of a "professional Paul Revere," spreading "the alarm prematurely," for "the enemy may be advancing, if it is the enemy, but he's a long way off and he is not numerous."[120]

Then he answered *seriatim* the charges concerning the benefit and utility of specific studies which "should magnify the educational functions of the library in the direction Mr. Thompson advocates," since, he added, "the individual studies mentioned in the foregoing paragraphs may be less impressive than the negations expressed so emphatically by Mr. Thompson." He concluded with the following "confession of faith":

1. The library profession is under an obligation to society to acquire whatever knowledge serves to justify public confidence. . . .
2. Librarianship has won and justified public confidence to the extent . . . that libraries know and provide "good books." . . .
3. The recent phenomenal increase in the total output of printed matter has made it vastly more difficult than formerly to select the best. . . .
4. The studies herein mentioned must simplify to some degree the problem of selecting good books. . . .
5. The studies may be justified by their contribution to theory given if practical applications are not yet apparent.[121]

On the last two points, Waples stressed that

bibliography and the "bibliothecal spirit" at best tell little more than what books there are and what books are about; . . . as the bibliographer looks to the specialist in the given field of literature for sources and for methods of investigation, so the librarian concerned with a definition of readers' needs should look to the social scientist for equivalent sources and methods.[122]

For Waples, the researcher and the practitioner "play different but supplementary roles,"[123] for which both are needed.

If I were compelled to vote for one or the other of two types of library schools, one devoted to specialized research and the other to the training of young people to operate libraries according to present methods, I should vote without hesitation against the research school and for the library school which teaches the conventional process.[124]

Nevertheless, he and his colleagues at Chicago believed there was "a place for both types of school." He expressed his expectation that, in the long run, "with due tolerance and the requisite amount of hard work current studies will eventually bear directly upon vital problems of library administration."[125] Waples concluded with a statement of his desire for future discussion on this subject, hoping that the matter would not be dropped, since, in his judgment, it was "perhaps the most significant issue confronting the profession today."[126]

Thompson was given the opportunity to comment in print on

Waples' reply, and it followed immediately in the pages of *LJ*. He regretted Waples' construing his remarks as a personal attack, although he acknowledged his "frank antagonism," which "was and is directed solely at principles and methods, in an absolutely impersonal spirit."[126] Showing himself to be a true humanist, Thompson suggested that he and Waples "dine together, discuss our differences of opinion as vigorously as we please, subject only to the ordinary principles of dining room decorum, and prove that men can differ irreconcilably in their opinions and still be good friends."[127] Thompson further attempted to answer Waples' charges regarding his conception of science, the burlesquing of educational research, and the misconstruction and misrepresentation of the character of Chicago's research.

Although by the time this appeared in print, Waples was in Europe, undertaking further research, congratulatory notes were sent to him by many of his colleagues at home and abroad.[128] Yet, as Sarah Bogle demonstrated in her account of the following incident, town-and-gown perceptions were not the same:

> At a meeting of North Shore [Chicago] Librarians following the dedication of Highland Park Library there was much discussion of the Chicago University Library School. The trained librarians openly expressed the opinion that they who are active in the profession should take some action of disapproval.[129]

However, one "trained librarian," active in his profession, felt strong enough in his disagreement to express his thought in print. Arguing that "every serious voice deserves a hearing," J. Christian Bay, librarian of the Crerar, listened to the Thompsonian thesis and the Waplesian antithesis and attempted to synthesize the two.[130] Librarianship, for Bay, was "the recognition, organization and utilization of printed and written records."[131] Adopting the analogy of the medical sciences, Bay proposed still another field of study, which he perceived to be "as definite as any within the exact sciences."[132] He argued that this field of study had a long history and a prescribed methodology, derived from many disciplines, "including philosophy, history, sociology (including education), linguistics, and the inductive sciences."[133] Whether one is instructed in a "school of library service" (e.g., Columbia) or in a school of the "science of librarianship" (e.g., Chicago or Osler's concept),[134] neither school contained the full sense of what Bay termed

> the library sciences; . . . Thus the terms
> library science
> science of library services

science of librarianship
the library (i.e., bibliothecarial) sciences,
may signify quantitatively different ideas, and varying
principles, methods—and academic treatment. . . . [However, the
end purpose of these is all the same.] To recognize, to
organize and to utilize books in accordance with social and
educational ideas, is, therefore, a function which requires
scientific thought and method. Its fundamental idea is to
provide the most direct and applicable form of enlightenment,—
i.e., the process of rousing the sense of, and the search for,
truth and fitness.[135]

Many will think it unfortunate that Bay did not push for a synthesis, an umbrella term for the cultural bookman and the scientific professional; otherwise, we might today speak of a "Bay bridge" between the two perceptions of the field. The *LJ* "Editorial Forum" for 15 September, also missing the opportunity to identify a synthesis, concluded that "whether it is based on science or is an art, service is the word which best indicates the usefulness of the library from whatever school or field the library assistant comes to her work."[136]

Two letters to the editor followed. The first was from C. C. Williamson, offering readers copies of his "The Place of Research in Library Service," to which Thompson had referred. Williamson had little further to say on the matter as Waples had, in his judgment, made an "admirable statement."[137] A letter also appeared from Marian C. Manley, a librarian of the Newark (N.J.) Public Library, in which she lamented "the mass of footless technical detail that cumbers methods of library training," hindering development of "the spirit of real library service."[138] Obviously, she did not appreciate what the Graduate Library School at Chicago was attempting to do.

The editor of *Libraries*, Mary Ahern, gave Thompson an opportunity to restate his position,[139] but preceded it with an editorial in the October issue on the purpose of the American Library Institute. In particular, she felt that

the whole flow from the fountain of wisdom should not be gathered from a restricted region, nor does truth lose by being questioned as to its source and extent. . . . If serious students on either side of the question [art or science] can sustain their contentions, they have a right to demonstrate their belief in the open forum of the Institute or anywhere else.[140]

Waples' colleague, Pierce Butler, responded to her editorial in an unpublished letter, dated 14 October, in which he singled out her third paragraph (quoted above in part) "as a *locus classicus* in our professional literature."[141] He went on to state that the possible mis-use of social sciences is not a strong enough consideration to offset the possible utility of the results of these methods. He felt that to say that the GLS

> attempts only two things:
> (1) to uncover new truths, and
> (2) to send in to the professional field men experienced
>   in scientific method . . .
> [but fails to train either] general or specialized practitioners
> is a disguised compliment.[142]

Butler then expostulated upon his belief in the "ample scope for the application of sociological, psychological, and historical methods of research."[143] At Chicago, he said,

> We are confident, moreover, that from these studies will emerge a cor-pus of knowledge akin to, but distinct from, the other social sciences. We believe that every increase in man's knowledge of himself, his society, and his world is worth the cost of its application.[144]

In a way, perhaps, it is just as well that the letter was not pub-lished; had it been, Butler might have been satisfied to let the matter drop, and would not have been motivated to write his *Introduction to Library Science*, which appeared in 1933 and employed the same tripartite scheme expressed in his letter to Ahern. In the intervening time, Butler had the opportunity to test these ideas on his students in courses 301, "Librarianship as a Field of Research," and 340, "The History of Scholarship."

Yet another individual was stimulated by Williamson's article. This time it was Jesse H. Shera, then the bibliographer for the Scripps Foundation for Research in Population Problems at Miami University. In the November issue of *Libraries* he had published an article playing off Williamson's title, "The Place of Library Service in Research: A Suggestion."[145] Shera was concerned that the recent awakening of self-consciousness among "educational librarians" (e.g., college, uni-versity, and research library workers) could result in a view of librar-ianship as an end in itself. "From being merely an important side issue in academic life, the library is now decidedly *in medias res*."[146] To balance this possibility, Shera proposed establishment of a permanent committee, to be chaired by a university librarian, comprising a repre-sentative from each of the learned societies. Its purpose would be to make recommendations, annually or biennially, which would improve library service. These recommendations would not only stimulate but also "freshen and revivify the outlook of the 'educational librarian.' "[147] Shera concluded:

> Essential as research should be in library service, it can be of use only when it is based on a thoro realization of the position which the library holds in relation to research in all its forms.[148]

As a final note on this debate before the American Library Institute, Randall later remembered the following incident:

> In 1932, I believe, Butler managed to get both Waples and myself elected to the Library Institute. This caused a schism in the Institute and in the "profession" generally. Several of the older members of the Institute, including Margaret Mann, immediately resigned. Both Waples and I refused to accept membership, but this will give [the reader] an idea of the bitterness which existed between the GLS and its proponents, and the older librarians who insisted that librarianship was an "art" and not a "science."[149]

Particularly revealing of this controversy were the published reviews of books written subsequently by members of the Chicago GLS faculty. Randall's *The College Library* appeared shortly after the ALA presentation and received mixed reviews. Reviewing it for *Library Journal*, Charles H. Brown termed Randall's book an impressionistic piece of art, not science, though it "may prove to be a landmark in the history of American college libraries."[150] A half-century later, Randall recalled that Milam had also asked him to call on him at ALA headquarters because he had some advice to give him about his research.

> "Bill," he said, "all this statistical work and correlations are a waste of time. If you want to write a good and useful book on college libraries, get together with Dr. Bishop, and "—then he named several well-known librarians—" and listen to what they have to say. You will find that their judgments will be much more valuable than all the so-called 'research' you can do." In other words, "Don't monkey with the status quo!"[151]

Other librarians came to the GLS defense. In a review in *Library Quarterly*, Henry Harap of Western Reserve University said of Waples and Tyler:

> Their work is no ruthless invasion by myopic manipulators of slide rules, logarithmic tables, and correlation machines. The investigators are "little more than kin and less than kind" in relation to the library world and so apply their measuring instruments with courtesy, sensitivity, and with a respect for literary values. Measurers and calculators that they are, they never lose sight of the personal and cultural nature of the situation with which they are dealing.[152]

The Next Dean, Scholar or Librarian?

In 1929 the new president of the University of Chicago decided to ignore the advice of the library establishment and offer the deanship of the GLS to Samuel P. Capen. As was mentioned in the last chapter, Capen declined the offer, and J. C. M. Hanson was appointed acting dean for the first summer term of 1929, to be followed by Douglas Waples during the second term. The deanship was then held eight different times, by four members of the faculty, before a permanent dean was appointed. The following paragraphs will discuss some of the issues involved in that search.

David Stevens, assistant to the university president, wrote to Works in July of that year that he expected Hutchins and Woodward would put off any decision on a permanent dean until late September.[153] Bishop and Keogh were already on record as supporting James I. Wyer,[154] who had been considered earlier, but when other librarians learned that the university now "proposed [a] repetition of an error [made] three years earlier,"[155] there was a minor outcry. Consequently, following Capen's rejection of its offer, the university again considered Henry Van Hoesen. Not only did Van Hoesen have the support of ALA headquarters,[156] but by late August he had gained the unanimous support of the GLS faculty.[157] George Works, now in Connecticut, continued to advise the University of Chicago on the matter, conveying his opinion that "it is more important to get the right man than it is to make the choice at once."[158] Evidently his advice was heeded. The administration took no action, except to appoint Van Hoesen as a lecturer in the GLS during the 1929/30 academic year—perhaps so the university could watch his development. Personally, Works thought that Pierce Butler should be considered, although his deafness would be a handicap in the position. Waples himself had no objection to Butler.[159]

Hutchins decided to test the support for Van Hoesen in a rather devious manner. First, he asked Bishop's opinion of the man and Bishop replied that he felt Van Hoesen to be a "good average man industrious and earnest; not outstanding nor unusually able."[160] Writing to Keogh at Yale and Gerould at Princeton, however, Hutchins misquoted Bishop to say that he had "highly recommended"[161] Van Hoesen. Keogh and Bishop had jointly stated their opinion against Van Hoesen earlier, but Gerould had not been consulted. Although Gerould may honestly have felt that Van Hoesen was a "man of high scholarly ideals and attainments, excellent administration ability, tactful in dealing with situations, [and a] keen judge of personalities,"[162] nevertheless Hutchins appeared to be pitting leading librarians against one another, because his manuscript note on Gerould's letter said "Look at this picture."[163]

Responding to Keogh's letter, which followed this stratagem, Hutchins explained that Chicago had no interest in holders of Ph.Ds per se. "We want a man," he wrote, "who will be acceptable to scholars and to librarians. (Please observe this distinction),"[164] he added. He felt that a temporary appointment was not satisfactory and that Wyer was too old. Hutchins, who wanted someone who would be able to serve for ten years, asked if Keogh would care to name someone. In the middle of all this, Works continued to advise on the GLS; he wrote to Stevens that the university should be careful in its consideration of Randall. Works wanted to advocate Randall, but he urged the consideration of Butler for a year as dean.[165]

By this time it was becoming obvious that something would have to be done to placate the library leaders. Hutchins therefore sent Stevens to talk about the matter in person with Keogh and Bishop.[166] The difficulty in filling the deanship stemmed from the rather extraordinary individual being sought by the university: someone with "the power to do research," the ability "to recognize unworked fields of library investigation," and "the technique of making the best curriculum."[167] Raney, in the university library, must have thoroughly enjoyed himself, for he had already informed the administration that he could carry both the librarianship and the deanship himself.[168] On 10 December, Stevens informed Van Hoesen that no appointment would be made even though Hanson would retire at the end of June.[169] Apparently Hutchins was going to wait for someone to "grow" into the position.

At ALA headquarters, as mentioned earlier, the mood was not good. As far as Milam was concerned, there was "not a person on the faculty who[m] we should want the young leaders of our profession to imitate."[170] At about the same time, Bogle also expressed her view to Harrison Craver, chairman of the BEL, that the school was not functioning "as we expected it to do when the Board voted on the University of Chicago as the appropriate recipient of the Carnegie grant."[171] She felt that it complicated the matter that the new university president talked only with Bishop and Keogh about it.

The Carnegie Corporation was also concerned about the GLS deanship. On 13 January 1930 Keppel wrote that "today the School needs a Dean worse than ever."[172] As a result of discussions at the corporation, it was decided that Keppel should approach Keogh, who in turn would talk with Hutchins about Learned as a potential candidate for the deanship. In reconsidering Learned, Hutchins also sought the counsel of Bishop. It is likely Bishop told Hutchins the same thing he told Keppel: neither the personnel nor the program of the GLS "measures up to what we have a right to expect."[173]

Hutchins became exasperated with the whole thing. Writing to Keogh, he said:

> I think the whole situation in the library field is a very serious reflection on those of you whose lives should have been devoted to the training up of your successors. With this mild and interrogative comment I beg to thank you for your interest in my University and for your great personal kindness to me.[174]

Keogh agreed with him, but gently directed Hutchins to consider that this was exactly "why the Library School at Chicago was started."[175] Hutchins was not appeased, but responded to Keogh:

> I applaud your foundation of the Library School at Chicago and would applaud it even more if you had been thoughtful enough to provide me with a number of candidates for its deanship. Meanwhile accept my assurances of continued reverence and esteem.[176]

Finally, Hutchins again seriously considered James I. Wyer. Perhaps as a trial run, Wyer was appointed a lecturer in the GLS during the 1931/32 academic year. Hutchins then suspended work on the matter.

In the meantime, George Works had returned to the University of Chicago from Connecticut Agricultural College, where his tenure as president had been undistinguished. Although, in his new position at Chicago, Works was dean of students and university examiner, Vice President Woodward asked that he do whatever he could for the GLS.[177] Works agreed to serve as dean *ex officio*, "with the understanding that I am not to be diverted from my primary responsibility —the work in higher education."[178] Woodward was gratified and agreed not to designate him as an official.[179]

Although Keppel had assured Bishop earlier that the corporation would not use any pressure on the GLS at Chicago,[180] Randall unknowingly raised the sleeping issue of the deanship when he asked Keppel to write an article for the first issue of *Library Quarterly*. Keppel did so and then told Randall, "Now it's the turn of the University of Chicago to do something about the Library School."[181] Randall relayed this statement to the administration. Discussing this comment with Hutchins, Woodward pointed out that its "most obvious inference" was to get a dean, though Keppel had said several times that the university should not rush to do so.[182] Apparently the presence of Wyer at Chicago, albeit as lecturer, had calmed some individuals' apprehensions about the direction of the GLS, though others were still "very much concerned about the situation."[183] Waples even commented to Charters on ALA's warmer attitude toward the school, saying of Bogle, "She seemed to understand our problem at the School so very much more clearly than she did two years ago."[184]

Waples himself now became the focus of attention. He had been the acting dean since the fall of 1930. At various times he had been mentioned as a possible candidate for the permanent deanship, but in March 1931 Charters expressed his opinion to Keppel that he did not think Waples should be the dean.[185] Next, Waples received another blow. Just before Wyer left, at the close of the summer term, Woodward interviewed him and later told Hutchins that Wyer "likes Waples and respects his work highly but thinks that it is being overemphasized in the Graduate Library School. It is a peripheral field."[186] Furthermore, Woodward explained, Wyer thought "Randall is very talented and promising"[187] but his work on the journal kept him from teaching. Examination of table 2 shows Wyer was correct.

By now, a decision had been made in the university administration which would mean a dean for the GLS would be decided upon before spring 1932.[188] Hutchins must have also decided that appeasement of ALA would only come if he could find a librarian for the deanship.

By the end of the summer, attention was thus focused upon one of the original consultants, Louis R. Wilson. His national reputation was growing because of his published articles and the two library buildings and several special collections he had built. Furthermore, Wilson was serving on the influential Board of Education for Librarianship. Conveniently, the November meeting of the Association of American Universities was being held in Chapel Hill. Wilson wrote his brother Edwin (at Haverford) that he had an appointment to see Hutchins and added that "recently [Douglas] Waples, a Haverford man, with special training in education has been acting dean, but evidently is not making a go of the job."[189] Most likely, Wilson had obtained some background information from George Works, who was then in North Carolina surveying aspects of the proposed consolidation of public institutions in the state. Wilson also mentioned that, although he originally had doubts "as to whether or not [he] could handle the work of organizing a school,"[190] he now had the experience of having established his own library school at North Carolina, although it looked little like the GLS at Chicago.[191]

The interview with Hutchins went well. Wilson wrote to W. W. Bishop that Hutchins had decided "it is necessary for him to secure some one acceptable to the library interests of the country or return the money to the Carnegie Corporation."[192] Wilson also identified Hutchins' plans for the GLS:

Hutchins is interested in seeing investigation carried on which has a fairly immediate and direct bearing upon the administration of the library and its utilization as a social and educational institution. He would like to see the school interest itself in the training of teachers of library science. He would also like for it to do whatever is required of it by way of giving essential training in bibliography and classification in cataloging insofar as they are involved in rather highly specialized situations.[193]

Wilson concluded his letter with an appeal for Bishop's suggestions. Wilson also sought the advice of Carl Milam,[194] James I. Wyer, H. W. Odum, and George Works.

In a letter written 30 November, Hutchins offered the position of dean to Wilson. Wilson acknowledged the offer, but wrote for additional opinions, this time of Jackson Davis of the General Education Board in Richmond and of M. R. Trabue of the University of Minnesota. To Trabue, Wilson mentioned that "a shift to Chicago would mean that I would have to tie myself up with the direction of investigation, I should have to do some teaching, for which I have had precious little preparation for thirty years."[195]

Carl Milam's letter to Keppel reveals that Wilson's state of mind was based on a conversation that Wilson must have had with Milam. First of all, Hutchins' salary offer was about the same as Wilson was already receiving in North Carolina. Secondly, "because of the permanent appointments—Waples and Butler—it is practically impossible for the University administration to give Wilson a free hand."[196] Milam said that "the question is still open but I am not very hopeful that Wilson will accept."[197] Keppel thanked Milam for his letter, adding his opinion that Wilson should accept Hutchins' offer as "it offers a real chance to make educational history."[198]

Just before Christmas 1931, Wilson wrote to his brother again, expressing doubts that were uppermost in his mind. In particular, he said:

Here [at Chapel Hill] I have my hand on a great many things of interest; at Chicago I will have one of the very smallest schools, that is not in good repute, that has not good physical quarters, and that has to work out its own salvation.[199]

At about the same time, Wilson wrote also to Hutchins, whose offer had been made in terms of the year's work comprising four quarters. Wilson did not object to being paid on a four-quarter basis, but he wanted to be able to take all or part of the winter quarter off, if he felt it necessary, "without having to effect a special arrangement through the President's Office."[200] Hutchins assented to this condition[201] and wrote again in early January, requesting Wilson's authorization to "report your acceptance at meeting of our board of trustees"[202] on 14 January. Wilson accepted the offer, under conditions that included a salary of $12,000 per annum, $3,000 toward retirement, and the winter quarters off.[203]

His appointment ended the nearly three-year-long search by the University of Chicago for a permanent dean of the GLS. President Hutchins had sought advice widely, but in the end he listened primarily to two leading librarians and selected a librarian, rather than a scholar, for the post of dean. Thus Wilson's "chance to make educational history" was about to commence.

5

The Wilson Era, 1932–42

The Dean as Administrator

Shortly after Wilson's acceptance, an announcement appeared to that effect in the newspapers.[1] He received letters of congratulations— "delighted," "very glad," "unanimous sigh of relief," "the Graduate Library School now has a chance"—from numerous individuals.[2]

Several items were on Wilson's mind as he contemplated his move to Chicago. His housing problem was solved by renting a house on Kenwood Avenue, near the campus, but other personal problems concerned the number of local bank failures; so he consulted several university officers for advice on this matter. Concerns more closely related to the GLS included students, faculty, and his own preparation for assuming the deanship. Concerning his preparation, Wilson wrote to Emery T. Filbey, an assistant to Hutchins, that "the change from merely administrative duties to those which involve the direction of investigation is not going to come easily, and therefore I am beginning to observe and to read in that field as quickly as possible."[3]

At Chapel Hill, Wilson had been acquainted with the officers and the work of the Institute for Research in Social Science since 1924. It is unlikely, however, that he considered social science methodology his forte, since he had written to Waples (concerning equipment purchases) that "unfortunately, I do not know the use of statistical apparatus myself, but I realize the great value of having that kind of aid close at hand."[4] Surely he was more comfortable with humanistic methods, since his Ph.D. was in English and, in his various notes[5] on Chicago, he referenced for special attention Tom Peete Cross's research methods in bibliography and English literary history.[6]

There were now four permanent appointments to the faculty, including Wilson, for between Wilson's acceptance and move to Chicago, Randall was promoted to full professor, though without additional compensation because of the Depression. Also, just before his arrival, Wilson allowed Waples' appointment of Leon Carnovsky as an instructor in the GLS at $2,750 a year. Carl Milam also encouraged Wilson to appoint an additional man in public library administration, but apparently this would have to await future funds because the original endowment was drawing less interest now.

Wilson had met with the GLS faculty before he arrived in Chicago, at the 1932 ALA New Orleans meeting. For tactical reasons, Wilson wanted to meet with all of them at the same time. Waples' reaction to this was "Each of us, no doubt, would like to talk with you about things near his heart, but those can wait"[7]—or would *have* to wait. Wilson, who had already sized up his new colleagues, told Robert Lester, who was attending the convention, that he, Wilson, had decided "how to handle Waples."[8] From his meeting with Wilson, Lester got the impression that Wilson "doesn't think much of Butler"[9] either. Lester informed Wilson, apparently on the basis of an earlier interview with Waples, that Waples was "beginning to see the light."[10] At the earlier interview with Waples, Lester recorded the following: "The present times are out of joint for elaborate statistical and mathematical studies such as he [Waples] had been doing, and he is shifting around to popular presentation."[11] Lester also told Wilson that Randall was "tractable."[12] Unfortunately, this brief, tantalizing memorandum is the only contemporary evidence of Wilson's thoughts on his new faculty.

Dean Wilson joined the faculty on 1 September 1932. Reminiscing, nearly fifty years later, Randall says:

> I remember very well the first faculty meeting at which he [Wilson] presided. We discussed various problems and some necessary decisions. We waited for him to ask for a vote on these decisions. He never did. Instead, he suddenly said, "Well, gentlemen, I think I know your attitudes toward what we have been discussing. That will be all. The meeting stands adjourned."[13]

Undoubtedly some of those "necessary decisions" concerned reassuring the profession vis-à-vis the GLS.

REASSURING THE PROFESSION

Wilson quickly learned the difference between administering a library and administering a library school. He observed in March 1933 that it isn't as easy to shape the course of a library school as it had been to direct the activities of a library. The latter stays put very much better than the former. Probably, this is due to the fact that every professor has a point of view and in the preparation of materials and in the shaping of policies he has a greater part than the usual staff member in a library.[14]

Among his first duties, Wilson sought to file reports with the university administration and the Carnegie Corporation on the GLS.[15] These reports discussed tasks such as accreditation, confidence in the school and its dean, articulating the program with other departments, diversifying the student body, and research and publication. Several of these will be expanded upon in sections of their own, following this section.

Later in his tenure as dean, Wilson reaffirmed the five original objectives of the GLS and offered seven additional objectives which the GLS should begin to work toward. The new objectives were development of a theory or philosophy of librarianship; extension and application of the search for guiding principles which might be applied to the various subdivisions of library science; training students to teach these principles, who would also be productive researchers; development within its students of a critical and experimental attitude toward librarianship; promotion of publication; increasing the educational effectiveness of the library in its various forms; and contributions to a better understanding of the means of communicating ideas through print, radio, and the moving picture.[16]

Whether he viewed it as a conflict of interest or simply an overextension of his responsibilities, Wilson resigned in November or early December 1932 as a member of the Board of Education for Librarianship, on which he had served since 1925.[17] In October of the following year, the board finished revising its Minimum Standards and these were adopted by the ALA Council.[18] Rather than quantitative, as the original 1925 Standards had been, the new ones "stipulate what, rather than how much, should go into a curriculum."[19] Whether the new qualitative Standards were a reaction to the question whether librarianship is an art or a science is not clear; nevertheless, the classification scheme was radically changed. The 1933 Standards defined a library school as "an agency which gives in a single academic year at least one coordinated professional curriculum in library science,"[20] and divided them into three "types." The basis for distinguishing type I, II, and III schools was admission requirements and academic programs. Type I, II, and III schools required a full academic year of the student's time, but the former also required a bachelor's degree upon entrance. However, it was more desirable to graduate from Type I schools "which require at least a bachelor's degree for admission to the *first full academic year* of library science, and/or which give advanced professional training beyond the first year" (emphasis added).[21]

The board went on to state, however, that the "Type I and Type II library schools shall be part of a degree-conferring institution approved by the Board . . . for giving professional instruction,"[22] but the GLS at Chicago still did not quite fit the BEL definition of a library school. Representing the Chicago school at the BEL meeting on 24 March 1934, W. W. Bishop stated that "the Graduate Library School seeks accreditation as a Type I school. It is different from other schools which fall within the group."[23]

First of all, none of the GLS faculty had completed the required two years of work in an accredited library school. Secondly, the standards applied primarily to schools with first-year professional programs, and as Brigham, chairman of the BEL, stated, the GLS offered "only courses leading to an M.A."[24] Executive assistant Hostetter pointed out that originally the BEL had "made a definite place for it [the GLS] in the [1925] Minimum Requirements."[25] According to her, Wilson had "said that his school would be very glad to be accredited under them [the 1933 Standards]."[26] The matter was settled by sending the BEL inspection team of W. W. Bishop and Keyes D. Metcalf to Chicago for its on-site visit on 22 March, and two days later the BEL approved the GLS accreditation as a Type I library school.

Accreditation, it seems, was part of Wilson's overall plan to establish a first-year program in library science at Chicago, for he mentioned both the lack of and the need for one several times in his 1933 annual report. Perhaps more importantly, accreditation made the Chicago school more like other library schools.

From the outset, Wilson was aware that the GLS at Chicago lacked the confidence of the profession at large. Writing to George Works, Wilson said his first task was to visit the other library schools, partially for the purpose of reassuring the field.[27] Of course, *Wilson's* appointment to the deanship went a long way to reassure the profession—at least Edward Henry, librarian at the University of Cincinnati, thought it did. He wrote:

> I think that you know that I had some hand in compiling a plan which secured the Carnegie endowment for the University of Chicago. I felt then and still feel that the library profession needs a school which shall be devoted to research. There are many things about our profession of which we have only a working knowledge with no understanding of the fundamental problems involved. Your present position and your experience and record eminently qualify you for the place. You

will enjoy the respect and confidence of librarians as Dr. Works could not, because of his lack of library experience, and you will be able to demand the respect of your academic colleagues as fully as he did, and more fully than almost any other librarian could. I am confidently expecting real progress for the school under your leadership.[28]

Wilson acknowledged, in his 1933 annual report, that the "School may be considered to have achieved reasonable success."[29] Whatever Works may have lacked in popularity with the profession, Wilson attempted to make up for; and with library educators he was clearly successful. In a survey of 10,000 university and college professors, conducted by Robert C. Cook in the summer of 1935, individuals in library service gave Wilson "the majority of all votes cast"[30] as the leading educator in the field. (The next leading educator was GLS graduate, Helen Martin of Western Reserve University.)

Wilson had equal success with the Carnegie Corporation and his own university. Reacting in the summer of 1933 to Wilson's recently submitted "Statement Concerning the Plans of the Graduate Library School," Keppel wrote:

> There's evidence that the general situation is being clarified and that the school is on the rails and not, as some people may have thought in other years, just bumping along the ties.[31]

A year later, Wilson learned from Vice President Frederick Woodward that

> it is the judgment of this office that the University was extremely fortunate when it secured your services. We are very happy about the Library School and have the utmost confidence in its future.[32]

While Wilson was receiving these accolades, Ralph Munn, director of the Carnegie Library in Pittsburgh, was assembling a pamphlet entitled *Conditions and Trends in Education for Librarianship*, which raised the familiar questions of a few years earlier. Specifically, his report was "a protest against the growing affection which many librarians are showing for the pseudo-scientific methods and jargon which they are borrowing from the schools of education."[33] Essentially, this "condition" was a repetition of Flexner's criticisms of 1930. Rather thinly veiled references were made to Chicago's attempt to produce leaders and statesmen—"the upper stratum," which included "those who are determined to professionalize librarianship at all costs, through advanced degrees, scientific research, and the formulation of an esoteric nomenclature,"[34] all of which was an attempt to become " 'academically respectable.' "[35]

A reply to Munn's statements came in the pages of *Library Quar-*

terly for April 1937 (the fiftieth anniversary of "Education for Librarianship"). Leon Carnovsky's response began with a comment on the confusion in librarianship over various terms, including "librarianship" itself. In rejecting the term "librarianship," Carnovsky did not suggest another (such as "library science"), but he stressed the differentiation of librarians on the basis of their respective functions. He suggested that fundamental questions be studied—that library *problems* be investigated rather than library *employees* be produced,[36] which he felt Munn had proposed to do. Carnovsky felt that Munn was "glued too firmly to the *status quo*" and that he saw "contemporary library forms as 'the best of all possible in this best of worlds.' "[37]

To support his contention that the profession still needed experimentation, Carnovsky mentioned such areas as library finance, book selection, and cataloging, wherein he felt that investigation would have immediate utilitarian consequences. In cataloging, for example, the profession had nearly forgotten its function in establishing the process. Studies of the effectiveness of the card catalog, he felt, had dramatic implications for the user. Not all studies needed to be applied, however; there was great opportunity for "exciting research"[38] by librarians in the areas of history, sociology, and psychology, he thought. Carnovsky concluded that

> librarianship as a field of research is still a relatively untried discipline. The opportunity for implementing it with significant investigations looms large before those who would be pioneers, provided they are willing to cast off too conventional modes of thought and have the courage to break new ground.[39]

The school received some compliments from abroad on its "courage to break new ground" when, in late 1935, the Carnegie Corporation made it possible for a European librarian to view "American Librarianship from a European Angle."[40] Dr. Wilhelm Munthe, librarian of the University of Oslo, was selected to perform the task, and his itinerary included a visit to the "A.L.A. Graduate School" in Chicago on 28 September 1936. His long-delayed report, which devoted an entire chapter to the GLS, appeared in 1939. In particular, Munthe discussed the "need for an institution for research in library science; the Carnegie Corporation's grant; aims and objectives of the graduate school; growing dislike and aversion [within the profession]; Pierce Butler's plea for library scholarship; Carnovsky's defense; influence of the Graduate School; and the Library Institute, 1936."[41] He singled out Carleton Joeckel's *The Government of the American Public Library* as a book "which at once placed American library research on a higher plane."[42]

By 1940, even Ralph Munn had begun to view the GLS differently. In an article written during his ALA presidency, he stated:

During recent years there has been a small but growing group of librarians, chiefly those connected with the Graduate Library School in Chicago, who have been concerned with research studies as a basis for determining library policies. They have not always had a full hearing from some of us busy librarians without academic aid. Now I am beginning to see more clearly that if our libraries are to respond effectively to changing roles we must have objective studies of every kind. We must all know far more about the basic needs of our communities, their relative importance, the obligations, interests, and resources of other agencies, and the possibilities of cooperation. Most of us know almost nothing about our borrowers in terms of their actual needs, their reading habits and abilities, and how they would respond to a policy which places stronger emphasis upon books of educational value.[43]

George Works must have had some satisfaction to know that the ten years which he predicted necessary for Chicago to demonstrate its worth was just about the right amount of time.

STUDENT BODY

The "paucity" of men in the GLS, a concern of George Works, was no longer an issue by the end of 1934, when the total number of men graduates was approximately equal to all women graduates (see table 3). By the end of Dean Wilson's tenure, however, another trend had become apparent. At the master's level, the number of women graduates was twice that of men, but at the doctoral level the reverse was true: there were twice as many men as women.

Paul M. Paine, a member of the Advisory Group on the Carnegie Fellowships, also felt that the ratio of men to women among the Carnegie Fellows was of significance.[44] The GLS had received thirty-six (or 37.5%) of the ninety-six fellowships awarded by the corporation between 1929 and 1942. (A list of the Carnegie Fellows at Chicago appears as table 4.)As a group, however, women at Chicago were 13 percent less likely to receive fellowships than their counterparts at other library schools.

Yet this apparent discrimination should not obscure the importance of the fellowships, even if most of the awardees were men. From the earliest discussions of the GLS, Works had recognized that the GLS needed to be established on "a very high plane"—the fellowships were to be the vehicle to attract top students. Works observed that the lack of financial incentive for students prohibited them from prolonging

TABLE 3

Chicago GLS Graduates by Year, Degree, and Sex, 1929–50

Year	Bachelor's M	F	All	Master's M	F	All	Doctorate M	F	All	Total M	F	All	Σ
1929					2	2					2	2	2
1930					1	1		1	1		2	2	4
1931					2	2	2		2	2	2	4	8
1932				1		1	2	1	3	3	1	4	12
1933					2	2	1		1	1	2	3	15
1934				2		2	2	2	4	4	2	6	21
1935				1	4	5	3	1	4	4	5	9	30
1936				1		1	2		2	3		3	33
1937					1	1	1	1	2	1	2	3	36
1938					3	3	1		1	1	3	4	40
1939				5	3	8	2	2	4	7	5	12	52
1940				4	6	10		1	1	4	7	11	63
1941				3	10	13	5	1	6	8	11	19	82
1942				5	4	9	6	2	8	11	6	17	99
1943				2	11	13		1	1	2	12	14	113
1944	3	22	25	2	4	6	4	1	5	9	27	36	149
1945	6	34	40	2	11	13	2	2	4	10	47	57	206
1946	11	38	49		11	11	3	2	5	14	51	65	271
1947	14	32	46	2	3	5	2	1	3	18	36	54	325
1948	12	23	35	4	7	11	3	3	6	19	33	52	377
1949	1	14	15	6	4	10	3	1	4	10	19	29	406
1950				2	6	8	1		1	3	6	9	415
Σ	47	163	210	42	95	137	45	23	68	134	281	415	

their training. As the new dean, Wilson also wanted the GLS to attract more librarians than it had previously.[45] Shortly, the GLS was able to obtain such well-qualified individuals as Frances Henne, Carleton Joeckel, J. Periam Danton, and Helen Martin, because the $1,500 grants were especially attractive during the Depression.

Carl Milam, chairman of the Committee on Carnegie Fellowships from 1929 to 1931, expressed the purposes of the fellowships:

1) for productive research
2) for preparation of research
3) training for high administrative positions (which may or may not contribute to either 1 or 2), and
4) for paving the way into the library profession for the exceptional man who may have had no previous library training.[46]

TABLE 4
Carnegie Fellows in the Graduate Library School at Chicago, 1929-42

Eliza Atkins (Gleason), 1938–40	Robert F. Lane, 1936–37
†Margrethe D. Brandt, 1930–31	Richard H. Logsdon, 1938–39
*Jack Ernest Brown, 1939–40	Mary R. Lucas, 1940–41
Charles E. Butler, 1937–38	Errett W. McDiarmid, 1931–32
Helen L. Butler, 1937–38	*Isabel G. McTavish, 1937–38
Leon Carnovsky, 1929–31	Helen Martin (Rood), 1931–34
*Mary Duncan Carter, 1931–33	Robert A. Miller, 1935–36
John M. Cory, 1939–40	Jeannette Murphy, 1933–35
J. Periam Danton, 1933–35	George F. Purdy, 1935–36
Helen H. Darsie, 1933–34	John C. Settelmayer, 1941–42
Ralph Dunbar, 1935–36	George D. Smith, 1937–38
Ethel M. Fair, 1934–35	Esther L. Stallman, 1938–39
Colman J. Farrell, 1932–33	Edward B. Stanford, 1939–40
William C. Haygood, 1936–37	*Jean E. Stewart, 1938–39
Frances E. W. A. Henne, 1938–39	Maurice F. Tauber, 1938–39
Mary E. James, 1934–35	Miriam D. Tompkins, 1929–30
Carleton B. Joeckel, 1933–34	John E. Van Male, 1940–41
Walter H. Kaiser, 1939–40	Lee Wachtel, 1932–33

*Canadian recipients.
†Died 1931.
Source: American Library Association, Committee on Fellowships and Scholarships, *Education for Librarianship, Grants-in-Aid Financed by the Carnegie Corporation of New York, 1929–1942* (Chicago: ALA, 1943).

His interest in the funding of "training for high administrative positions" is clearly evident when table 5 is examined. By the end of Wilson's tenure, the GLS had accomplished one of its objectives, as stated in the 1932–33 *Announcements:*

> The opportunities of the School should be directly useful to those attracted by such positions as the following: *administration of public, college, and university libraries, teachers in library schools and training classes, headships of departments* in libraries . . . [emphasis added].[47]

This is exactly the order in which Carnegie Fellows at the GLS accepted positions. When the male Carnegie Fellows of the GLS are compared to all other Carnegie Fellows, it is clear that almost half of them took positions as head librarians of college or special libraries. There is no clear pattern for other Fellows, as they seemed equally likely to accept headships of departments, library school professor-

TABLE 5
Carnegie Fellows' Positions upon Graduation, 1929–42

Type of position	Other Library Schools			Graduate Library School		
	% Female	% Male	% Total	% Female	% Male	% Total
Head Librarian	17 (5)	17 (4)	17 (9)	21 (3)	48 (10)	37 (13)
College and special	(3)	(3)	(6)	(2)	(9)	(11)
Public	(2)	(1)	(3)		(1)	(1)
School				(1)		(1)
Associate librarian		4 (1)	2 (1)		5 (1)	3 (1)
Head of department	48 (14)	17 (4)	35 (18)	21 (3)	14 (3)	17 (6)
Assistant librarian	10 (3)	4 (1)	8 (4)	14 (2)	14 (3)	14 (5)
Library school	24 (7)	13 (3)	19 (10)	43 (6)	10 (2)	23 (8)
Special services		17 (4)	8 (4)		5 (1)	3 (1)
Armed forces		17 (4)	8 (4)			
Unclassified		9 (2)	4 (2)		5 (1)	3 (1)
Total	100 (29)	100 (23)	100 (52)	100 (14)	100 (21)	100 (35)

Source: Derived from tables in American Library Association, Committee on Fellowships and Scholarships, *Education for Librarianship, Grants-in-Aid Financed by the Carnegie Corporation of New York, 1929–1942* (Chicago: ALA, 1943). Totals may not equal 100 as percentages are rounded to nearest unit; numbers in parentheses = "raw numbers."

ships, or to serve in the army as they were to accept the head librarians posts of college or special libraries. Women Fellows at Chicago most frequently accepted library school positions whereas their counterparts at other schools accepted headships of departments in libraries.

Reflecting on the thirteen years of grants, the committee took "particular pride in the original and constructive work done by two of the fellows."[48] The two singled out were both Chicago students:

> Dr. Carleton B. Joeckel was enabled to complete his meritorious "Government of the American Public Library" which received the James Terry White award in 1938 for "notable published writing." Proceeding rather directly from his sponsored project on reading studies, Dr. Carnovsky has done much to standardize community analyses of reading and libraries to the point that such analyses have become indispensable to any realistic approach to the larger questions involved in public library service.[49]

Although Dr. Works had been confident that the fellowships would benefit the profession because the GLS holders would return to the field and act as "leaven," these two men became instructors, influencing the next generation of librarians.

In 1930, however, Douglas Waples spoke confidently: there were "four librarians [who had graduated from the GLS], who can be relied upon to approach library problems from the basis of trustworthy evidence."[50] Thus it may be interesting and significant to examine this leavening influence by the type of library or kind of positions the graduates accepted.

The categorization of positions, by type of library, that the Ph.D. graduates accepted upon graduation (table 6) indicates that the objective of training students to teach library science was least-well fulfilled during Wilson's tenure; the school did substantially better in

TABLE 6
Chicago Ph.D. Graduates' Positions upon Graduation

Type	1928–32 N = 6		1933–42* N = 30		1942–51† N = 32	
College and university	50%	(3)	57%	(17)	44%	(14)
Public and other	17	(1)	23	(7)	6	(2)
Library school faculty	33	(2)	20	(6)	44	(14)
Undetermined					6	(2)

*1933–Aug. 1942.
†Sept. 1942–1951.
Numbers in parentheses = "raw numbers."

the periods immediately preceding and following his administration. The large number, equaling the college and university positions accepted from 1942 to 1951, may be indicative of the increased status, prestige, or compensation associated with library school faculty positions. At the M.A. level (table 7), the decreasing trend of graduates

TABLE 7
Chicago M.A. Graduates' Positions upon Graduation

Type	1928–32 N = 6		1933–42* N = 46		1942–51† N = 84	
College and university	50%	(3)	37%	(17)	42%	(35)
Public and other	33	(2)	50	(23)	39	(33)
Library school faculty	17	(1)	11	(5)	7	(6)
Undetermined			2	(1)	12	(10)

*1933–Aug. 1942.
†Sept. 1942–1951.
Numbers in parentheses = "raw numbers."

who accepted faculty positions is probably best explained by the increasing tendency of library schools to upgrade their faculties' educational qualifications, thereby attempting to answer criticisms ranging from Williamson's 1923 *Report* and Munn's 1936 *Conditions* to comments in *Education for Librarianship* (1948).

The other pertinent observation to be made from consideration of these two tables concerns public librarianship. Several individuals, but especially Carl Milam, recommended that Wilson focus attention on this area by appointing a faculty member with these research interests. Carleton Joeckel was appointed, and the school's response or recognition of public librarianship as a field in need of scholarly inquiry is most clearly reflected in the M.A. graduates during Wilson's tenure. The fact that public librarianship never seems to have come of age may result from the deemphasis of this area by the GLS following Wilson's retirement from Chicago in June 1942.

After dean Wilson retired, statements were solicited from students to the following questions:

1) What were your original motives for going into library work as a profession?
2) Has your concept of library work changed during your period of graduate work? How? Why?[51]

Fourteen M.A. and Ph.D. students responded, and three motives (all received equal emphasis) emerged from their responses to the first question. The opportunities, especially for men and for advancement —as contrasted with the poor economic outlook in other pursuits— were cited. An equal number mentioned the "atmosphere," or the academic or bookish character of library work. Third, the service aspect or social and educational objectives of librarianship were given for going into library work. Less consensus was reached on the influence of friends and relatives, pregraduate experience in library work, the variety of encounters in the work situation, and the encyclopedic nature of library work.

Regarding the "change" in their concepts of library work, nine agreed; four said it was more "growth" than change, and one went so far as to say he had had no valid concept when he began. As to *how*, almost two-thirds viewed the library as a social or educational institution (in contrast to emphasis on routines or techniques); nearly half also mentioned the necessity of scientific investigation or research into library problems. Less consensus was reached on the interdisciplinary nature of library work, defining library problems, evaluating library work, emphasizing people over books, and a critical or questioning attitude toward library work. In answer to *why*, the major influences were the faculty, colleagues, and curriculum. Particular faculty members who were mentioned were Waples, Joeckel, and Wilson; specific courses in the curriculum were 310 and 383. Less consensus was reached on a critical or inquiring atmosphere and "time to think."

FIRST-YEAR PROGRAM

Wilson's interest in a first-year program stemmed from his membership on the BEL. The 1925 Minimum Standards allowed an "advanced graduate library school" to offer instruction toward the degree of B.S.L.S.[52] Although the GLS required this degree or its equivalent for admission, it did not offer the formal coursework at the time that Wilson accepted the deanship. Writing in February 1933, Wilson expressed his feeling that an "undergraduate school" (by which he meant a postgraduate program) was needed to supply "students of exceptional and proved ability."[53] In his first annual report, he recommended that provision for "elementary training in library science . . . be given thoughtful consideration."[54] In a sense, this change in the original objective of the GLS was a move to rationalize the GLS program to the profession. For example, Wilson wrote to Hostetter (of the BEL) that we more or less deliberately eliminated the statement that we do not give general training such as is given in other library schools for two reasons. The first was that we are trying to overcome the idea that we are necessarily "highbrow," which, it seemed to me, was pretty prevalent and due in part to the fact that in our statements in previous years we had so many expressions that we were totally unlike anything that had been seen on this planet before![55]

Accreditation, in 1934, finally brought the GLS into line with the four other Type I schools: California, Columbia, Illinois, and Michigan. Yet Wilson did not envision a first-year program like the programs other schools had. He intended, rather, that the first year be liberated from the stress on technique. The reason why many public librarians were "unaware of the part they could play in society today . . . is due both to the nature of the first year curriculum and the narrow limits of subject matter which it embraces."[56] According to Wilson, Ralph Munn (in his *Conditions and Trends*) "has missed the significance of library training if it is placed on an appropriate basis such as it can be given in the first year school."[57]

Early in 1937, Wilson was still approaching President Hutchins regarding additional faculty members for the first-year program. Filbey, in the president's office, found in a file a commitment, made before the original Carnegie grant, that the University of Chicago would not compete with other library schools but would stress "research and advancement of knowledge."[58] Basically, this allowed only two alternatives, as Filbey saw it: (1) offer the program to University of Chicago BA students who wanted advanced work and (2) offer it to students who had incomplete library training before coming to Chicago.[59] By late 1937, the first-year program was under active consideration by the university and by the Carnegie Corporation; and Wilson informed Keppel that $25,000 would probably be needed to start it.[60]

Wilson wrote Hutchins that there was "pressure in the Chicago area for a library school which gives first year instruction"[61] and would emphasize the educational role of the library, not technique. He recommended asking for $25,000 from Carnegie initially and another $25,000 to $50,000 later. Some of the pressure on the GLS to establish the program came from Carl Roden at the Chicago Public Library, who thought it would help solve some of his personnel problems.[62] However, Franklin Hopper of the New York Public Library, and adviser to the corporation, was not convinced; besides, he felt that the "inevitable tendency would be to follow up the first year work with the graduate work without practical experience intervening."[63] Discussion of the first-year program bogged down on the issue of further endowment for the GLS. The corporation had just endowed the Melvil Dewey professorship at Columbia with $250,000,[64] and the GLS was desirous of its fair share. By 1941, however, Wilson allowed that monies for the one-year course would be "the most acceptable temporary gift"[65] in lieu of an endowment grant.

During this time, Isabel Nichol, who held a certificate in library science from Denver (where Harriet Howe was experimenting with the curriculum), was recruited as a master's student. For her thesis at Chicago, she studied "The First-Year Library School Curriculum."[66] Under Carnovsky's direction, Nichol reviewed library literature regarding the curriculum, compared the current (1940) content of twenty-nine accredited programs, and surveyed the alumni of the University of Denver's program. In a chapter entitled "Changing Curricula of Library Schools," she reported four trends: (1) emphasis on "social content," as opposed to technical skills, (2) educational measurement, (3) integration of courses, and (4) specialization.[67] Analysis of programs found: (1) five basic courses: book selection, reference work, bibliography, cataloging and classification, and administration; (2) "an integration of the curriculum through large subject units";[68] (3) "topics frequently included in basic courses"[69] were introduction to librarianship, reading interests of adults, history of libraries and printing, library techniques, and college/university, public, regional, and special libraries; and (4) specialization. Seven schools gave some kind of attention to research and statistics: Denton, the use of libraries for research; Denver, statistics as part of administration; Louisiana, research methods; North Carolina, statistics; Syracuse, tests and measurements. (The last four offerings were electives.) Nichol's last chapter surveyed the opinion of Denver alumni regarding the curriculum, much as Charters' earlier study had employed job analysis.

Based in part on Nichol's study, Wilson was prepared to recommend (1) a one-year curriculum, following two years in the university's divisions or an A.B. from another institution, or (2) a three-year curriculum, based on the new degree of the college or its equivalent, equaling six quarters in divisions followed by three quarters in the school.[70] Hutchins read the two proposals ("Proposed Curriculum for the Bachelor's Degree in Library Science in the GLS" and "Proposed Curriculum for the Professional Degree of Bachelor of Library Science in the GLS") and took the matter under advisement, although he stated that it would have to be considered from a financial angle.[71] Filbey wrote to Wilson that the awarded degree would have to distinguish clearly between the A.B. and the B.S.L.S.[72] At the Carnegie

Foundation for the Advancement of Teaching, William Learned was pleased:

> I have nothing but admiration for Wilson's proposed library training curriculum. We have long needed something to break the strangle hold of the narrow, exaggerated, professional interests on the library training group. Wilson's prospectus subordinates the technical aspects of this profession to its proper level and gives an opportunity for the librarian to turn his thoughts outward where the people are. The whole thing sounds very promising to me.[73]

On the Chicago campus, Wilson scheduled four courses in the new program for 1942/43, two of them to be taught by Joeckel and Carnovsky and two by Frances Henne, a new instructor who had been the University High School librarian (and who was later to earn her doctorate in the GLS). Although Wilson seemed to expect an "adverse vote"[74] from the University Senate, which considered the new degree on 9 April 1942, that body approved it.[75] Consequently, parts of the new program went into effect in 1942/43 and the program was in full swing by 1943/44. Before Wilson retired from the GLS in 1942, he recommended that Carnovsky "be appointed assistant dean and should give special consideration to the first year curriculum."[76] It was the new dean, Carleton Joeckel, who expressed one of the difficulties of the new program.

> A good many inquiries are coming in about the first-year curriculum, but I must confess that the persons I have talked with individually have not been unusually impressive. I can see that there is going to be a considerable group of the refugee type of student.[77]

The difficulty of "relating the old graduate curriculum to the work of the first year"[78] persisted for the next occupant of the dean's chair, Ralph A. Beals, and these persistent problems have been identified by some as resulting in degradation of the academic program in the GLS. In fact, William Randall cited this degradation as his reason for not returning to the GLS after the war:

> Fortunately, I had left . . . before Wilson's plan for the school came to full fruition. But we realized the direction it was taking very soon after his arrival.
>   You must understand two things: (1) Dr. Wilson did not really believe in research. He used to joke about his own PhD in English from U. of North Carolina, which he received for "counting the number of relative pronouns in Chaucer's 'Canterbury Tales' "; and (2) he was not at all in sympathy with the concept of the GLS, as it had been developed before his arrival, and he let us know that in his opinion, it

would never amount to much until it included an undergraduate library school. Of course, Waples, Butler, and I strongly opposed this from the beginning. Dr. Wilson's first move in that direction was to recruit Carleton Joeckel, first as a PhD candidate under his own (Wilson's) direction, and then, after his degree was awarded, as a member of the faculty. He succeeded Wilson as Dean. So, he acquired a strong ally. He also partly took Carnovsky into his camp, since Leon was interested, as was Joeckel, in public library administration. But it was only after Waples and I had both taken leave for WWII that the school Dr. Wilson wanted was included formally.

This, of course, completely altered the original concept and purpose of GLS.[79]

Research and Publication

CONCEPT OF RESEARCH

The GLS at Chicago rejected the broad term "librarianship" as not satisfactorily describing its field of study, preferring "library science," by which it meant the scientific study of the relationship between people and books within the context of libraries. Much of the effort of the GLS may be viewed as attempting to imbue a largely hollow phrase with meaning. Operationally, the field of study at Chicago included adult and adolescent reading, education for librarianship, cataloging and classification, history of libraries and printing, and the administration of libraries. Butler, in his *Introduction*, considered these to be part of either the sociological, psychological, or historical problems in library science. Undoubtedly, the GLS did not need to be told by the *New York Times* that merely calling it a science did not make it so (see the discussion, below, on *Library Quarterly* monographs).

The GLS faculty was strongly united in believing that prospective students should have a "problem" (as distinguished from a "topic") to study before entering the program. In a particular case, related by Hazel B. Timmerman (an assistant in the ALA Personnel Division), Ellyn Beaty had come into her office, quite upset because she had to have a "problem" before she could enroll in the GLS to study high school library work and children's literature. Beaty explained this to Timmerman as meaning that

> apparently the Graduate Library School is not interested in giving people anything but is only interested in those who can contribute something towards the School.[80]

This statement reveals the divergence between the school's concept of research and the concepts of many practicing librarians. Further evidence of the divergence is provided in the BEL's "Alphabetical List of Library Terms," in which "research" was defined as

> in general limited to finding the facts, and . . . not concerned with their interpretation or ultimate utilization.[81]

A few months before, Douglas Waples, as acting dean, had defined what the BEL called research as *searching*. "This important distinction between research and *search*," he pointed out, "is not apparent to many prominent librarians."[82] While he could have argued that, etymologically, research means "to search again and again," instead he chose illustrative examples. Waples considered the compiling of an index to be a "search," and "*evaluating* source materials in our own field and in other fields as well"[83] to be closer to the GLS ideal of "research." In further contrast to the BEL statement, Donald Slesinger and Mary Stephenson, in the *Encyclopedia of the Social Sciences* (1934), state:

> Research is the manipulation of things, concepts, or symbols for the purpose of generalizing to extend, correct or verify knowledge, whether that knowledge aid in the construction of a theory or in the practice of an art.[84]

This definition was implicit in Waples' 1931 discussion, "The Graduate Library School at Chicago."[85]

Another aspect of the work of the GLS which set it off from the rest of the profession was the nature of the problems that were studied, which took the form of questions. William Randall has related a series of disquieting questions, which concerned cataloging, that were asked at Chicago during his tenure:

> In general, in making catalogs, librarians have said, in effect, "what can we say about this *book*?" Well, you know the answer. "How tall is it?" "How many pages does it have?" "Who wrote it?" "When was he born?" etc.; all *this* set out on the catalog card according to strict rules of spacing and punctuation, which are supposed to take a year of intelligent study to learn, and are sacro-sanct and never, never to be deviated from, because "it has always been done this way."
>
> Now, the question I asked myself in studying cataloging is quite different. "What do readers or library patrons need to be told about this book?" The answer is not simple. Different people need to be told different things, in different ways. The bibliophile needs (or wants) one type of information; the person . . . looking for a book to read for recreation only, doesn't really care about knowing anything we tell him in a catalog, but would like to know things we don't tell him.[86]

Thus members of the GLS faculty were often considered by librarians to have inapposite answers in this early period, but it was because they were asking different questions. Waples' research on "what people want to read about" was a good example; on more than one occasion, Carl Milam asked Wilson to "put his [Waples'] work where it belongs in relation to the whole picture."[87] It was still too early to speak of a shift in the consensus concerning relevant sets of questions to be asked and studied to the GLS position, since, for a long time, other library schools had been teaching students to ask and to answer an entirely different set of questions.

The GLS faculty did not perceive its developing discipline as independent but as strongly interdisciplinary. Thus its members and their students most often sought sources of solutions to library problems from the social sciences. Specific, identifiable interactions of faculty and students occurred with individuals on the university faculty, such as Beardsley Ruml, dean of the Social Sciences Division; Donald Slesinger, Robert Redfield, Ernest W. Burgess in sociology; Charles H. Judd of educational psychology; Floyd W. Reeves in educational survey; L. L. Thurstone of psychology; Simeon E. Leland of political science; and Louis Brownlow in public administration. Humanities professors who were contacted included John Manly of the English Department and William A. Nitze in Romance languages. In particular, the departments of sociology, political science, and education were singled out as the most significant sources of relevant methods, and as a result, "cross-fertilization"[88] with library science occurred. More importantly, perhaps, this interaction with other departments led to further integration of the Graduate Library School with the university —one of the earliest stated objectives of the new school.

Douglas Waples was largely responsible for the emphasis on the social sciences as he taught 310, "Methods of Investigation," during this period. Unfortunately, there are no locatable early syllabi for the course, although much can be reconstructed from his *Investigating Library Problems* (1939).[89] The first chapter of that book discusses the statement of the problem, directing attention toward (1) the definition of terms, (2) external validity, and (3) a checklist for selecting a problem. The second through the fourth chapters discusses evidence; chapters five through seven explicate rules of evidence, including historical criticism. The last three chapters are a synthesis, evaluation, and summary of necessary elements in a research proposal. Each chapter concludes with discussion and application.

The GLS at Chicago was also at variance with most other library schools in the use of particular instruments and techniques of analysis to solve the problems, but primarily in the use of questionnaires and statistical analysis. Although the GLS was often characterized during this period as interested solely in this type of research, the school seemed to be following Slesinger's counsel when he advised, in the *Encyclopedia*, that the "recent tendency to identify research with a particular method of investigation"[90] (such as surveys) should be avoided. Similarly, in his *Introduction to Library Science* Butler recognized that

> the experiment is important, not because it is an experiment, but because it furnishes favorable opportunity for accurate observation: disturbing factors are eliminated, instrumental manipulation is simplified, and endless repetitions are possible.[91]

The experiment was desirable because it allowed an additional measure of control; yet it would be an inappropriate, if not impossible, technique to apply to certain library problems, such as historical questions. The historical areas, however, received little support.

The humanities contrasted with the flourishing social sciences. Despite repeated calls for research support and effort, first by Waples and then by Carnovsky, research in the humanities ("bibliography, historical method, paleography, advanced reference work and rare book-room and museum practice")[92] languished, mostly due to lack of support rather than lack of effort. As acting dean in 1931, Waples had recommended that Butler's status be changed to a full-time professorship so that "our efforts in bibliography"[93] would be less limited. Yet these efforts were largely unsupported due to lack of interest at the Carnegie Corporation.

During this period, the corporation supported the GLS by additional grants of $656,000, but less than 10 percent of this amount went directly to any of the humanities mentioned above. Butler's proposals, such as "preparation of a source book and treatise on the invention of printing" or "a treatise on the spread of printing and the establishing of it as a definite industry,"[94] were rejected at the corporation. The former idea had been developed at the Newberry, cited as being in progress in 1930, and finally published in 1940 as *The Origin of Printing*.[95] Just prior to his death in 1953, Butler (still unsupported) was working on a manuscript concerning rare-book librarianship.[96] James Westfall Thompson's work fared about as well; he worked intermittently for twelve years before *The Medieval Library*[97] was published in 1939.

In the *Encyclopedia of the Social Sciences*, Slesinger had also observed that statistical method has supplemented and replaced experimentation, but because of the pressure of demand few statistical workers have acquired the theoretical background necessary for an understanding of the significance of the formulae with which they work. Since anyone can learn a correlation formula and how to run an adding machine, the qualifications for research have been reduced to a point where little more than high school education is required. The result has been a selective lowering of the type of intelligence attracted to the social sciences and thus a serious danger to their advancement. The depression may have a salutary effect in cutting off some of these less intelligent fact finders and in forcing the surviving workers to think more about the material in hand and to collect new material in terms of specific problems.[98]

Waples' course in methods was a first-line defense against a similar degradation of library *science*. The second was evaluation of students' work.

As a response to Waples' interest in evaluation of theses, Hester Hoffman, for her master's thesis, studied 470 master's theses and the twenty-four Chicago doctoral theses (or 92% of the 535 postgraduate degrees awarded between 1926 and 1940).[99] As a necessary antecedent to evaluation, she inductively classified their methodologies. She defined the three categories (see table 8) and cited examples. Table 8 demonstrates that, during the period, Chicago discouraged bibliographies, or what she termed "Case I" theses, despite the fact that Waples called for more "critical bibliographies"[100] in his *LQ* columns.

Compared to other library schools, the GLS employed the most "current survey" methodologies, although it is second to California when historical methodology is added. Examples of Type IIA research at Chicago are the theses of Mary K. Armstrong or Thomas S. Harding ("A Comparison of Student Library Use" and "The John Crerar Library as a Regional Center"). At the M.S. level, the GLS was also second to George Peabody College in the percentage of theses devoted to the "solution of unknown variables," for example, those theses that employ a hypothesis and are forward looking (as opposed to surveys and histories). Examples of Type III research are the theses of Leon Carnovsky, Lester D. Condit, J. Periam Danton, Jeannette H. Foster, Carleton Joeckel, Robert Miller, and James Wellard (e.g., "An Experiment in Classifying Fiction" or "Bases for a Theory of Book Selection"). For further comparisons, see table 9.

As part of the evaluation of research, the GLS faculty began in 1939 to distinguish between theses, reports, and papers. By the term master's *report*, it meant "fact gathering," and the term master's *thesis* meant "constructive analysis";[101] *paper* appears to be nearly synony-

TABLE 8
Library School Theses Classed by Type, 1926–40

School	Bibliography I Simple IA	Annot. IB	Total	Survey II Current IIA	Hist. IIB	Total	Unknown Variable III	Grand Total
California		2	(8) 2	8	13	(84) 21	(8) 2	25
Chicago (M.A.)				21	5	(76) 26	(24) 8	34
Columbia	5	21	(12) 26	97	60	(74) 157	(14) 29	212
Illinois	2	11	(11) 13	32	56	(73) 88	(17) 20	121
Michigan	4	9	(26) 13	21	15	(72) 36	(2) 1	50
George Peabody				1	2	(60) 3	(40) 2	5
George Washington	4	4	(57) 8	2	4	(43) 6		14
Western Reserve				2	5	7	2	9
Total Master's	15	47	(13) 62	184	160	(73) 344	(14) 64	470
Chicago (Ph.D.)				4	5	(38) 9	(68) 15	24
Total M.A.s and Ph.D.s	15	47	(13) 62	188	165	(72) 353	(16) 79	494

Source: Tables 4 and 5 of Hester E. Hoffman, "The Graduate Thesis in Library Science" (M.A. thesis, University of Chicago, 1941).
Numbers in parentheses = percentage of grand total.

TABLE 9
Percentage of *Library Quarterly* Contributors by Occupation

	Period Covered				
Occupation	1931–36	1937–42	1943–48	1949–54	Total
University and college librarians	30% (47)	35% (62)	29% (37)	39% (50)	33% (196)
Library science educators	31 (49)	17 (30)	16 (21)	21 (27)	21 (127)
Special librarians	14 (23)	15 (27)	16 (20)	20 (25)	16 (95)
Other educators	13 (20)	10 (17)	12 (15)	14 (18)	12 (70)
All others	13 (20)	22 (40)	27 (35)	6 (8)	17 (103)
Total articles	159	176	128	128	591

Source: Based on table 3 in Ruth O. Rehfus and Eugene I. Stearns, "The Library Quarterly, 1931–1966: An Index with Commentary" (M.A. thesis, Kent State University, 1967).
"All others" includes public libraries, students, school librarians, those employed in some phase of the book industry or publishing, and other occupations. Numbers in parentheses = "raw numbers."

mous with *report*. (Further discussion of this distinction and the pro-portion of theses, reports, and papers are presented in the last section and table 12, respectively.) Papers or reports tended to be what Sle-singer, in *Encyclopedia of the Social Sciences*, called "the material in hand,"[102] Robert Burgess's master's paper, "The Sources of Library Statistics" (1942), being an example. It had been Waples' desire, since at least as early as 1931, that individuals who were interested in the contributions of the GLS would "take the trouble to read our theses. I think that anyone who reads these theses should see a connection between studies of that character and the advance of the library profession."[103]

Unfortunately, some of the techniques, especially questionnaires, were annoying to the profession they were supposed to help, and Dean Wilson had encountered a similar response when the BEL sent out a questionnaire. Wilson wrote to Waples in 1932 that "question-naires do irritate, particularly if the letter asking for cooperation is not carefully phrased."[104] Even after Wilson left Chicago, one of his suc-cessors was still getting comments about students' questionnaires. Warner G. Rice, the new librarian at the University of Michigan, wrote to Berelson complaining about a particular piece of Chicago "research":

In the social sciences and education the number of dissertations based upon raw and untested data assembled by the questionnaire method is growing rapidly. We do not find that the conclusions reached amount to much more than statistical summaries; we think that there is little originality or penetration required for the production of such results; and we doubt very much whether a study of this kind deserves the name of research.[105]

Wilson also received comments on the increased use of statistics, even from the Carnegie Corporation. On one occasion, Robert Lester waggishly referred to the work emanating from Chicago as "the 6-point-decimal-square-root type of library research."[106] W. W. Bishop, at Michigan, also was "anxious to avoid . . . these pseudo-statistical studies with an air of great learning which emanate from Chicago at intervals and which show nothing."[107]

Some instances were not without humor, such as the one related by Ralph Ellsworth, which occurred circa 1936:

Harper E10 was full of clacking Monroe calculating machines and crews of National Youth Administration workers being managed by a few graduate students. Billy Haygood had been working at ALA headquarters on some statistical project that required the use of a calculator. His comments on the reaction of the ALA staff to the machine were somewhat as follows:
"Why, those women really thought there was a devil in the machine. They gathered around me and were filled with awe and wonder as I ground out percentages."[108]

Equally revealing of the school's "spirit of inquiry" was a 1933 incident told to Maurice Tauber by Wilson:

One day as he [Wilson] was walking in front of the [Rockefeller Memorial] chapel with Leon Carnovsky, one of the first Ph.D.'s of the school, several buses rolled up and the Midway vendors of ice cream and other articles began to hawk their wares. One, who was selling some sort of inexpensive cigarette lighter, bellowed: "Right this way, gents; get your everlasting match; one for fifty cents, three for a dollar!" Infused with the school's spirit of letting no statement, however sound it seemed, go unchallenged, Carnovsky stopped and said, "See here, Mister, there is something wrong with that assumption. If one match is everlasting, why get three?"[109]

These statements help to exemplify the divergence in understanding of what the GLS was attempting to do, as well as the magnitude of Wilson's task in explaining the school to librarians. Not surprisingly, Wilson frequently used the library press as the vehicle for such explanations of its perceived mission as "The Development of Research in Relation to Library Schools," "The Development of a Program of Research in Library Science in the Graduate Library School," and "The American Library School Today."[110]

"LIBRARY QUARTERLY" AND ITS MONOGRAPH SERIES

At the end of Wilson's first year, he filed a report with the Carnegie Corporation on the use of the grant monies for *Library Quarterly* during 1931–33. He pointed out that 1,300 pages had been published for 934 subscribers (882 paid, 52 free); of those subscriptions, 761 were domestic and 121 foreign. Geographically, seven states accounted for nearly half of the subscriptions: New York 93, Illinois 62, California 55, Massachusetts 48, Pennsylvania 48, Ohio 35, and Texas 22.[111] The following year, however, he had to report a net loss of a dozen subscriptions, due perhaps to the Depression.[112]

In 1935, Wilson requested a further subvention of $15,000 from the corporation for the next five years (in 1931, the GLS had received $5,000 for five years).[113] He emphasized six studies or series of studies that he felt were especially outstanding in the 137 major articles published to date. Whereas three areas (reading, education for librarianship, and academic libraries) had been concentrated upon to that time, the editor and the editorial board were now looking forward to publishing "to a greater extent useful and authoritative material concerning public libraries."[114] The addition of Carleton Joeckel to the faculty and the board of editors was mentioned as contributing to this intention. Viewing the history of the journal, Wilson thought the "first few numbers [had been] made up of articles written largely by members of the faculties of library schools."[115] He anticipated that this policy would change, although "there was still some difficulty in acquiring publishable and interesting manuscripts."[116]

He was correct. From 1931–36 to 1937–42, the contributions by library science educators dropped 14 percent. As shown in table 9, the most frequently published contributions during this period came from college and university librarians, outnumbering those of library science educators by more than two to one. If we assume that the "all others" category primarily comprised writings by public librarians, Wilson's intention of publishing their articles, at least in the 1937–42 period, appears to have been fairly well accomplished. Unfortunately, the original investigators, Ruth O. Rehfus and Eugene I. Stearns, did not present findings in their thesis on the subject matter directly.

Rehfus and Stearns, however, presented a table on the "types of articles" published in *Library Quarterly*; this information is recast into percentages by period and by category in table 10. Wilson himself commented on the types of material that appeared in *LQ*. First, there were critical reviews of current publications; second, scholarly articles of professional interest; and third, the results of research were published. The last category accounted for approximately 35 percent of the articles published in volumes 1 through 3. The largest number of these, six in all, were in the area of education for librarianship (all of E. J. Reece's articles qualified). As the second-largest number (5) concerned public libraries, Wilson might have been satisfied to stop there, without going out of his way to get more such articles. Douglas Waples' articles on reading made up the largest part of the third-most-frequent area of research. Although there were almost as many articles on the history of libraries and printing (12) as in education for librarianship (14), only two of them qualified as re-

TABLE 10
Percentage of *Library Quarterly* Articles by Type, 1931–54

Type of Article	Period Covered									
	1931–36		1937–42		1943–48		1949–54		Total	
Bibliographic essays	2%	(3)	3%	(6)	7%	(9)	4%	(5)	4%	(23)
Bibliographies	2	(3)	4	(4)		(0)	1	(1)	1	(8)
Biographies	6	(10)	6	(10)	13	(16)	9	(11)	8	(47)
Descriptive articles	23	(38)	21	(37)	21	(27)	37	(47)	25	(149)
Historical articles	13	(20)	12	(21)	9	(11)	12	(15)	11	(67)
Library science research descriptive studies	21	(34)	20	(35)	18	(23)	9	(11)	17	(103)
Library science research experimental studies	3	(4)	2	(3)	6	(8)		(0)	3	(15)
Opinion articles	19	(30)	25	(44)	16	(21)	27	(34)	29	(129)
Review articles	7	(11)	6	(11)	5	(7)	3	(4)	6	(33)
Sociological studies	2	(3)	1	(2)	3	(4)		(0)	1	(9)
Textual criticism	2	(3)	2	(3)	2	(2)		(0)	1	(8)
Total articles		159		176		128		128		591

Source: Based on table 1 in Ruth O. Rehfus and Eugene I. Stearns, "The Library Quarterly, 1931–1966: An Index with Commentary" (M.A. thesis, Kent State University, 1967).

"Articles which are simply listings of graduate theses, or introductions to conferences, were omitted from this table." Numbers in parentheses = "raw numbers."

search: Ruth S. MacKensen's "Four Great Libraries of Medieval Baghdad" (July 1932) and Duncan Black MacDonald's "A Bibliographical and Literary Study of the First Appearance of the *Arabian Nights* in Europe" (Oct. 1932). Since only 16 percent of the articles in this area were considered research, Carnovsky (as quoted earlier) was quite right about historical research in librarianship being an area of "great opportunity."[117]

In comparing these comments with the data in table 10, at least one caution should be heeded. Rehfus and Stearns do not define for the reader "library science research," either descriptive or experimental. Since their columns—collectively for the 1931–36 period—do not equal Wilson's categorization of research articles for the 1931–33 period alone, one may conclude either that Wilson had a broader definition of research than later writers or that there was a sharp decline in research during 1934–36. The latter supposition might be borne out by the fact that there was a 6 percent increase in articles of opinion (the most frequent in 1937–42), while descriptive articles, which had been the most frequent in the earlier period, took second place, behind the opinion pieces. The recast chart of Rehfus and Stearns indicates only a slight decrease in research. An alternative explanation—that Wilson inflated the articles considered to be research—seems less likely since he enclosed an index of the articles published, marking those which in his judgment, were research pieces.[118]

Finally, Rehfus and Stearns investigated the number of *LQ* contributions per author. Table 11 shows that, save for two individuals, the most prolific authors of articles were GLS faculty and students. One-time contributors, however, account for nearly half of all *LQ* articles. Rather ironically, Leon Carnovsky was prompted to write to Wilson, following his address on the twenty-fifth GLS anniversary in 1951, that

> one point on which we all felt pretty strongly was that the LQ was not and should not be the mouthpiece of the Graduate Library School, any more than it should so serve for any other library school.[119]

Leon Carnovsky had become the most frequent contributor to *LQ* in the intervening years. However, identified GLS contributors account for only 11 percent of all articles between 1931 and 1966.

In 1940, subscriptions to *Library Quarterly* increased to more than 1,000, despite "fears expressed in last year's report that the new American Library Association publication, *College and Research Libraries*, might perhaps prove to be a serious competitor of the *Quarterly*."[120] Leon Carnovsky replaced William Randall as the man-

TABLE 11
Library Quarterly Contributions per Author, 1931–66

No. of Authors		No. of Articles
1	Leon Carnovsky	27
1	W. W. Bishop	16
1	Howard W. Winger	14
1	Douglas Waples	13
1	J. C. M. Hanson	11
1	Pierce Butler	10
1	Lester Asheim	8
2	L. S. Thompson and H. Goldhor	7
4		6
10		5
16		4
31		3
74		2
434		1
578	Total Identified	Total Articles 926

Source: Recast table 2 from Ruth O. Rehfus and Eugene I. Stearns, "The Library Quarterly, 1931–1966: An Index with Commentary" (M.A. thesis, Kent State University, 1967).

aging editor of *LQ* in 1942; another change that was considered was solicitation of articles, as opposed to reliance upon voluntary contributions. "This," according to Wilson, "should result in a better balanced distribution of articles than has been true heretofore."[121] In the 1943–48 period, the number of published biographies increased. Meanwhile, descriptive, opinion, and historical articles decreased, although descriptive articles accounted for roughly the same percentage of the total as in the earlier two periods. Finally, the Second World War caused a marked drop in the number of foreign subscriptions. The number of domestic subscriptions boosted the total circulation slowly, but at a satisfying rate. At the end of this period, *LQ* was "substantially self-sustaining."[122]

At about the time the first issue of *Library Quarterly* was sent to press, Douglas Waples wrote to Frederick Keppel at the corporation, asking if the journal might consider publishing occasional longer papers as monographs. Waples proposed to call them "Library Quarterly Monographs" and to use the monies appropriated by the corporation to finance them, at least in part.[123] Robert M. Lester, however, advised Keppel against it, recommending that the money be used solely for the journal and that the GLS find some other source for funding the proposed monograph series.[124] Keppel agreed and informed Waples that it was a good idea, but he should look elsewhere for the required financial support.[125]

Deciding they could do it alone, arrangements were made with the University of Chicago Press. William Randall, a member of the press's selection committee, "which determined what books the Press would publish,"[126] most likely was also consulted. Consequently, "the results of more extensive studies than can appropriately be presented through the pages of the Library Quarterly"[127] formed the University of Chicago's new Library Science Series, which was to be published "from time to time."[128] The first in the series was Pierce Butler's *An Introduction to Library Science*.

As was mentioned in the last chapter, although Pierce Butler's letter to Mary Ahern, editor of *Libraries*, was not published, he still had his classes as a vehicle for presenting his ideas. Butler, then acting dean, shared a copy of his letter to Ahern with Wilson soon after it was made known that he was being considered for the deanship.[129] The basic ideas in his letter were expanded to book length, and in March 1933 Wilson, the new dean, wrote a foreword to Butler's manuscript. The book's jacket indicated that it was "a new approach to librarianship,"[130] although this did not appear as the subtitle. Of his approach, Wilson wrote:

> Dr. Butler sets forth the essential nature of science as he conceives it, and shows how the problems of the modern library as an important social institution may be studied in accord with its spirit and methods. *In this respect it reflects the approach made by the School to librarianship and the attitude assumed by it in the study and investigation of library problems* [emphasis added].[131]

Accordingly, Butler's work is discussed at length in the following pages because it was acknowledged by the new dean to be a guide to the new intellectual discipline of library science as perceived by the GLS at Chicago.

Addressing himself to practitioners, Butler adopted the role of a speculative philosopher who has only empirical knowledge with which to start. His first task, to define the nature of science, was hard, if not hazardous, "for nothing is so difficult as definition, nor anything so severe a test and exercise of mental clarity and skill."[132] Yet with clarity and lucidity Butler revealed its nature in terms of observation, rational explanation, and evaluation. He fully expected that the new science of librarianship would "become scientific only as it conforms

in essentials to the habitual methods of thought in the modern temper."[133] Accepting Waples' strongly interdisciplinary view of librarianship, Butler further thought that

> in the course of the new departure librarians will win a new outlook.
> They will transfer their attention from process to function. They will
> come to strive for accurate understanding just as ardently as they now
> do for practical efficiency. They will temper their ideals with realistic
> considerations and discover standards in the nature of their elements
> rather than assume them as *a priori* values. They will seek for knowl-
> edge in typical phenomena instead of in particular occurrences. They
> will study librarianship rather than single libraries. Their enthusiasm
> for vocational unanimity will give way to a recognition of real differ-
> ences in operative levels, but their quest they will still regard as a co-
> operative enterprise of the whole profession.[134]

Such was Butler's Utopia. As he further conceived librarianship,
"library science in particular can embrace only the rational side of the
fundamental phenomenon of librarianship which is the transmission
of the accumulated experience of society to its individual members
through the instrumentality of the book."[135] The rational aspect of
librarianship, he felt, has a tripartite division, which he termed the
sociological problem, the psychological problem, and the historical
problem.[136]

Having established the importance and significance of reading,
Butler raised the question of the effect of reading on society as part
of the sociological problem. He urged community analysis, for "selection with reference to the kind of people served is the sole criterion of social efficiency"[137] in librarianship. Coincident with an
analysis *en masse* is the principle that learning through reading is
a solitary or individual intellectual activity. Essentially, this section
of Butler's book is a discussion of the problem of motive, which can
be defined as action which is preceded by will which is preceded by
desire. Butler categorized three types of motives for reading: for information, for esthetic appreciation, and for direct pleasure.

The question, again, is What is "the effect of reading on the mental
life of the reader?"[138] In the last division of the book, Butler wrote
that "the form of the book through the ages and the various methods
of its fabrication are basic historical problems for library science."[139]
Furthermore, he proposed that "the development of the library as an
institution is also an essential chapter in library science."[140] Of the
various kinds of history, Butler named three. The first, the history of
knowledge, he divided into the esthetic, which is the history of literature, and the factual, which he called the history of science. In dis-

cussing these, he pointed out the different types of library service rendered by subscribers to different schools of historical thought. His last two kinds of history are the history of education and the history of scholarship. Both are important to understand, he felt, for "the scholarship of a community will determine the character of its library."[141] Providing a history of scholarship became the life work of Butler.

In his final chapter, on "practical considerations," Butler identified four possible benefits of library science. The first was that "a professional philosophy would give to librarianship that directness of action which can spring only from a complete consciousness of purpose."[142] A professional philosophy would mean, for library education, that library schools would view their activity as "the administration of a public trust" rather than "the correct supervision of a routine procedure."[143] Secondly, the "responsibility which [the librarian] assumes with his office is to exploit those archives for communal advantage to the utmost of his ability."[144] Another benefit is that library science "will establish that theoretical framework without which no deliberate extension of knowledge is possible."[145] "A third probable benefit which may be expected to result from the development of library science will be the way in which it will distinguish between the various professional activities."[146] Adopting a medical analogy, Butler equated clerical, technical, and professional "librarians" with orderlies, nurses, and physicians respectively. He believed that the profession to that time had, unfortunately, not clearly distinguished these tasks, and in some cases had simply promoted nurses to the office of physician. Finally, Butler believed that professional unity would be promoted by the establishment of a library science. None of these benefits, however, was possible "until librarianship turns its attention from process to function."[147]

As an *apologia pro libro suo*, Butler hoped the essay would be simply "a tract for the times . . . no better fate can be hoped for what is here written than that it should quickly become obsolete."[148]

M. E. Walker, who reviewed the book for the *New York Times Book Review*, took Butler to task. First, he pointed out that "the mere statement that librarianship is a science does not make it so."[149] Perhaps the reviewer did not recognize the emerging discipline or the context within which the book was written; nevertheless, he pointed out that the first section lacked "the simplicity and directness of the others."[150] Second, Walker felt that, in the statement of the psychological problem, Butler refused "to speak of the effect of reading on the mental life of the reader."[151]

"This," he [Butler] says, "is so obscure that any attempt to analyze its complexities on the basis of general observation alone is quite futile." Obscure? Futile? Surely Dr. Butler meant that had he touched upon that one detail alone he might have filled volumes.[152]

The review concluded that the book was nevertheless a "worthy undertaking."[153]

At the Carnegie Corporation, Nathaniel Peffer reviewed the work and summarized it for Keppel. Peffer's concluding comment was, "I confess I do not quite see the application."[154] On the other hand, Frank K. Walter of the University of Minnesota, reviewing it for *LQ*, thought that "the book should do real service in hastening, even if it does not actually inaugurate, a more scientific approach to a real library science."[155] Ernest J. Reece, of Columbia's School of Library Service, concluded that "those who realize that any new order comes not by observation of course will not anticipate an immediate recreating of librarianship's professional outlook."[156] Yet he would probably agree that the GLS had what was required for this re-creating, and that was a disciplined community of scholarly inquirers.

During Wilson's tenure, twenty-seven titles, or an average of three books annually, were published in the University of Chicago Studies in Library Science. Beginning in 1937, the annual conference—or Library Institute, as it came to be called—began publication as a part of this series. Aside from these volumes, however, the majority of titles dealt with reading or public librarianship. Douglas Waples, the most prolific author in the series during this period, wrote five titles, and his books account for the strong emphasis on reading. A complete list of titles in the series through 1951 is presented in appendix E.

ANNUAL CONFERENCE

The idea of the library institutes did not originate with Dean Wilson, since there was a series of summer institutes at the GLS underwritten by the Carnegie Corporation, beginning in 1926. It is to Wilson's credit, however, that they were revived and the proceedings published, beginning with the 1936 Institute for Librarians and Teachers of Library Science. Ninety-seven participants[157] were attracted from twenty-two states,[158] and for the first time a much wider audience could participate by reading the addresses. Incorporating the institutes into the Studies in Library Science Series also meant that many more libraries would obtain them on standing orders.

The purpose of this "first" annual conference was to present the social trends which were affecting the development and administration of libraries so that planning could take place before such social changes actually occurred. The subject was prompted because the National Commission on Social Trends completely overlooked libraries in its *Recent Social Trends in the U.S.* (1932). The underlying assumption gave recognition to the fact that

> the library [according to William Ogburn, professor of sociology at Chicago], is a part of society as a whole and does not exist in any sense in a vacuum, nor does it pursue its own course isolated from the happenings around it. The corollary of this assumption is that libraries are, on the other hand, largely molded by the events that are occurring outside their walls, in society as a whole.[159]

This institute set a pattern of selecting topics concerning the developments which would likely have impact on libraries in the near future. As such, they were probably of interest to library administrators.

Dean Wilson was most frequently listed as the editor of the individual institute proceedings, although Professor Randall has pointed out that

> the history of this Institute and the publication of its proceedings show another facet of Dr. Wilson's character. This year before [1939], Leon Carnovsky had organized the Summer Institute, supervised it, and prepared the proceedings for publication. But Dr. Wilson was named as the Editor, and Leon received no credit whatever. When I began to edit the papers of 1941 [*sic*], Dr. Wilson called me to his office and informed me that, as Head of the School, the same thing would of course apply for the 1941 [*sic*] Institute. I believe I was polite, but I told him flatly that if he wanted his name on the title page, he would do the editing. First, I was a full professor, and an Assistant Dean in the University; I had tenure, which Leon at that time did not have. There was no way Dr. Wilson could coerce me except by bringing formal charges before the University Senate, which I knew he would not do, because he had none to bring.[160]

Evidently, from that time on the individual responsible for the institute was the editor, and his name appeared on the title page. A complete listing of the institutes appears in Appendix F.

No less significant were the annual summer seminars and workshops for college librarians, which were held on the Chicago campus, beginning in 1936 and continuing throughout this period. Although the seminars and workshops did not result directly in publication, they were useful periods of time, spent in interaction and using the GLS faculty as resource people.

Epilogue, 1942–51

The onset of the Second World War was the cause for dispersal of the major portion of the original GLS faculty. At the close of the war, a succession of deans had held that office, although in 1952 Lester Asheim took over the deanship for a period of eleven years. Also, there were several deaths of influential individuals involved with the Graduate Library School at Chicago.

At the Carnegie Corporation, Keppel wrote to Wilson in August of 1940 that the "critical state of things" would mean no support for the GLS, as the corporation was marshaling its resources for "some enterprise."[161] Wilson's reply indicated that he understood; he feared, however, that the American public would only want to solve the problems at hand rather than to promote scholarship.[162] Records at the corporation concerning the GLS from 1943 to 1947 seem to be nonexistent, due (presumably) to the war efforts and Carnegie's other interests. In this period, Frederick Keppel retired and shortly thereafter died, on 8 September 1943. Writing from Chapel Hill, Wilson eulogized him thus in the pages of *LQ*:

> As president of the Carnegie Corporation of New York from 1923 to 1941, Dr. Keppel directed with rare wisdom and skills the affairs of that organization; its fundamental aim—the advancement and diffusion of knowledge and understanding—gave range and life to his vision and constantly guided him in the formulation of policies.[163]

Of course, Wilson singled out Keppel's interest in education for librarianship as typical of the kind of consideration he gave to an area. However,

> upon all of them, whatever their nature, he brought a rich experience, a keen mind, a retentive memory, a wide knowledge, and a rare genius for quick understanding that insured such development as to contribute most to the achievement of the trust he so successfully administered.[164]

Another loss was J. C. M. Hanson, by death in 1943. He was eulogized in a memorial issue of *Library Quarterly* the following January.

DISPERSAL OF THE ORIGINAL FACULTY

The war also made itself felt on the Chicago campus. The Graduate Library School had to give up its typewriters to the effort in November 1942.[165] The next month, Douglas Waples joined the army with the rank of major; he had been in Washington earlier in the year, consulting with the Bureau of Intelligence, Office of War Information. His army assignments took him to Lexington, Virginia; the Pentagon; London; Paris; Bad Homburg; and finally to Berlin. If the war was a period of great atrocity, it was also a time of great adventure. On VE Day, 8 May 1945, Waples and Hellmut Lehmann-Haupt were in Leipzig,

> one week before the Russians took Leipzig over from the U.S. Seventh Corps. We went down publishers' row in that city and picked some ten publishers whom we considered the best compromise between the most important pre-war German publishers and those most likely to be cleared by our own Intelligence Branch, which had a veto on all of our recommendations to license. Those we picked were moved out of Leipzig on the eve of the Russian occupation and across Germany by military convoy to Wiesbaden on the Rhine where they have prospered ever since.[166]

Waples remained in Nuremberg until December 1948. When he returned to the United States, the University of Chicago reappointed him professor of researches in reading in the GLS. However, he left the GLS in 1950 for the Committee in Communication, and became its chairman in 1951.[167]

Dr. Randall joined the army as a major in 1942. Particularly because of his knowledge of Arabic and the Middle East, he saw service in Cairo and Casablanca, ending with the North Atlantic Division in October 1945. "Upon leaving the service, [he] became manager of the Library Division of Snead & Company" in Virginia and was promoted to vice president of the Angus Snead Macdonald Corporation in 1946.[168] In June 1947 Randall accepted the directorship of the University of Georgia Libraries. After a brief tenure there, he joined the U.S. Merchant Marine Academy, but because of a federal investigation that "show[ed] what may be slight communistic tendencies"[169] he was forced to resign. He became dean at Wilmington College in North Carolina, from which he retired in 1968, after ten years as the school's president. Although his position in the GLS had been available to him upon his leaving the service, he returned only once, to deliver a paper on library buildings at the eleventh annual Library Institute in the summer of 1946.[170]

The other original faculty member was Pierce Butler. Undoubtedly due to his hearing loss and the fact that he was closer to retirement than other members of the faculty, Butler was not drafted. (Furthermore, his being an Episcopal priest may have entered into his decision not to volunteer.) Butler retired in 1952, and the July issue of the *Library Quarterly* was a tribute to his twenty-five years of service at the GLS. A year later, Pierce Butler died in an automobile accident, returning from the dedication of a new library building in Winston-Salem, North Carolina.[171]

The dispersal of the original faculty appears to have had some effect on research in library science, especially at the doctoral and master levels. First, the number of doctorates granted in the three years following the dispersal of the faculty (roughly contemporary with U.S. involvement in the Second World War) was 50 percent greater than in the preceding three-year period (see table 4; 1939–41 compared to 1942–44). The so-called "leavening" influence of the GLS, however, may have continued, as students of former GLS students were now desirous of studying at Chicago. A faculty composed of Butler and Carnovsky, assisted by Bernard Berelson, Herman Fussler, and Lowell Martin, under the deanship of Joeckel or Beals, became available to direct their work. However (as shown in table 12), a significant decline occurred in the amount of research done in the GLS, as defined by the thesis, from 1940 until 1945. This may be a reflection of the new emphasis on the first-year program and/or a return to the original deemphasis of the master's program, as stated by Works and Waples in the late 1920s and early 1930s.

TABLE 12
Percentage of Masters' Theses, Reports, and Papers

Year	Thesis		Report		Paper		Total	
1939	50%	(4)	38%	(3)	13%	(1)	100%	(8)
1940	50	(5)	50	(5)				(10)
1941	46	(6)	54	(7)				(13)
1942	44	(4)	22	(2)	33	(3)		(9)
1943	38	(5)			62	(8)		(13)
1944	33	(2)	17	(1)	50	(3)		(6)
1945	15	(2)			85	(11)		(13)
1946	36	(4)			64	(7)		(11)
1947	60	(3)			40	(2)		(5)
1948	73	(8)			27	(3)		(11)
1949	90	(9)			10	(1)		(10)
1950	63	(5)			38	(3)		(8)
Total	49	(57)	15	(18)	36	(42)		(117)

Numbers in parentheses = "raw number"; "report" and "paper" may be treated as synonymous.

SERIES OF DEANS

The selection of Carleton Joeckel, Wilson's hand-picked successor, was discussed earlier. As was also mentioned above, Herman H. Fussler and Lowell Martin joined the faculty during his tenure. Joeckel served until mid-1945, when he left for a professorship in the University of California's School of Librarianship. Several candidates were then considered for the deanship, including Warner G. Rice of the University of Michigan's Department of English Language and Literature. A stronger candidate, however, was already on the scene.

Randall had commented in 1939 on the "danger that efforts may be made to make a library science professor out of Beals,"[172] the University of Chicago library director. Indeed, his foresight was acute, for Ralph Beals was appointed dean of the GLS in 1945. During his brief tenure, he deemphasized administration and wrestled with "the problem of relating the old graduate curriculum to the work of the first year."[173] Perhaps Beals may also be credited with reversing the decline in the amount of research at the master's level, because, beginning in 1946, the number of theses increased. Unfortunately, however, he too left; this time for the New York Public Library as its director.

Later, Beals wrote a brilliant conceptual article on education for librarianship in which he proposed a truly interdisciplinary program.[174] Following the students' sophomore year in college (they would be admitted to college upon completion of their junior year of high school), they would be admitted to a three-year curriculum, the model for which would come from a similar applied science, such as medicine or engineering. The former required a common groundwork whereas the latter allowed early specialization. The three-year curriculum, as Beals conceived it, would consist of

1. Subject field, 30 per cent
2. The theory of communication . . . 20 per cent
3. The formation and use of book collections, 20 per cent
4. Seminar and thesis, 20 per cent
5. Directed practice, 10 per cent[175]

Since schools of librarianship had been unsuccessful in determining entrance requirements,[176] Beals proposed entrance and exit examinations, for only in this way, he thought, would the degree mean something. Beals concluded that this program was possible at Chicago, but unfortunately, he was no longer there to oversee its adoption.

After a brief time with Clarence H. Faust, dean of the University College at Chicago, the deanship settled on Bernard Berelson, who had earned his Ph.D. at the GLS in 1941 and had joined the faculty as an assistant professor. Writing to Wilson, Berelson said in August of 1947, "The chair of the Dean . . . has another occupant, namely me. . . . Since you of all people must know the Rules on How to Be a Good and Lasting Dean, I hope you will communicate them to me!"[177]

During Berelson's three and a half-year tenure, Jesse Shera joined the faculty. Shera had been in Washington as head of the U.S. Census Library Project and then as deputy chief, Central Information Division, Research and Analysis Bureau of the Office of Strategic Services. Most recently he had served as Beals's assistant director in the University Library. Also during this time, Fussler was promoted to professor and Martin left for Columbia's School of Library Service.

Two significant events occurred during Berelson's tenure, one inside and the other outside the school. Beginning in 1948/49, a course in documentation (the precursor of information science) was offered as "Bibliographic Organization" by Margaret E. Egan, an assistant professor in the GLS since the autumn quarter, 1946. The other event, outside the school, was the establishment of doctoral programs by other library schools. Berelson himself commented on the growing number of them (Illinois, Michigan, Columbia, and, he thought, California would likely be added to the list shortly). While he thought it a mistake for only one school to give the degree, he thought that too great a number would mean "the deterioration of the quality of the degree; it looks to me as though some schools are going to give a Master's degree for the old Bachelor's program and then give a doctorate for the old Master's program."[178]

Noting the growth of yet another intellectual discipline within librarianship, Berelson articulated potential areas for research which included "research on the use of mechanical, especially electronic, equipment in solving bibliographic problems."[179] The 1950 Institute on Bibliographic Organization addressed some of the problems of this new research area. However, when he resigned in May 1951, to devote more time to his personal research, Berelson cited his major contribution to the GLS at Chicago as the "Books Course materials."[180]

Although Wilson expressed the hope of several alumni, that Lowell Martin would be appointed the next dean, the appointment of Lester Asheim in 1952 gave the University of Chicago someone with the "longevity for deaning" that Wilson himself had possessed (see Appendix D). Wilson concluded:

> With you and Waples out permanently, with Carnovsky away on leave, and Butler retiring next year, the School gives the impression

to librarians generally of having suffered a great loss which it should make every effort to remedy as quickly as possible. A strong appointment or two should be made as quickly as possible if Illinois and Columbia are not to be allowed to edge ahead in favorable professional opinion.[181]

From the discussion in the first section, it should be apparent that Dean Wilson subordinated research early in his tenure; yet it would also appear that he was tempered by his new environment. The stance of the GLS, his new base of operation, on the side of librarianship as a science made it imperative that he effect a reasonable defense against the external attacks of individuals such as Thompson. Consequently, Wilson published a series of articles on (though not of) research, such as "The Development of a Program of Research in Library Science in the Graduate Library School" (1934). Wilson's assumption of the decision-making role at the beginning of his tenure supports Berelson's and Steiner's observation that "an organization is more likely to be strongly centralized during external crises than during normal periods."[182] It is less clear, though still apparent, that Wilson's understanding of and respect for academic freedom[183] allowed the faculty to continue its search for a research base throughout his tenure, as presented in the second section. It should be noted, however, that Wilson had to make the best of the new situation he found himself in, for it was difficult, if not impossible, to radically alter the composition of the GLS faculty; Butler, Randall, and Waples were all tenured upon Wilson's arrival in Chicago. Also, the organizational leadership in the GLS shifted from a charismatic leader, George Works, who was characterized as possessing an "unusual personality,"[184] to a bureaucratic leader, Louis R. Wilson, who was characterized as possessing administrative skills.[185]

Finally, Wilson's emphasis on administration and creation of the first-year program ran counter to the Laing Committee's original conception of the GLS. Both changes in the direction of the program had their support, if not their origin, in President Hutchins' thinking; he had articulated at least the former direction to Wilson in 1931 while he was at Chapel Hill. Needless to say, training students to administer libraries found favor with Carl Milam at ALA and thereby probably reassured the profession of Chicago's intentions.

6

Conclusions

The preceding five chapters are a detailed analysis of the development of the graduate library school concept in relation to the academic milieu and education for librarianship, and their ample evidence should allow reasonable assessment of the contribution of the Graduate Library School at Chicago, examined in light of the accomplishment of its objectives.[1] In summarizing its accomplishments, the author has identified and selected "critical incidents"[2] which have aided or hindered the work at the GLS. But several questions need to be answered before we address its accomplishments.

One of the first questions is how the profession's definition of "library science" and conception of "research" differed from those of the GLS. Within the profession, the following definitions are representative:

> Library science is that branch of human knowledge which treats of the production, care and use of the records of human knowledge [H. H. B. Meyer, 1925].[3]
>
> Library science is the knowledge and skill by which printed or written records are recognized, collected, organized and utilized [J. Christian Bay, 1928].[4]

At the University of Chicago, Edward Henry described library science

> as the science of the care and the use of books both for the control of knowledge already in existence and for the discovery of new knowledge through researches in books themselves or with books in connection with other sources of information.[5]

144

By late 1929, Douglas Waples was able to articulate further distinctions between the broadly understood "library science" (better understood today as *librarianship*) and the new "library *science*." Basically, "library science" was to him a human science or humanistic pursuit which lacked content or subject matter *per se*. Thus the sources of a science had to be found in other disciplines, which he named: bibliography, education, history, law, literary criticism, philosophy, political science, psychology, social service administration, sociology, and statistics. By the end of Wilson's tenure, "library science" at the GLS was understood as the scientific study of the relationship between people and books. Whether "books" was too narrowly understood to mean the codex rather than the "generic book," thus ignoring scientific report literature and giving rise to the new intellectual discipline of information science, is outside the scope of this study (although there appears to be evidence for this hypothesis).

The generally conceived scope of research in the library profession prior to the early years of the GLS at Chicago was bibliography, more specifically enumerative bibliography. Evidence for this view was presented in chapter 1, and particularly in the *honoris causa* M.L.S. awarded by the Albany State Library School. The affiliation of a graduate library school with a university such as Chicago, and the increasing interest in social science methods, relegated bibliography to the role of the "parent" of research in library science. Waples, as acting dean, in 1931 defined research in library science as

> extending the existing body of knowledge concerning the values and practices of libraries in their many aspects, and including the development of methods of investigation whereby significant data are obtained, tested, and applied.[6]

Waples' concept of research also carried utilitarian baggage: the worth of research in library science was to be established in the marketplace of use. Research was a "source," until the practitioner adopted it, and then it became "content." Utilitarianism is still present today in such a dictum as "maximizing the social utility of the graphic record." Nevertheless, when the GLS conception of research is compared to that in the *Encyclopedia of the Social Sciences*,[7] it is obvious that the GLS had truly adopted the university or scientific sense of research.

A second question, "What was the origin of the intellectual technique and the underlying 'science' of librarianship?" can be answered by examination of the backgrounds of members of the GLS faculty and their relationships with other departments of the University of

Chicago. George Works conceptualized library science as strongly interdisciplinary: " 'There is no justifiable demand for . . . the building of high fences about intensive professional interests.' "[8] Works's and Waples' backgrounds in statistics and education caused them to seek sources of a science of librarianship in those disciplines. The resources of the University of Chicago, with an especially strong social science division, also determined that library science would utilize social science methods. An expected side benefit from adoption of such an interdisciplinary perspective was the ability to recruit better-qualified students than if the school recruited only practicing librarians.

The third question relates to the roles of the Chicago Library Club, the University of Chicago, the Carnegie Corporation, and the GLS deans in formulating and redirecting the school's objectives. As discussed in chapter 2, the CLC attracted the Carnegie Corporation's attention to the city of Chicago as early as 1921. Carl Roden, as chairman of the CLC's Committee on a Library School, appears responsible for positing the sociological aspects of librarianship as an objective in the committee's 1923 memorandum. At the University of Chicago, Ernest D. Burton, first as librarian and then as president, assisted by J. C. M. Hanson, but more importantly by Edward Henry, developed a series of memoranda containing objectives of the proposed school. Significant drafts of the proposal, dated 23 January 1924, 20 May 1924, and 30 December 1924, may be taken as critical incidents in the formulation of the school's objectives.

Another critical incident was the selection as Burton's successor in the university presidency of Max Mason, who held a traditional view of bibliography as the appropriate research method for the GLS. However, Mason sought the opinion of distinguished members of the faculty. Their report, on 7 January 1926, is a critical incident in the decision of the University of Chicago to pursue the corporation grant and to develop objectives. Bishop's and Wilson's reports to the committee in April and May 1926 (respectively) are further critical incidents in the formulation of objectives.

The major incident in the formulation of objectives was the selection of George Works as dean in 1927. He articulated four major objectives, which will be discussed in detail later.

Dean Louis R. Wilson reaffirmed these objectives several times during his tenure, but most importantly he emphasized, beginning in 1932, the training of students for administrative posts as an objective. The major addition or change in the original objectives, development of a theory of librarianship (as compared to "library science"), was stated in 1940.

The fourth question deals with the GLS's objectives, what purpose they were prepared for and how widely they were promulgated within the profession. As presented in chapter 2, the original objectives of the GLS—to undertake research, to cooperate in investigations, to promote publication, and to train students in education for librarianship —were all stated before the school opened in the fall of 1928. The first public statements of these objectives, by George Works, appeared in *Library Journal* in December 1927 and in *Libraries* in February 1928. Since these were the two major journals in this period, it may be concluded that the statements were widely read. (An in-house publication, *University Record*, also carried an article on the subject in January 1928.) During the second or third quarter of instruction, a paper entitled "The Graduate Library School at the University of Chicago" was presented to the Chicago Library Club and was subsequently published in *Libraries* for July 1929. During the interregnum, Douglas Waples presented two more public statements, which appeared in the *ALA Bulletin* for August 1929 and the *Library Quarterly* for January 1931. Overall, these were consistent with in-house actions presented in chapters 3 and 4. In other words, GLS attempted to do what it said it was going to do.

The last question, "Did the GLS meet, modify, or change objectives over time?" is the central question in this study. The accomplishment of the GLS's objectives is elaborated upon in the following section, but one modification to these objectives should first be stressed. Early in Dean Wilson's tenure, administration came to be emphasized above training for library science education. The first public statement of this modification appeared in the 1932/33 *Announcements*. The major change in the original objectives occurred near the end of Dean Wilson's tenure with the additional intent to develop a theory or philosophy of library science. This new objective was publicly stated in *New Frontiers in Librarianship* (1940). In a sense, this objective grew out of the attention given this area by the GLS and its graduates, for instance, by Butler (1933), Carnovsky and E. McDiarmid (1934), Wellard (1934), Merritt (1936), R. Miller (1936), and Joeckel (1939).[9]

Evaluation of the Accomplishment of Objectives

There are a few difficulties with the data developed in the course of this study. First, in some cases potentially useful data were simply lacking, and there were many cases when minor questions could not be answered. The limited nature of the data is also apparent in considering the students; undoubtedly, for example, there were dropouts from the GLS[10] about whom no information was available in our material. Furthermore, the availability of students' entrance examinations (not developed until the 1940s) would have allowed the investigator to study the effects of the GLS program more carefully. Third, it is obvious that recruitment procedures changed during the period under investigation. In its early years, more women were found in the program than men; however, Dean Wilson was able to attract more men to the program (due to the effects of the Depression and the availability and attractiveness of the Carnegie fellowships).

Finally, it is apparent that much of the program's effectiveness was due to the personalities of members of the faculty, especially Douglas Waples and Pierce Butler. Their maintenance of a critical, inquiring atmosphere and an innovative approach to dealing with library problems and procedures is likely to have been more important than the content of any of their courses. Therefore the following statements are made with a caveat, that the GLS's contributions appear to be wider than the mere accomplishment of any particular objective. Yet these objectives provided structure for the spirit of inquiry in library science.

INSTRUCTION ON A GRADUATE BASIS
IN SPECIAL PHASES OF LIBRARY SCIENCE

This objective had its origin in the 1925 Standards adopted by the Board of Education for Librarianship. In creating a category for an advanced graduate library school, the BEL stipulated that it be "an integral part of a university which meets the standards for graduate study laid down by the Association of American Universities."[11] Thus the work of the Chicago Library Club in 1923 and Ernest D. Burton and his staff, especially J. C. M. Hanson and Edward Henry, as articulated in various memoranda, should be credited with focusing attention on the University of Chicago as a possible site. However, major credit for selecting the University of Chicago as the site is due to Frederick Keppel at the Carnegie Corporation. Max Mason's Committee on the Library School, headed by Gordon Laing, which reported on its concept of the proposed school early in 1926, also was critical in assuring instruction on a graduate basis.

The association of the school's first dean, George Works, with education, and Dean Wilson's later interactions with other departments, such as political science and sociology, were collective critical incidents which led to the GLS being an integral part of the univer-

sity. Accreditation by the BEL in 1933 reflects this agency's satisfaction with the school as an integral part of the university. By 1940,
the Carnegie Corporation was also satisfied that the school had met
the terms of the original grant—that it was indeed a "school of a new
type."[12] In this respect, the school was intended to undertake investigation rather than be a model of education for librarianship, although
in the late 1940s other library schools established programs to award
doctorates in librarianship on the basis of original contributions to the
solution of library problems as well. This was anticipated by the BEL
and the University of Chicago in that BEL expected to accredit other
library schools as advanced graduate library schools and the university
and the faculty consistently referred to their school as "The Graduate
Library School at Chicago," apparently with the expectation of GLSs
in other cities. Whether library science outside the GLS was fully in-
tegrated into the social sciences is another question. Compared to Beals's
1946 conceptualization,[13] library science was only beginning to be fully
interdisciplinary.

At Chicago, the special phases of library science were operationally
defined, by George Works in 1928, as cataloging and classification;
adult education, which included reading; the history of libraries and
printing; education for librarianship; and the administration and financial problems of public librarianship. Other areas were covered
by visiting lecturers. Undoubtedly there were additional areas, but
the GLS at Chicago had neither the interest nor competency to deal
with them. After his acceptance of the deanship, Wilson began to
emphasize administration generally. This emphasis was due in part
to President Hutchins' articulation of that objective to Wilson at
Chapel Hill in 1931.

Secondly, as the GLS became an integral part of the university,
it began to reflect the strengths of the University of Chicago in public
administration and government. College library administration, as a
fully self-conscious area of investigation and study, may be traced
to the University Press's publication of Randall's *The College Library*
(1932) and to Randall and Goodrich's *Principles of College Library
Administration* (1936). Public librarianship was also a focus of Wilson's interest which led him to recruit Carleton Joeckel, who wrote
The Government of the American Public Library (1935). However,
a general deemphasis of administration occurred after Wilson's successor, Joeckel, left the GLS (this is discussed more fully in a following section).

Degradation of the graduate program occurred when the first-year
B.L.S. was fully implemented in 1943/44. Although the Laing Com-

mittee in 1926 had expressly advised against it, Dean Wilson pursued this new objective from the very beginning of his appointment. Several individuals, especially William Randall, viewed its introduction as having "completely altered the original concept and purpose of GLS."[14]

TRAINING STUDENTS FOR TEACHING LIBRARY SUBJECTS

The next objective, articulated by George Works in 1928, was reaffirmed by Louis R. Wilson on several occasions, the last time in 1940. Several critical incidents which preceded establishment of the GLS at Chicago bear on the accomplishment of this objective. The first is Williamson's Report of 1923, which found that 93 percent of library school instructors in the nation had had no training in teaching. In response, the BEL recommended, in its first annual report, that a summer institute be established for teachers of library science; and such institutes were held at the University of Chicago beginning in 1926.

Following establishment of the GLS, the next critical incident was selection of a faculty member whose primary interest was education for librarianship, Harriet E. Howe. Although she was appointed as a "peace offering" to ALA (where she had been executive assistant to the BEL), her background as a professionally trained librarian and her earlier professorial posts at Western Reserve and Simmons apparently were strong influences on students in her course, 350, "Organization and Methods of Teaching Library Science," offered in 1928/29. During this period, 33 percent of the doctoral graduates and 17 percent of the master's graduates went into library science education. During Wilson's tenure, however, library science education was deemphasized. Doctoral graduates who went into library schools decreased by 13 percent and master's graduates decreased by 7 percent. After Wilson's retirement, the number of doctoral graduates who accepted such positions doubled.

Apparently, critical negative incidents were Howe's departure from the GLS to accept the directorship of the library school at the University of Denver and Wilson's decision not to seek a strong replacement for the GLS with her interest. Douglas Waples appears to share some of the responsibility for this decision, as he recommended Carnovsky to Wilson in 1932 as an instructor. As indicated in chapter 5, the decreasing proportion of M.A. graduates who accepted library school positions was outside the control of the school, reflecting the upgrading of library school faculties throughout the nation.

If the GLS is compared to other library schools over the entire period (1929–42), at least on the basis of Carnegie fellows, 4 percent more of the Chicago school's graduates went into library science education than those of other schools. At the GLS, more female (43%) than male (9%) fellows accepted teaching positions. Thus the Carnegie fellowship program may be considered another critical, though less significant, incident in the accomplishment of the objective to train students to teach library subjects.

This, however, appears to be an unanticipated outcome of the GLS program. Throughout the period under investigation, roughly 50 percent of the graduates accepted positions in college and university libraries. Strictly speaking, the primary objective of the GLS was to train students to teach, and Works, in January 1928, placed it first in the order of positions for which the school was to prepare graduates. In the 1932/33 *Announcements*, however, Wilson reordered them, placing administration first. Yet, in the 1940 *Frontiers* statement, he still paid homage to the teaching objective. This situation is not necessarily to be interpreted negatively, as it placed many GLS graduates in positions to employ scientific methods in solving library problems; however, this was never expressed as of equal importance to teaching library subjects.

Acceptance of the Carnegie fellowships, as mentioned above, was treated as a positive critical incident, although there was a negative aspect to it as well. One of the major purposes of the grant money was "to train students for high administrative posts,"[15] and as long as the fellowships were available (through 1942), the GLS was committed to this objective. In this respect, the fact that the majority of GLS Carnegie fellows accepted positions as head librarians or heads of departments (54% of the total) is completely explicable. The oft-heard statement that the GLS was a training ground for high-level administrators probably has its origin in this fact, and it has some validity.

A quantitative criterion for attainment of this objective has been avoided thus far; rather than offer one, the following qualitative points are raised. By 1951 the GLS was a strong influence on other library schools. First of all, other programs had begun to offer doctoral degrees. Second, and more important, was the direct influence on members of other library schools' faculty. For instance, in 1951 at the University of Illinois alone, Professors Thelma Eaton, Herbert Goldhor, Rose Phelps, and Mary A. Lohrer were alumni of the GLS; Gwladys Spencer and Lewis Branscomb had also been members of the Illinois faculty. During the Works era and the interregnum, the GLS graduated Carnovsky and several outstanding women who accepted library school positions; these included Susan Akers at the University of North Carolina, Helen Martin at Western Reserve University, and Ruth Worden at the University of Washington, Seattle. During Wilson's tenure, J. Periam Danton went to the University of California, Carleton Joeckel to the University of Chicago and then to the University of California, and Bernard Berelson to the University of Chicago, reflecting the opportunities for males and the stress on recruiting males to the GLS. The post-Wilson period saw such educators as Jesse Shera at Chicago and Western Reserve, Ralph Shaw at Rutgers, and Lowell Martin at Chicago, Columbia, and Rutgers.

TRAINING STUDENTS IN THE METHODS OF INVESTIGATION

Teaching methods of investigation is an obvious adjunct to the school's original objective of undertaking research in librarianship. Its origin may be traced to Louis R. Wilson's 1926 Memorandum "in which the handling of statistics and methods of research and investigation would receive specific consideration"[16] and to John Dewey's *The Sources of a Science of Education* (1929), in which he viewed education as a discipline lacking content or subject matter *per se* and, therefore, emphasized method instead. Waples, coming from education, recognized that this distinction applied as well to library science, and he quoted Dewey extensively in his own 1929 address, "The Graduate Library School at Chicago" (1931). Consequently, each member of the faculty had an opportunity to instruct in the various methods of investigation, but especially in 410, "Individual Research." In particular, Waples and Butler set the tone of scholarly investigation at the GLS and their course offerings may be cited as critical incidents in the accomplishment of the objective. The primary contribution was Waples' 310, "Methods of Investigation," first offered in 1928/29; then Butler's 301, "Librarianship as a Field of Research," first offered in 1931/32.

Two publications may be singled out as additional critical incidents which enhanced accomplishment of this objective: Pierce Butler's *Introduction to Library Science* (1933), which argued for a scientific approach to solving library problems, and Douglas Waples' *Investigating Library Problems* (1939), a textbook on methods of solving library problems.

The view of library science as interdisciplinary, acquiring methods from other disciplines, is supported by the additional contacts, outside the GLS, established during Wilson's tenure. Besides education (which resulted in Flexner's 1930 criticisms), the GLS worked primarily with the departments of sociology and political science. Work with these departments led to further integration of the GLS with the university and its sense of research. The next critical incident, a negative one, was C. S. Thompson's 1931 criticism of the adoption of scientific methods. Waples' countering of that position (1931), as well as Butler's *Introduction* (1933), may also be cited as critical incidents.

Apparently the utility of social science methods in answering the types of questions the GLS asked led to the relative neglect of humanities research, especially historical methodology. While it is conceivable that a faculty that was more aggressive in this area could have balanced this situation, the lack of development of humanities research methods, as they apply to library problems, may be a shortcoming of the GLS program. Although many academic university library positions were held by GLS graduates, the head librarians' posts at Yale, Princeton, Michigan, Pennsylvania, and two research libraries (the Newberry and the Library of Congress) were filled by cultural bookmen or subject specialists in the humanities. Had the GLS equally emphasized humanities research, it is possible that the GLS might have succeeded in filling these positions as well, thus adding to its dominance in administration. It would be pure conjecture to suggest that, had the Carnegie grant been awarded to the proposed National School of Library Science, H. H. B. Meyer and George F. Bowerman might have stressed humanities research and the library as a cultural institution. In this respect, Frederick Keppel must "accept the responsibility,"[17] to use his words, of favoring the orientation proposed by the GLS. Whether graduates of the GLS continued in their subsequent careers to employ the methods of investigation and to publish the results is addressed in the next two sections.

ORGANIZING AND CONDUCTING INVESTIGATIONS

The origin of this objective may be traced to George Works's experience during 1926–27, when he led a Carnegie-funded study which resulted in his book *College and University Library Problems* (1927). Not surprisingly, his recognition that librarianship needed service studies or a problem-solving orientation led to his positing a cooperative endeavor in research as an objective for the new GLS in 1927. Two critical incidents may be mentioned in this connection. The first was Hanson and Randall's joining the Carnegie International Peace Commission's study of the Vatican Library in 1928, and the second was Randall's survey of liberal arts college libraries for the Carnegie Corporation, beginning in 1929. During his tenure, Wilson reaffirmed this objective, and with Edward Wight undertook a survey of county library service in the South, resulting in a book that was published in 1935.

Slowly, the value of the GLS and its scientific methodology, such as the survey, was recognized by practitioners. Critical incidents in the accomplishment of this GLS objective are Wilson and Wight's study (1935), Haygood's study of the New York Public Library (1938), Carnovsky and Amy Winslow's Cleveland Public Library appraisal study (1939), and Joeckel and Carnovsky's study of the Chicago Public Library (1940). Such formal surveys of libraries allowed the practitioner to observe the spirit of inquiry firsthand.

Works's service obligation to practitioners in the field also was reflected in the theses by students in the GLS. In 1931 Carl Milam encouraged Wilson to lower the standard of thesis work to allow service studies to be conducted. Figures for the last three years of Wilson's tenure indicate that roughly half of the manuscript work was fact gathering as opposed to rigorous hypothesis testing. Nevertheless, valuable service studies resulted; examples are Robert Burgess's M.A. report, "The Sources of Library Statistics" (1942), and Herman Fussler's M.A. report, "Administrative Aspects of Photographic Reproduction for Libraries" (1941). The publication of these cooperative investigations (and research generally) is discussed next.

PUBLISHING THE RESULTS OF INVESTIGATIONS

The promotion of publication had its origin in George Works's understanding of the necessity to communicate findings to other researchers and to practitioners in the field. This reflects adoption of the university model of research, as presented in chapter 1. As mentioned in chapter 3, Works also observed that publication is a strong "stimulus to research."[18] A critical incident or stimulus in the accomplishment of this objective was Waples' 1930 suggestion that a Library Quarterly Monograph Series be established, a suggestion that was realized in 1933 as the "University of Chicago Studies in Library Science." The Carnegie Corporation subventions for the *Library Quarterly*—$25,000 in 1931, $15,000 in 1935, and $6,000 in 1940 are also identifiable critical incidents. Wilson's revival of the summer institutes in 1936 and the subsequent publication of their proceedings (as part of the "Studies" series) are another critical incident.

"Studies in Library Science" contained twenty-seven titles by 1942; an additional fourteen had appeared by 1951. Included in the series were such significant works as Pierce Butler's *Introduction to*

Library Science (1933), Carleton Joeckel's *The Government of the American Public Library* (1935), LeRoy Merritt's *The United States Government as Publisher* (1943), and Jesse Shera's *Foundations of the Public Library* (1949). Obviously, Works's "freedom for research,"[19] provided to members of the faculty in the form of reduced teaching loads (as discussed in chapter 3), helped accomplish the publication objective.

Further evidence that the GLS accomplished its objective of promoting publication is contained in Nancy Lane's study, "Characteristics Related to Productivity among Doctoral Graduates in Librarianship."[20] Studying 289 of the 307 scholars who took doctorates in librarianship between 1930 and 1969 (a broader period than the one under study here), she found that 25 to 50 percent had no subsequent scholarly publications to their credit, although another 25 percent had regularly and consistently published. GLS graduates accounted for 34.3 percent of her population, but they constituted 56.9 percent of her "high-sum productive subset."[21] Of the seven M.L.S. institutions that she reviewed, GLS ranked fifth in percentage of nonproductive Ph.D. graduates.[22] In her predictive model (a multiple regression formula), she found a plus .30 correlation (at the .9995 confidence level) between graduation from the GLS and the "weighted publication total."[23] She interpreted this, however, as a result of the length of time the GLS was the sole doctoral-granting institution and the consequently longer careers of Chicago graduates.[24] While this relationship accounts for only 9 percent of the variance, no other school in her study could claim a positive predictive value in postdoctoral publication.

Lane also found a slight correlation, plus .19, between predoctoral publication total and graduation from the GLS, which she believed to be indicative of the GLS's attempt to attract individuals to its student ranks who were "active" in scholarship.[25] (The present study tends to collaborate these findings.) Finally, Lane found an equally weak correlation between graduation from Chicago and the scholarly productivity of the dissertation adviser.[26] She attributed this to the fact that the Graduate Library School at Chicago had outstanding faculty members,[27] which is further evidence that faculty members responded to George Works's "freedom to research."

In general, it may be observed that members of the GLS faculty experienced greater success in publishing the results of their social science research than research of other kinds—although some completed research, such as Randall's "Measurement of Vocabulary Difficulty in A.L.A. Subject Headings" and his study of academic library buildings, was never published. Examples of unpublished research in the humanities are Randall's history of Muslim libraries and scholarship during the Middle Ages of Europe (begun in 1930) and Butler's "A Bibliography of Sources and More Important Secondary Material Relating to Early American Libraries" (also begun in 1930) and his monograph on rare-books librarianship. This situation may simply indicate the general support of social science research in the world of scholarship from the late 1920s through the 1940s, but further investigation would be needed to substantiate this hypothesis.

It should be noted that the University of Chicago Press, the *Library Quarterly*, and the "Studies in Library Science" series were strong stimuli for research at the GLS.

The success that the Graduate School achieved in accomplishing its objectives may be summarized as follows (in order of the previous discussion). During the Works and interregnum era, a high degree of success was achieved on the first, third, and fifth objectives, and a moderate degree on the second and fourth. During Wilson's tenure, success on the fourth objective increased while success on the second category decreased; the first, third, and fifth remained essentially unchanged. After Wilson's retirement, success in accomplishing the first objective decreased considerably while success on the second objective increased considerably, for the reasons presented earlier. Success in achieving the second, third, fourth, and fifth objectives remained high. Overall, throughout the periods under investigation the Graduate Library School sustained a moderate to high level in accomplishment of its objectives, although there were extreme fluctuations after Wilson's retirement.

Assessments of the Impact of the Graduate Library School

For the twenty-fifth anniversary of the GLS, Dean Berelson invited Dean Emeritus Wilson to address a commemorative dinner of GLS alumni on "the historical impact of the School,[28] and preparing his speech, Wilson solicited assessments from twenty individuals. Of the nineteen who responded during a two-week period in June 1951, ten were GLS graduates. Eight of these were university librarians and the other two were library-school faculty members. Of the nine non-GLS graduates, seven were university library directors and the other two were directors of public libraries.

Most responded to Wilson's request for a simple list of contributions in order of significance, but many elaborated upon their lists. Nearly three-fourths of the respondents singled out, as of major significance, the GLS's application of research methods to solving library problems. Several applied adjectives, such as "graduate," "statistical," or "social science," to the research method; others termed it an "objective," "critical," "scholarly," or "inquiring" method.

The second most significant aspect, in the view of the respondents, was the work of graduates of the GLS program. This answer was proposed by more than half of the respondents, and some specifically mentioned graduates in the field of education for librarianship or in college and university library positions. One said "administrative positions generally"; one stressed the early women graduates; and another referred to "a good group of young men." Two expressed belief that GLS graduates had arrived at their most productive periods earlier, as a result of the program, than they would have otherwise. Another individual, pointing to the posts these graduates held, thought they were the most influential group of library school alumni since those of the earlier Albany Library School.

Almost half of the assessors felt that the third most important impact of the GLS was that it tended to relate the problems of librarians to other disciplines. Three mentioned special subject fields, such as sociology and higher education. Several believed that this wider understanding of librarianship was due to the GLS's integration into a university, and one specifically mentioned the University of Chicago.

Less consensus (listed in declining order) was achieved on (1) the *Library Quarterly*, for valuable contributions or as a medium for publication of research; (2) the summer institutes; (3) publishing research literature, possibly definitive; and (4) progress on developing a philosophy of librarianship. Fifteen other contributions were mentioned.

Finally, several respondents listed shortcomings or negative aspects of the GLS, and since they were not solicited, greater weight might be given to these comments. The eleven shortcomings were mentioned primarily by non-GLS graduates. Two areas, cited at least twice, related directly to the GLS objectives of training students in methods of investigation and offering graduate instruction in special phases of library science. As for the special phases, one individual wondered why the psychological study of readers was not continued after Waples' departure, while another pointed out that public librarianship never "came of age" due to GLS neglect. The latter comment may be a function of graduates' stopping at the master's level, rather than continuing through the Ph.D. (see table 3). A second concern was that the objective of training students in the methods of investigation was accomplished with emphasis on statistical method and the social sciences, which tended to obscure the validity and usefulness of other approaches.[29]

In conclusion, the Graduate Library School at the University of Chicago was a scholarly meritocracy, powered by scientific methods and techniques—a small, disciplined community of intentionality (a prerequisite for change) in the midst of a bibliophilistical population, held together by an almost religious conviction of the gospel of scholarship, that ruled the new intellectual discipline of library science.

These pages in the new history of library science have not been intended as a vain "search for a scientific profession" nor, to paraphrase Plato, do they pine for what is not. The movement was a Dream, emboldened by the spirit of inquiry, which took concrete form. Perhaps the preceding pages have been only a representation of reality; nevertheless, they "may serve as a goal and model of our movement and behavior."

In this particular Chicago lies the universal, scientific Utopia. It can occur again and again, but this spirit, unlike the wind, blows where someone wills.

Appendixes

Appendix A

Chicago Library Club Memorandum (12 Apr. 1923) with cover letter of Carl B. Roden (20 Apr. 1923)

Twentieth
April, 1923

Mr. James Bertram,
Secretary, The Carnegie Corporation,
522 Fifth Ave., New York City, N. Y.

My dear Mr. Bertram:—

I have the honor to transmit, herewith, a communication addressed by the Librarians of Chicago to the Trustees of the Carnegie Corporation.

We should be grateful to you if you would, at the proper time, bring it to their attention.

Very truly yours,
[signed] C. B. Roden
Librarian.

159

CHICAGO LIBRARY CLUB
CHICAGO

To the Trustees of the Carnegie Corporation of New York.
Gentlemen:—

The subscribers to this communication, representing the several public, reference and university libraries in the metropolitan area of the city of Chicago, and representing, also, the membership of the Chicago Library Club, comprising a large majority of all persons engaged in Chicago and vicinity in the practice of librarianship as a profession, respectfully ask leave to submit to your Board the following recommendations for the establishment and endowment of a professional school for librarians within the area mentioned.

It is not here proposed to recommend the establishment of a school to be in any sense restricted to, or designed for, the training of librarians for the libraries of Chicago alone. On the contrary, the plan and purpose of such a school must be conceived upon very much broader lines, and must contemplate an organization capable of offering systematic and thorough instruction in two separate though related fields:

First, in the field of practical librarianship, comprising the several subjects commonly included in the curriculum of the modern library school.

Second, in the far more important field, for which no satisfactory provision has hitherto been made, of the cultural, literary, bibliographical and sociological aspects of librarianship as a learned profession built upon ideals and charged with responsibilities as definite and as vital in their implications as those of any other learned profession, and requiring similar academic preparation to ensure its highest development.

It is obvious that, to fulfill these functions adequately, the School for Librarians must become an organic member of a university group, with the background, atmosphere, resources and equipment afforded by such affiliations.

It is therefore recommended that such a School for Librarians be established under the authority and direction of the trustees of one of the universities in or near Chicago, or under a separate directorate in close affiliation with one or possibly with both of these universities.

Attention is called, in this connection, to the generally recognized need for the extension of library training along lines that lead to the establishments of higher standards and a wider realization of the inter-relations of librarianship with the other learned professions. It is further pointed out that the establishment of courses of study and research along these lines, offered to librarians already employed as well as to library students, in the form of supplemental or graduate work, must inevitably exert a widespread influence upon the whole structure and trend of modern library administration. Especially in the Middle West, where the growth of public libraries, in number as well as in influence, has admittedly been more rapid than the supply of adequately trained librarians, the provision of facilities for such courses of study would be of extreme value and importance.

Attention is called, also, to the peculiar fitness of Chicago as the place for such a school, which would be unique in character, aims and organization. Exceptional wealth in the materials of research, as offered by three large and splendid public libraries, two university libraries, and a multitude of smaller specialized institutions; the presence of two great universities, one of which is about to establish a campus of professional schools in the heart of the city upon a scale of unprecedented completeness, and an extraordinary variety of public foundations and institutions for the promotion and cultivation of the arts and sciences, combine with its commanding geographical and commercial position to make this city the logical and natural site for a school designed to afford proper facilities for the development and study of the principles composing a body of professional doctrine as a basis for the practice of librarianship upon a plane of professional dignity.

It is submitted that, with the exception of the library schools on the Pacific Coast and of one in St. Louis, whose appeal is of necessity purely local, there is no institution west of Chicago offering instruction, however elementary, in the processes of library management, and that the two schools nearest to Chicago are admittedly unable to supply the constant demand for trained library personnel in the Middle West. Moreover, these two schools, in common with all other existing library training schools, have been impelled, by the very exigency of this demand, to place greatest emphasis upon purely technical processes in order to equip their graduates with a maximum of practical proficiency in a minimum period of time. The development of a library school curriculum upon broad lines of cultural and theoretical principles remains to be undertaken. The need for such a course has long been obvious and is daily growing more insistent. Granting the truth of this assertion and assuming the propriety and practical wisdom of making proper provisions for meeting that need, it is submitted that no other place offers so many advantages, so many favorable conditions and so strong a probability of success in the conduct of a School of Librarianship as outlined above, as are offered by the City of Chicago.

The maintenance and conduct of such a School of Librarianship as is here proposed would require the services of a highly competent and experienced Director and a staff of thoroughly trained and expert instructors. It would involve the institution of courses in all branches of practical librarianship, with adequate facilities for laboratory and experimental work. It would further involve arrangements for the admission of students, upon a full credit basis, to courses in several of the departments of one or both of the universities. It would be desirable to maintain independent quarters for such a school at a point from which all classes of libraries would be easily accessible, and it might prove feasible and desirable to arrange for such quarters in the building of one of the great libraries of the city.

The budget for the maintenance and conduct of such a school, upon lines substantially as indicated herein, would require an expenditure of not less than $20,000 to $25,000 a year, which sum could be only partially met by fees paid by students.

The undersigned, therefore, in presenting the foregoing particulars, beg leave to add, as a final recommendation, that such an annual sum as may be determined to be necessary, or a sustaining fund capable of producing such a sum, be provided by the Carnegie Corporation upon such terms and for such a period of years as may be agreed upon by all parties in interest after a full survey, investigation and discussion of all aspects of the proposition hereby

Very respectfully submitted,

The Executive Committee of
The Chicago Library Club:

Sarah C. N. Bogle
President

Theodore A. Mueller
Secretary

William Teal
First Vice President

Sue M. Wuchter
Treasurer

Alice M. Farquhar
Second Vice President

The foregoing communication is fully endorsed and supported by the undersigned:

Clement W. Andrews
Librarian, The John Crerar Library

Theo. W. Koch
Librarian, Northwestern University
Library

Ernest D. Burton
Director, University of Chicago
Libraries

C. B. Roden
Librarian, The Chicago Public
Library

J. C. M. Hanson
Associate Director, University
of Chicago Libraries

Geo. B. Utley
Librarian, The Newberry Library

Chicago, 12th April, 1923.

Appendix B

Graduate Library School at the University of Chicago: Suggestion and Recommendations (the Laing Committee Report) of 7 January 1926

GRADUATE LIBRARY SCHOOL AT THE UNIVERSITY OF CHICAGO. SUGGESTION AND RECOMMENDATIONS.

I. OBJECTIVES.

Recent study of the library situation in America has shown the urgent need for a school of library science of graduate standing and standards, in which college graduates who look to a library career may find the opportunity for the broadest possible professional education, and where those already in the profession may be given opportunities for general or specialized courses which shall fit them for higher and more valuable service.

To be more specific, there is needed a school

1) which shall in its administration, faculty, curriculum, and requirements, correspond to the graduate professional schools of our leading universities.

2) which shall be open only to those who have a bachelor's degree from an approved institution, including or supplemented by a year's training in library science.

3) which shall offer in the field of library science the same opportunities for study and research, leading to advanced degrees, now open to advanced students in other fields.

4) which shall offer opportunities for study on a part-time basis to experienced librarians employed in the vicinity of the school.

5) which shall supervise research in library problems in Chicago and elsewhere, thus utilizing the facilities of the American Library Association and other library organizations as opportunities for field work.

6) which shall train teachers for the faculties of institutions giving instruction in library science.

II. ADVANTAGES AFFORDED BY THE CITY OF CHICAGO FOR A GRADUATE LIBRARY SCHOOL.

1) Chicago is centrally located. It is the headquarters of the American Library Association, and the meeting place of the Council and various sections of that Association.

2) Chicago is a very important Library center with all types of libraries represented, including the Chicago Public, John Crerar, the Newberry, the libraries of the Art Institute, the Chicago Historical Society and the Field Museum, two great university libraries, several large theological libraries, the libraries of the American Medical Association,

The Chicago Law Institute, the Western Society of Engineers, a number of Club libraries, several bank libraries and many scores of special business libraries. These libraries offer opportunity for study of many phases of library work.

3) Chicago offers exceptional opportunities for adult education and for the many other socializing activities of a public library. It is a great social laboratory for the study of the relation of books and libraries to people of varied classes and racial types.

III. ADVANTAGES AFFORDED BY THE UNIVERSITY OF CHICAGO FOR A GRADUATE LIBRARY SCHOOL.

1) The University of Chicago has graduate and professional schools of high standards.

2) The University of Chicago has the fourth largest university library in America and one of the best reference and bibliographical collections in the Central States.

3) The four quarter system at the University of Chicago makes it possible for librarians to take advantage of the opportunities of the Library School with great freedom as to periods of attendance.

4) The University of Chicago is primarily interested in research, and a Library School maintained in it will profit greatly by this dominant interest.

5) The University Press constitutes one of the divisions of the University and offers unique facilities for the dissemination of the results of the investigations carried on by the Graduate Library School.

6) The Graduate Schools of Arts, Literature and Science and the Professional Schools offer many courses which would be available for properly qualified students in the Graduate Library School.

7) Through cooperation with various other departments, a Library School at the University of Chicago could offer special courses, as for example courses in the laws affecting libraries or in the legal and business aspects of the control and use of endowment.

IV. SUGGESTED ORGANIZATION AND FACULTY MEMBERSHIP.

The Library School should be organized as a Graduate School of the University and the members of its staff should be members of the Graduate Faculty. It should have its own budget. The following administrative, instructional, and research personnel should be provided:

1) A dean of the School who shall be responsible for the general administration and for the organization of research work. The dean shall also be a professor of library science.

2) A secretary of the School (who may be an instructor in the school).

3) Two professors (in addition to the dean).

4) One associate professor.

5) One assistant professor.

6) Research assistants and fellows.
7) Provision for a Research Institute.
8) Provision for fourth quarter instruction.
9) Clerical and stenographic service.

V. THE CURRICULUM

The following curriculum is based on the admission requirements already given on page 1 of this Report, namely a bachelor's degree including or supplemented by a year's training in library science. It is the opinion of the Committee that the School should not provide the preliminary year of library training since a year of such training is one of the requirements for admission. At the same time it recognized that some provision should be made to enable students whose preliminary course has not been complete in all respects, to make up their deficiencies. Such courses as might be offered for this purpose would not be undergraduate courses.

The curriculum will fall into three divisions:

1. Professional technical courses.
   1) Library architecture and building problems.
   2) Filing methods.
   3) Library administration (boards, staff, budget, etc.)
   4) Relation of the library to its constituency (e.g. to college or university, town or city, professional groups, etc.)
   5) Book acquisition and ordering (study of book reviews, sales catalogs, trade lists, bibliographies, purchase, exchanges, gifts.)
   6) Advanced classification (general history of classification, e.g. the Dewey system and those of the Library of Congress, the University of Halle, etc.)
   7) Advanced cataloguing (author catalog, subject catalog, combination or dictionary catalog.)
   8) Advanced reference work (study of encyclopaedias, indexes, periodicals, bibliographies, catalogs, year books, biography, bio-bibliography, scientific and learned society publications, government publications, (national, state, and municipal)).
   9) Copyright and copyright legislation.
2. Professional Cultural Courses.
   1) History of the book in manuscript.
   2) Paleography.
   3) Arrangement of manuscripts.
   4) Diplomatics and archives.
   5) History of Great Libraries.
   6) History of the printed book.
   7) History of paper and paper making.
   8) History of printing
      (1) Block books
      (2) First half century of printing.

9) Book collections and book collectors.
10) Bind, book illustration and decoration.
11) Modern fine printing.
12) Care of the book.
3. General Cultural Courses.
1) Introduction to the Study of Language.
2) Languages. (ancient and modern)
3) Survey courses in literature (classical, medieval and modern)
4) Outline courses in history and geography.
5) Survey of the physical and biological sciences.
6) Survey of philosophy and psychology.
7) History of religions.
8) History of aesthetics. (art and music).
9) Anthropology and the history of society.
10) Political economy, political science, and government.
11) History of education.

VI. LOCATION

The administrative offices of the Library School together with suitable classrooms and work rooms should be as near to the General Library of the University as is practicable. It is recognized that this space must be provided by the University preferably in a separate building. As a temporary measure, it seems desirable, in the present lack of space, to secure one of the houses now available on Woodlawn Avenue. It is imperative, in the interest of the unity of the organization, that the administrative offices and the students' workrooms and library should be under the same roof. In order to facilitate cooperation with the American Library Association and with libraries other than the University of Chicago Library, it is recommended also that workrooms be provided downtown preferably near the quarters of the American Library Association.

VII. BUDGET MEMORANDUM

1. Personnel and Organization (Annual cost for first
   five years[1]):

Dean of School (who is also a professor of library science).	$10,000
Secretary of School (an instructor)...................	1,000
Clerical and stenographic service (12 months at $150)....	1,800
Printing and office supplies........................	2,500
Professor library science (the dean above)............	
Two other professors of library science (at $7000 each)..	14,000
One associate professor............................	4,500
One assistant professor............................	2,500
Two research assistants (at $1,500 each)..............	3,000
Fourth quarter instruction.........................	5,000
Fellowships and scholarships.......................	4,500

Occasional lecturers of distinction.   2,000
Organization and initiation of the work of a
Research Institute[2]   5,000

Total Annual Expenditure   55,800[3]

2. For permanent Equipment:
1) Library   14,000
2) Furniture   6,000

Total Expenditure for permanent equipment   20,000

---

1. As the School would doubtless grow, a larger endowment would be necessary for its maintenance in subsequent years. It does not, however, seem possible for the Committee to make a satisfactory estimate beyond the first five year period.

2. The Research Institute is an organization designed to initiate and carry through research projects in the library field. Our inquiries lead us to believe that there are many problems confronting libraries the investigation and solution of which would prove of the utmost service not only to universities and colleges but also to the cause of adult education. The $5,000 appropriation which we suggest would of course be only a nucleus to which other sums could be added as the necessity of this or that investigation should be made clear. The Institute would be under the general direction of the Dean of the School, who would avail himself of the services of his staff and, as the occasion might arise, of the assistance of outsiders.

3. Of this sum five or six thousand dollars would come from students' tuition fees.

Appendix C

Memorandum concerning Advanced Graduate Library School by Louis R. Wilson (24 May 1926)

MEMORANDUM CONCERNING ADVANCED GRADUATE LIBRARY SCHOOL

I. *Nature of school.* The proposed school should be an advanced graduate school conducted in accord with the best standards of American university graduate instruction and open to students who hold bachelor degrees which include, or are supplemented by, one year of technical training in library science.

II. *Curriculum.* The curriculum outlined by your committee seems to me to include, in the academic field, subjects that are quite appropriate and essential. It would seem to me, however, that a fourth division should be added in which the handling of statistics and methods of research and investigation would receive specific consideration. By way of differentiation from the work done at Illinois and Columbia in the second year it is hoped that specialization may be emphasized rather than adding more of the same kind of subject material. In the case of students going on for the Ph.D. degree, specialization of a high degree, with investigation and field work is desired. Considered from the point of view of positions, training should be provided for the following groups of library workers:

1. Administrators and executives for:
   a. Public libraries. The American public library is a distinctive institution with a wide variety of administrative problems.
   b. College and university libraries. It is generally recognized, I believe, by the library profession, that the public library has outdistanced the college and university library in efficiency of administration.
   c. School and children's libraries. Knowledge of the school curriculum and educational methods would seem to be desirable, as well as educational and child psychology and children's literature.
   e. Library commissions, charged with the formation of libraries and specialized library service for the entire state, including library legislation, library certification and the conduct of library institute work.
   f. Library schools and departments charged with the duty of providing instruction in library science.
      Note 1. It is greatly to be hoped that administrators who have already had experience may take advantage of courses in these fields and that scholarships and fellowships may be provided.
      Note 2. I do not know to what extent publishing houses and bookstores draw upon library schools for recruits. It may or may not be appreciable.

2. Teachers for positions in:
   a. Library schools.
   b. Normal schools giving instruction in school library methods.
   c. Summer schools giving instruction in school library methods.
   d. Training classes in public libraries.
   e. Colleges and universities;
      i. To provide instruction for freshmen and undergraduates in the use and meaning of books, history of books and libraries, etc.
      ii. To offer courses in bibliography in the graduate school similar to those now given by members of graduate faculties, such as that given at Chicago by Dr. Cross. Dr. Keogh, at Yale, for example gives a general course in bibliography in the field of language and literature, particularly in the Romance languages and literatures.

3. Bibliographical experts to administer:
  a. Special collections outside large libraries:
    i. The Clement Library of Americana at Michigan.
  b. Special collections in large libraries:
    i. Manuscripts at the Library of Congress, New York Public, State archives and historical societies, etc.
    ii. Prints, maps, etc.
  c. Libraries of research institutes in special subjects:
    i. The institute of research in social science at the University of North Carolina.
  d. Legislative reference libraries.

4. Investigators and conductors of surveys in the library field. This is in recognition of the fact that the American public library is a great social and educational institution whose functions, practices, and effectiveness have not in any sense been subjected to close, scientific scrutiny. At present the following investigations, which are illustrative of the need, are being made: (1) Data for the basis of text books on circulation and cataloguing, by Dr. Charters, for the A. L. A.; (2) Data for findings concerning qualifications for library personnel, etc., by Mr. Telford and Mr. Thompson, for the A. L. A.; (3) College and university library administration, by President Capen, of Buffalo, and Dr. Works, of Cornell, for the Carnegie Corporation; and (4) (Three years ago) Data concerning library schools, by Mr. Williamson, now of the Columbia library, for the Carnegie Corporation out of which the Williamson report came with vital suggestions concerning the whole subject of library school organization. The relation of the library and the school is a tremendously vital question which as yet has had no comprehensive consideration.

5. Library inspectors for state and city departments of education. They are essential if library standards for schools are to be carried out properly and the school libraries made effective teaching agencies.

6. School librarians.

7 Children's librarians.

III. *Investigations and theses.* Subjects for theses growing out of the courses suggested in the three sections of your curriculum will readily occur to your committee. I append a list of suggested subjects for investigation prepared by representatives of A. L. A. headquarters. The list could be extended almost indefinitely.

IV. *Methods of instruction.* A number of the courses will probably be formal. In the case of research investigations subjects will probably be considered which will involve the cooperation of several departments and schools as well as extensive field work.

V. *Degrees.* I believe it is the hope of the profession that the work, when satisfactorily completed, may lead to the M. A. and Ph.D. degrees. In the case of the master's degree it would seem that M. A. would be more appropriate than M. S. It is hoped that the qualifying phrase *in library science* may not be employed in connection with degrees.

VI. *Plan of organization.* The school should have distinct administrative and financial entity, but at the same time it should be closely coordinated with other schools and departments. This coordination should probably admit of more flexibility than is permitted in some other fields.

It would seem to me that the directorship of the school should be separate from that of the library. The fact that the two offices are combined at other institutions should not obscure certain differences which inhere in the Chicago situation. The Columbia school will probably include in its staff a number of the more effective members of the faculties of the two former schools which it is combining. In the immediate future its work will be largely with first year students and at present it is not giving much consideration to the third year of work. At Chicago the whole matter of personnel, curriculum, school and departmental relationships involved in a strictly graduate school, and equipment, has to be considered. It will require the full time of any one to develop the school properly. On the other hand, the development of your enlarged library according to your present plans and in such way as to yield you more effective service, will require the full time of your librarian. In both instances, in my opinion, direct responsibility to the President of the University is desirable, as it stimulates initiative and definitely fixes responsibility. There is, of course, the possibility of friction, but it is to be remembered that administrators drawn from the library field usually have an institutional rather than a departmental point of view, their objective being the effective service of as many groups and individuals as possible.

VII. *Personnel.* I mentioned the following persons for consideration for the following positions:

1. Directorship of school: Bishop, Wyer, Mitchell, Strohm, Reece.
2. Librarian: Strohm, Lydenberg, Raney, Utley.
3. Professorships: Reece, Van Hoesen, Cleavinger, Miss Mann, Miss Curtis, C. B. Shaw.

Respectfully submitted,

(Signed)   *Louis R. Wilson*

Appendix D

CHRONOLOGY OF CHICAGO GLS DEANS, 1927–62

George Works	June 1927–July 1929*
J. C. M. Hanson	1st summer term, 1929
Douglas Waples	2d summer term, 1929
J. C. M. Hanson	Oct. 1929–June 1930
Douglas Waples	1st summer term, 1930
William Randall	2d summer term, 1930
Douglas Waples	Fall 1930–Sept. 1931†
Pierce Butler	Sept. 1931–Mar. 1932†
Douglas Waples	Apr. 1932–Aug. 1932
Louis R. Wilson	Sept. 1932–Aug. 1942
Carleton B. Joeckel	Sept. 1942–Aug. 1945**
Ralph A. Beals	Sept. 1945–1946
Clarence H. Faust	Oct. 1946–Aug. 1947
Bernard R. Berelson	Sept. 1947–July 1951
Frances Henne (acting)	July 1951–Apr. 1952††
Lester E. Asheim	May 1952–Sept. 1961‡

*Harriet E. Howe served the 2d summer term, 1928.
†George Works served *in camera*, Nov. 1930–Nov. 1931.
**Leon Carnovsky was assistant dean during this period.
††Associate dean and dean of students, 1947–50.
‡Dean of students, 1951–52.

Appendix E

UNIVERSITY OF CHICAGO STUDIES IN LIBRARY SCIENCE, 1933–51

Pierce Butler, *An Introduction to Library Science*, 1933. 118 pp.

William S. Gray and Bernice E. Leary, *What Makes a Book Readable*, 1935. 358 pp.

Carleton B. Joeckel, *The Government of the American Public Library*, 1935. 393 pp.

Louis R. Wilson and Edward A. Wight, *County Library Service in the South: A Study of the Rosenwald County Library Demonstration*, 1935. 259 pp.

Library Trends; see Library Institute, 1936, v. 1.

William M. Randall and Francis L. D. Goodrich, *Principles of College Library Administration*, 1936; 2d ed., 1941. 245 pp.

Douglas Waples and Harold D. Lasswell, *National Libraries and Foreign Scholarship: Notes on Recent Selections in Social Science*, 1936. 151 pp.

Role of the Library; see Library Institute, 1937, v. 2.

Current Issues; see Library Institute, 1938, v. 3.

William C. Haygood, *Who Uses the Public Library: A Survey of the Patrons of the Circulation and Reference Departments of the New York Public Library,* 1938. 137 pp.

Douglas Waples, *People and Print: Social Aspects of Reading in the Depression,* 1938, 228 pp.

Louis R. Wilson, *The Geography of Reading: A Study of the Distribution and Status of Libraries in the United States,* 1938. 481 pp.

The Practice of Book; see Library Institute, 1939, v. 4.

Lester Condit, *A Pamphlet about Pamphlets,* 1939. 104 pp.

J. C. M. Hanson, *A Comparative Study of Cataloging Rules Based on the Anglo-American Code of 1908,* 1939. 144 pp.

James W. Thompson, *The Medieval Library,* 1939. 682 pp.

Douglas Waples and Leon Carnovsky, *Libraries and Readers in the State of New York,* 1939. 160 pp.

The Acquisition and . . . ; see Library Institute, 1940, v. 5.

Pierce Butler, *The Origin of Printing in Europe,* 1940. 155 pp.

Carleton B. Joeckel and Leon Carnovsky, *A Metropolitan Library in Action: A Survey of the Chicago Public Library,* 1940. 466 pp.

Douglas Waples, Bernard Berelson, and Franklyn R. Bradshaw, *What Reading Does to People: A Summary of Evidence on the Social Effects of Reading and a Statement of Problems for Research,* 1940. 222 pp.

Print, Radio; see Library Institute, 1941, v. 6.

Eliza A. Gleason, *The Southern Negro and the Public Library: A Study of the Government and Administration of Public Service Library to Negroes in the South,* 1941, 218 pp.

Arnold Miles and Lowell Martin, *Public Administration and the Library,* 1941. 313 pp.

Reference Function; see Library Institute 1942, v. 7.

Herman H. Fussler, *Photographic Reproduction for Libraries: A Study of Administrative Problems,* 1942. 218 pp.

The Library; see Library Institute, 1943, v. 8.

LeRoy C. Merritt, *The United States Government as Publisher,* 1943.

Gwladys S. Spencer, *Chicago Public Library,* 1943.

Library Extension; see Library Institute, 1944, v. 9.

Edward B. Stanford, *Library Extension under the WPA,* 1944.

Personnel Administration; see Library Institute, 1945, v. 10.

Louis R. Wilson and Maurice F. Tauber, *The University Library: Its Organization, Administration, and Functions,* 1945; 2d ed., 1956. 641 pp.

Library Buildings; see Library Institute, 1946, v. 11.

Youth (communication); see Library Institute, 1947, v. 12.

Education for . . . ; see Library Institute, 1948, v. 13.

A Forum; see Library Institute, 1949, v. 14.*

Jesse H. Shera, *Foundations of the Public Library,* 1949.

Bibliographic Organization; see Library Institute, 1950, v. 15.

Librarians, Scholars; see Library Institute, 1951, v. 16.

*Strictly speaking, volume 14 is not part of the series, as it was published by Columbia University Press.

Appendix F

ANNUAL LIBRARY INSTITUTES HELD IN THE GLS AT CHICAGO, 1936–51

v. 1   *Library Trends.* 3–15 Aug. 1936. Louis R. Wilson, ed. Mar. 1937.

v. 2   *The Role of the Library in Adult Education.* 2–13 Aug. 1937. Louis R. Wilson, ed. Dec. 1937.

v. 3   *Current Issues in Library Administration.* 1–12 Aug. 1938. Carleton B. Joeckel, ed. Apr. 1939.

v. 4   *The Practice of Book Selection.* 31 July–13 Aug. 1939. Louis R. Wilson, ed. Feb. 1940.

v. 5   *The Acquisition and Cataloging of Books.* 29 July–9 Aug. 1940. William M. Randall, ed. Dec. 1940.

v. 6   *Print, Radio, and Film in a Democracy.* 4–9 Aug. 1941. Douglas Waples, ed. Feb. 1942.

v. 7   *Reference Function of the Library.* 29 June–10 July 1942. Pierce Butler, ed. 1943.

v. 8   *The Library in the Community.* 23–28, Aug. 1943. Leon Carnovsky and Lowell Martin, eds. June 1944.

v. 9   *Library Extension: Problems and Solutions.* 21–26 Aug. 1944. Carleton B. Joeckel, ed. 1944.

v. 10   *Personnel Administration in Libraries.* 27 Aug.–1 Sept. 1945. Lowell Martin, ed. 1946.

v. 11   *Library Buildings for Library Service.* 5–10 Aug. 1946. Herman H. Fussler, ed. 1947.

v. 12   *Youth, Communication, and Libraries.* 11–16 Aug. 1947. Frances Henne, Alice Brooks, and Ruth Ersted, eds. 1949.

v. 13   *Education for Librarianship.* 16–21 Aug. 1948. Bernard Berelson, ed. 1949.

v. 14   *A Forum on the Public Library Inquiry.* 14th Annual Conference, 1949. Lester Asheim, ed. 1950.

v. 15   *Bibliographic Organization.* 24–29, July 1950. Jesse H. Shera and Margaret E. Egan, eds. 1951.

v. 16   *Librarians, Scholars, and Booksellers at Mid-Century.* 16th Annual Conference, 1951. Pierce Butler, ed. 1953.

Notes

Chapter 1

1. Daniel C. Gilman, *The Launching of a University and Other Papers: A Study of Remembrance* (New York: Dodd, Mead, 1906).

2. Richard Hofstadter and Walter P. Metzger, *The Development of Academic Freedom in the United States* (New York: Columbia University Press, 1955), p. 373. An alternative view, that Johns Hopkins developed a "uniquely American curriculum rather than transplanting the German Ph.D. program," is provided by Francesco Cordasco's *Shaping of American Graduate Education: Daniel Coit Gilman and Protean Ph.D.* (Totowa, N.J.: Rowan and Littlefield, 1972).

3. Hy Baker, "University Teaching and Research," *Journal of Education* 55 (Jan. 1923): 13.

4. H. E. Roscoe, "Original Research as a Means of Education," *Nature* 8 (23 Oct. 1873): 559.

5. J. C. Irvine, "Development of Research in Universities," *Nature* 110 (22 July 1922): 131–33.

6. G. Stanley Hall, "Research, the Vital Spirit of Teaching," *Forum* 17 (July 1894): 558–70.

7. Arthur T. Hadley, "To What Extent Should Professors Engaged in Research Be Relieved from Teaching?" *Educational Review* 31 (Apr. 1906): 325.

8. Ibid.

9. William James, "The PhD Octopus," *Harvard Monthly* 36 (Mar. 1903): 1–9; reprint ed., *Memories and Studies* (New York: Longmans, Green, 1934), pp. 329–47.

10. G. Stanley Hall, "What Is Research in a University Sense, and How May It Best Be Promoted?" *Pedagogical Seminary* 9 (Mar. 1902): 74–80.

11. Homer C. Hockett, *The Critical Method in Historical Research and Writing* (New York: Macmillan, 1955), p. 232.

12. Hall, "What Is Research?" p. 74. "Half the problem is to select a good topic." To help his students, he maintained a "book of problems, which [was] always at hand, where [he] set down such thoughts and references that occur." Hall considered three things to be important in undertaking research. First, doubt the authorities; "criticize, evaluate, relate, and perhaps first of all make a concise digest of all the important work that precedes, whether or not it be later printed. Second, there must be data collected." But the third is most important: "The third and main stage is to think it all out."

13. Albion W. Small, "Some Research into Research," *Journal of Applied Sociology* 9 (Sept.–Dec. 1924): 3–11; 98–107.

14. G. Stanley Hall, "How Can Universities Be So Organized as to Stimulate More Work for the Advancement of Science?" *Journal of the Proceedings and Addresses of the 18th Annual Conference of the Association of American Universities* (1916), pp. 25–38.

15. James R. Angell, "Report of Committee O on Requirements for the PhD Degree," *American Association of University Professors' Bulletin* 5 (Jan.–Feb. 1919): 12–18.

16. Frederick P. Keppel, *Columbia* (New York: Oxford University Press, 1914), p. 7.

17. Chester Kerr, *A Report on American University Presses* (Washington, D.C.: Association of American University Presses, 1949), pp. 15–41.

18. Frederic A. Ogg, *Research in the Humanistic and Social Sciences: Report of a Study Conducted for the American Council of Learned Societies* (New York: Century, 1928), p. 13.

19. J. Periam Danton, "Corrigendum and Addendum to a Footnote on the History of Library Education," *Journal of Education for Librarianship* 18 (Fall 1977): 93–98; reprint ed., *Essays and Studies in Librarianship Presented to Curt David Wormann* (Jerusalem: Magnes Press, 1975), pp. 73–78.

20. The three other schools that offered formal instruction were Pratt, Drexel, and Armour.

21. Laurel Ann Grotzinger, *The Power and the Dignity: Librarianship and Katharine Sharp* (New York: Scarecrow, 1966), p. 38.

22. *106th* [1891–92] *Annual Report of the University of the State of New York* (Albany: James B. Lyon, State Printer, 1893), pp. 62–85.

23. Ibid., p. 141.

24. A. G. S. Josephson, "A Post-Graduate School of Bibliography," *Library Journal* 26 (Aug. 1901): 197–99; reprint ed., *Papers and Proceedings of the American Library Institute Atlantic City Meeting, 1916* (Chicago: American Library Association, 1916), pp. 127–30.

25. Ibid., p. 128.

26. *New York State Library School Register, 1887–1926* (New York: New York State Library School Association, 1928), p. iv.

27. Maurice F. Tauber, *Louis Round Wilson: Librarian and Administrator* (New York: Columbia University Press, 1967), p. 142.

28. For example, Walter Lichtenstein, "The Question of a Graduate Library School," *Library Journal* 42 (Apr. 1918): 233.

29. To Western Reserve University in 1903; Carnegie Library in Pittsburgh, also in 1903; the Carnegie Library of Atlanta in 1905; and the New York Public Library in 1911.

30. Alvin S. Johnson, *A Report to the Carnegie Corporation of New York on the Policy of Donations to Free Public Libraries* (New York: Carnegie, 1917).

31. Sarah K. Vann, *The Williamson Reports: A Study* (Metuchen, N.J.: Scarecrow, 1971), p. 18; see also George S. Bobinski, *Carnegie Libraries: Their History and Impact on American Public Library Development* (Chicago: American Library Association, 1969), esp. pp. 143–60.

32. Professor Paul A. Winckler has provided a detailed biographical study of Williamson's background, report, and subsequent contributions as head of Columbia University's library, which interested readers may profitably consult: "Charles Clarence Williamson (1877–1965): His Professional Life and Work in Librarianship and Library Education in the United States" (Ph.D. dissertation, New York University, 1968).

33. C. C. Williamson, "Some Present-Day Aspects of Library Training," *ALA Bulletin* 13 (July 1919): 120–26.

34. Vann, *Williamson*. Professor Vann has made an extensive study of his report, and readers are advised to consult her book for more detailed information, especially regarding the omissions.

35. Charles C. Williamson, *Training for Library Service* (New York: Carnegie, 1923); "[Summary of Findings and Recommendations in] Training for Library Service," *Library Journal* 48 (1 Sept. 1923): 711–14.

36. Carl M. White, *A Historical Introduction to Library Education: Problems and Progress to 1951* (Metuchen, N.J.: Scarecrow, 1976), p. 157.

37. William S. Learned, *The American Public Library and the Diffusion of Knowledge* (New York: Harcourt Brace Jovanovich, 1924), p. [iii].

38. Ibid., p. 76.

39. Ibid., p. 79.

40. Keppel to Milam, 23 Mar. 1925, Graduate Library School Papers, 1923–26, Carnegie Corp. (hereafter cited as GLS Papers, 1923–26, CC).

41. Quoted in Vann, *Williamson*, p. 7, and in Winckler, "Charles Clarence Williamson," p. 304.

42. *Christian Science Monitor*, 2 July 1924, p. 7.

43. American Library Association, *Annual Report of the Board of Education for Librarianship* (Chicago: American Library Association, 1925), p. 15; see also p. 25.

44. Ibid., p. 9.

45. Frederick P. Keppel, "[Report to the Executive Committee of the Corporation Trustees]," p. 38, GLS Papers, 1923–26, CC.

46. American Library Association, *Second Annual Report of the Board of Education for Librarianship* (Chicago: American Library Association, 1926), p. 8.

47. There are several chronologies of the Board of Education for Librarianship in the ALA archives, e.g., in Series 28/50/6, Boxes 1 and 2 (hereafter cited as ALAA Series 28/50/6, 1-2). Although the historical records are extant, no one has thoroughly or extensively investigated this agency; consequently, the profession is poorer for not knowing the full role that the board played in American education for librarianship.

48. Bogle to Williamson, 23 Sept. 1921, C. C. Williamson Papers, Box 49, Columbia University (hereafter cited as Williamson MSS, CU 49).

49. Dewey to Milam, 27 Dec. 1924, ALAA Series 28/50/6-1.

50. "Graduate Library School: Attitude of Faculty of Graduate Schools Indicated by Answers to Form Letter of December 19, 1923," 17 Oct. 1924, ALAA Series 28/50/6-1.

51. Ibid.

52. "For the President, Extract from Minutes, Academic Senate," Mar. 8, 1926; Report of the University Council: "Proposed School of Librarianship," 12 Mar. 1926, Office of the President Papers, 1926, University of California, Berkeley (hereafter cited as Presidents' MSS, UCB, 1926).

53. James Sutton, recorder of the faculties, to W. W. Campbell, 19 May 1926, Presidents' MSS, UCB, 1926.

54. Campbell to Keppel, 12 Apr. 1926, Presidents' MSS, UCB, 1926.

55. Keppel to Campbell, 24 May 1926, Presidents' MSS, UCB, 1926.

56. W. W. Bishop, "Memorandum on Instruction in Library Methods in the University of Michigan," 30 Dec. 1922, Board of Education for Librarianship Papers, 28/50/6-1. Bishop stated that library schools needed "the atmosphere of the seminar and laboratory far more than that of the cataloging room and the loan desk." Furthermore, "the chief defect of the second year courses now given at Albany, New York and Illinois (as I view it) is exactly the absence of the spirit of research and of respect for the methods of research."

57. W. W. Bishop, "Tentative Outline of Courses of Instruction for Graduate Students in Library Science and Bibliography" (not after 19 Dec. 1923).

58. Andrew Keogh, "Advanced Training for Research Workers," *ALA Bulletin* 13 (Sept. 1919): 165–67; *Library Journal* 44 (Sept. 1919): 581–82.

59. "A Department of Bibliography in the Graduate School" (c. 1923), Library School at Yale, 1919–23 Papers (Library Records, Series 1, Box 136, Folder 1617), Yale University.

60. J. C. M. Hanson to Ernest D. Burton, 4 Dec. 1924, Presidents' Papers, 1889–1925, Box 19, Folder 8, University of Chicago (hereafter cited as 1889–1925 Presidents' MSS, UC, 19-8).

61. Cf. Charles D. Churchwell, *The Shaping of American Library Education*, ACRL Publications in Librarianship, no. 36 (Chicago: American Library Association, 1975), pp. 5, 13, 14–15, 25.

62. American Library Association, Board of Education for Librarianship, "Digest of Discussion [at Open Meeting]," 31 Dec. 1924, p. 2; "An Advanced School of Librarianship," *Library Journal* 50 (15 Feb. 1925): 171.

63. On 17 Dec. 1924, Andrew Keogh, Malcolm Wyer, Elizabeth Smith, and Harriet Howe met with Meyer and President Schmidt in Washington, D.C. (ALAA Series 28/50/6-1).

64. Robina Rae, secretary of the District of Columbia Library Association, to Milam, 12 May 1925, ALAA 28/50/5-3.

65. Frederick Keppel to Ernest D. Burton, 14 Apr. 1925, 1899–1925 Presidents' MSS, UC, 19–9.

66. Board of Education for Librarianship Minutes, 12 Mar. 1925, ALAA Series 28/50/5-3.

67. John B. Kaiser, director of University Libraries at State University of Iowa, to Jessup, 15 Oct. 1924, President's Office Correspondence, Library, July 1924–June 1926, University of Iowa, Iowa City.

68. Tse-Chien Tai, *Professional Education for Librarianship*, with introduction by John B. Kaiser (New York: H. W. Wilson, 1925), p. viii.

69. F. K. W. Drury, acting librarian of Brown University, to Kaiser, 15 June 1925, President's Office Correspondence, Library, July 1924–June 1926, University of Iowa, Iowa City.

70. "Final Examination of Tse-Chien Tai . . . for the Degree of Doctor of Philosophy, Friday, June 5, 1925, 8:00 A.M." (Iowa City: Graduate College of the State University of Iowa, 1926), p. [3].

71. Werrett W. Charters, *Curriculum Construction* (New York: Macmillan, 1924).

72. "Memorandum of Interview between Tai and FPK," 24 June 1925, GLS Papers, 1923–26, CC.

73. Julia A. Robinson, executive secretary for Library Commission, to Jessup, 24 May 1926, President's Office Correspondence, Library, July 1924–June 1926, University of Iowa, Iowa City.

74. [New York State Library School Faculty], "Advanced Library Training and the New York State Library School" (ca. 1923/24), ALAA Series 28/50/6-1.

75. "Graduate Library School; Attitude of Faculty of Graduate Schools Indicated by Answers to Form Letter of December 19, 1923," 17 Oct. 1924, ALAA Series 28/50/6-1.

76. "Board of Education for Librarianship Minutes," 12 Mar. 1925, ALAA Series 28/50/5-3.

77. Frederick P. Keppel, "Report to the Executive Committee of the Corporation Trustees," p. 38, GLS Papers, 1923–26, CC.

78. "Memorandum of Conversation between F. P. Keppel and M. A. Cartwright," 11 June 1925, GLS Papers, 1923–26, CC.

79. Interested readers may consult Ray Trautman's *A History of the School of Library Service* (New York: Columbia University Press, 1954) for in-depth coverage of this period.

Chapter 2

1. The committee members were Carl B. Roden, Theodore W. Koch, and J. C. M. Hanson.

2. Chicago Library Club, "Memorandum on the Establishment of a School for Librarians in the City of Chicago," [28 Feb. 1923], 1889–1925 Presidents' MSS, UC, 19-7.

3. "Chicago," *Public Libraries* 28 (May 1923): 150–51.

4. Ibid., p. 251.

5. Chicago Library Club, "To the Trustees of the Carnegie Corporation of New York," 12 Apr. 1923, GLS Papers, 1923–26, CC.

6. Ibid., p. 5. The revised memorandum was signed by the executive committee of the Chicago Library Club: Sarah C. N. Bogle, president; William Teal, first vice president; Alice M. Farquhar, second vice president; Theodore A. Mueller, secretary; and Sue M. Wuchter, treasurer. In addition, "the foregoing communication is fully endorsed and supported by the undersigned": Clement W. Andrews, librarian, John Crerar Library; Ernest D. Burton, director, University of Chicago Libraries; J. C. M. Hanson, associate director, University of Chicago Libraries; Theodore W. Koch, librarian, Northwestern University Library; Carl B. Roden, librarian, Chicago Public Library; and George B. Utley, librarian, the Newberry Library. The proposal was sent with a cover letter, written by Carl B. Roden, to James Bertram, secretary of the Carnegie Corporation, on 20 Apr. 1923.

7. W. S. Learned to Carl B. Roden, 1 May 1923, GLS Papers, 1923–26, CC.

8. Chicago Library Club, "To the Trustees."

9. "Memorandum on Interview between CHM and Walter D. Scott of Northwestern University," 8 Dec. 1923, ALAA Series 28/50/5-3.

10. D. R. Curtiss, secretary, "Northwestern University Minutes of the University Council," 15 Dec. 1923, Northwestern University. This committee consisted of Koch, Franklyn B. Snyder of the English Department, and Frederick S. Deibler, a professor of economics.

11. "Northwestern University Minutes of the Board of Trustees," 2 Jan. 1924, Northwestern University.

12. [Theodore Koch], "Extract from a Memorandum on Library Schools Submitted to the Council of Northwestern University," prior to 8 July 1924, Northwestern University.

13. D. R. Curtiss, secretary, "Northwestern University Minutes of the University Council," 16 Feb. 1924, Northwestern University.

14. W. S. Learned to F. P. Keppel, 1 Mar. 1924, GLS Papers, 1923–26, CC.

15. E. A. Henry to Hanson, 23 Oct. 1924, 1889–1925 Presidents' MSS, UC, 19-7.

16. [Theodore Koch], "Extract."

17. "Minutes of the Board of Education for Librarianship Meeting," 30 Dec. 1924, ALAA Series 28/50/5-3.

18. Since Carl Milam has recently been the subject of an intensive biographical examination, readers may refer to that work for many aspects of his life; see Peggy Sullivan, *Carl H. Milam and the American Library Association* (New York: W. H. Wilson, 1976). On the other hand, no one as yet has studied Sarah Bogle, a strong personality whose biography would

surely shed light on the role of women in librarianship. Lucile F. Fargo, associate director of the Peabody Library School, proposed such a biography in 1932, along the lines of Thomas Beer's [Mark] Hanna (New York: A. A. Knopf, 1929), but never followed through on it; see Fargo to Louis R. Wilson, 29 Feb. 1932, Louis R. Wilson Papers (Series II, Folder 32), in Southern Historical Collection, University of North Carolina Library, Chapel Hill (hereafter cited as Wilson MSS, UNC, II–32).

19. Bogle to Williamson, 18 July 1922, Williamson MSS, CU, 49.

20. Sarah K. Vann, The Williamson Reports: A Study (Metuchen, N.J.: Scarecrow, 1971), p. 164.

21. "Notes on Dr. Williamson's 'Training for Library Work' by Sarah C. N. Bogle and Carl H. Milam, Dictated by C. H. M.," after 18 Aug. and before 5 Sept. 1922, Williamson MSS, CU, 49. In the BEL's second annual report, the question of geographical distribution of schools, raised by Milam and Bogle, can be answered by examining the statistics on the "enrollment of the 14 accredited library schools . . . analyzed to show geographical divisions from which students entered." The United States was divided into four divisions: East, Central, South, and West. Of the 526 enrolled students, 40% came from the Central division, which was represented by only four library schools. Thus approximately two more schools could be added in the Central division. The South and the West were appropriately distributed; the East had an overabundance.

22. Milam to Charters, 21 Feb. 1924, W. W. Charters Papers, Folder Cal-6, Ohio State University (hereafter cited as Charters MSS, OSU, Cal-6).

23. "Conference between Charters, Dr. Russell, C. H. Milam, L. L. Dickerson and Howe," 16 Dec. 1924, ALAA Series 28/50/6-1.

24. Howe to Charters, 14 Feb. 1924, ALAA Series 28/50/6-1. These notes addressed such questions as the organization of such a school, its administrative and instructional staff, financial status, requirements for admission, length of curriculum, and degree awarded.

25. "Board of Education for Librarianship," American Library Association Bulletin 19 (May 1925): 83.

26. Laing and Charters had known each other from an encounter in 1922, when Laing, as dean of the Faculty of Arts at McGill University in Montreal, had asked Charters to consider the headship of McGill's Department of Education, an invitation which was later withdrawn. See Laing to Charters, 16 May 1922, Charters MSS, OSU, YD28.

27. Adolf C. Noé, "Our University Libraries," School and Society 10 (19 July 1919): 70–72.

28. Dr. Noé was born in Gratz, Austria, on 28 Oct. 1873. He received his A.B. degree from the University of Chicago in 1900 and the doctorate in 1905, also from Chicago. Noé held a post in the Department of German Literature from 1903 to 1923; he later became a paleobotanist.

29. Noé, "Our University Libraries," p. 70–72.

30. Burton to Williamson, 7 July 1920, Williamson MSS, CU, 49.

31. Vann, Williamson Reports, p. 75.

32. Burton to Judson, 30 June 1921, 1889–1925 Presidents' MSS, UC, 19.

33. Judson to Burton, 5 July 1921, 1889–1925 Presidents' MSS, UC, 19.

34. Ahern to Burton, 25 Jan. 1923, Ernest D. Burton Papers, Series II, Box 15, Folder 9, University of Chicago.

35. "Chicago," *Public Libraries* 28 (May 1923): 250–51.

36. "Memo on Burton," 26 Nov. 1923, GLS Papers, 1923–26, CC.

37. Hanson to Burton, 19 Jan. 1924, 1889–1925 Presidents' MSS, UC, 19-7.

38. Burton, "A Tentative Plan for an Evening School of Library Science in Chicago," c. 1902, 1889–1925 Presidents' MSS, UC, 19-7.

39. Hanson, "Courses," 23 Jan. 1924, 1889–1925 Presidents' MSS, UC, 19-7.

40. More recent assessments of Burton's brief tenure as president indicate that his attention to the undergraduate programs kept them from being abolished; see William M. Murphy and D. J. R. Bruckner, *The Idea of the University of Chicago: Selections from the Papers of the First Eight Chief Executives of the University of Chicago, 1891 to 1975* (Chicago: University of Chicago Press, 1976), p. 274.

41. "Memo on Burton," 20 Feb. 1924, GLS Papers, 1923–26, CC.

42. Learned to Keppel, 1 Mar. 1924, GLS Papers, 1923–26, CC.

43. Henry to Burton, 13 May 1924, 1889–1925 Presidents' MSS, UC, 19-7.

44. "A Library School in Chicago," [20 May 1924], 1889–1925 Presidents' MSS, UC, 19-7.

45. Ibid.

46. Henry to Bogle, 20 June 1924, ALAA Series 28/50/5-3.

47. Andrews to Keppel, 25 July 1924, GLS Papers, 1923–26, CC.

48. Henry to Burton, 16 Sept. 1924, 1889–1925 Presidents' MSS, UC, 19-7.

49. Henry to Burton, 18 Sept. 1924, 1889–1925 Presidents' MSS, UC, 19-7.

50. Ibid.

51. Keppel to Burton, 27 Oct. 1924, GLS Papers, 1923–26, CC.

52. Henry to Burton, 14 Nov. 1924, 1889–1925 Presidents' MSS, UC, 19-7.

53. "Memorandum in Regard to a Possible Library School in Chicago," [30 Dec. 1924], ALAA Series 28/50/5-3.

54. "Extract of Keppel Letter to Corporation," 11 Jan. 1925, GLS Papers, 1923–26, CC.

55. "Memorandum on Keppel Interview in Chicago," 1889–1925 Presidents' MSS, UC, 19-8.

56. "Minutes of the Board of Education for Librarianship," 12 Mar. 1925, ALAA Series 28/50/5-3.

57. "Minutes of the Chicago Library Club Committee on a Library School in Chicago," 14 Mar. 1925, 1889–1925 Presidents' MSS, UC, 19-8.

The committee members present and voting were: C. B. Roden, C. W. Andrews, G. B. Utley, T. W. Koch, and J. C. M. Hanson. It is highly probable that Carl Milam was also present; besides being invited by Roden, he was going to New York on 17 March and would likely be asked by Keppel about the CLC opinion.

58. Keppel to Milam, 23 Mar. 1925, GLS Papers, 1923–26, CC.

59. "Memorandum of Conversation with Burton," after 17 Mar. but before 14 Apr. 1925, GLS Papers, 1923–26, CC.

60. Henry to Burton, 1 Apr. 1925, GLS Papers, 1923–26, CC.

61. *New York Times*, 27 May 1925, p. 23; 29 May 1925, p. 17.

62. "Conversation between Keppel and Cartwright," 11 June 1925, GLS Papers, 1923–26, CC.

63. Keppel to Milam, 23 Mar. 1925.

64. Swift to Tufts, 25 June 1925, 1925–45 Presidents' MSS, UC, 112.

65. Tufts to Keppel, 4 Aug. 1925, GLS Papers, 1923–26, CC.

66. Mason to Keppel, 30 Aug. 1925, GLS Papers, 1923–26, CC.

67. Tufts to Mason, 3 Sept. 1925, 1925–45 Presidents' MSS, UC, 112.

68. William E. Scott to Henry, 17 Sept. 1925, 1925–45 Presidents' MSS, UC, 112.

69. Bogle to Keppel, 24 Oct. 1925, ALAA Series 28/50/5-3.

70. "Memorandum of Conversation between Mason and Keppel," 27 Oct. 1925, GLS Papers, 1923–26, CC.

71. Joining him were Harlan H. Barrows, chairman of the Geography Department; Professor Charles H. Judd, head of Education, whose research interests were in the field of reading; Shailer Mathews from the Divinity School, whose catholic interests were widely known; James Westfall Thompson, a noted medievalist; Ernest H. Wilkins, dean of the University College and known for his able administration of educational experiments; and Professor John M. Manly of the English Department (*in absentia* after 2 Jan.). A last-minute addition to this group of influential men, who supposedly had their fingers on the pulse of the university, was Edith Abbott, dean of the School of Social Service Administration.

72. John M. Manly to Andrew Keogh, 22 Dec. 1925, Library School at Yale, 1919–23 (Library Records, Series 1, Box 136, Folder 1617), Yale University.

73. Bishop to Laing, 17 Dec. 1925, 1925–45 Presidents' MSS, UC, 112.

74. For master's work in library science he suggested "at least two seminars running throughout the year—in 1) early printed books, 2) national and regional bibliography, 3) advanced cataloging, 4) government documents, 5) library administration, and 6) advanced subject bibliography and reference work," besides "practice in compiling several select and one exhaustive bibliography." Bishop to Laing, 17 Dec. 1925.

75. Roden to Laing, 19 Dec. 1925, ALAA Series 28/50/5-3.

76. Utley to Laing, 19 Dec. 1925, 1925–45 Presidents' MSS, UC, 112.

77. Henry to Laing, 21 Dec. 1925, ALAA Series 28/50/5-3.

78. Ibid.

79. Hanson to Laing, 21 Dec. 1925, 1925–45 Presidents' MSS, UC, 112. In the first section, Hanson emphasized languages, history and geography, literature and art, philosophy and education, theology and religion, and history of the sciences and arts as composing the cultural course offerings. Professional course offerings should include administration; bibliography; book acquisition, ordering, selection and rejection; cataloging; classification; and reference. Many of these areas were subdivided by five or six sub-headings and included a selected bibliography.

80. Rockwell to Laing, 18 Dec. 1925, 1925–45 Presidents' MSS, UC, 112.

81. Association of American Universities, "Report of the Committee on Academic and Professional Higher Degrees," *Journal of Proceedings and Addresses* 26 (31 Oct.–1 Nov. 1924): 25–26. The AAU committee was advised by James I. Wyer, chairman of the Association of American Library Schools' Committee on Degrees, and by Harriet E. Howe on behalf of the Board of Education for Librarianship. Reports were received in Dec. 1919, June 1923, and May 1924 (the date of the final report of the Temporary Library Training Board). In adopting the AALS proposals, the AAU report stated, in essence, that "two years should be required for a Master's degree; . . . but that the Master's degree does not stand solely or exclusively for research. It is appropriate for scholarly work on a graduate basis, and a thesis may often prove desirable as giving evidence of ability to write clearly and constructively, but need not be treated as a general requirement. It is probably not desirable for the present to plan curricula and work beyond the Master's degree, at least until problems concerning Bachelor's degrees and Master's degrees have been solved. Students wishing higher degrees should be advised to seek these in scholarly fields" (p. 26).

82. Rockwell to Laing, 18 Dec. 1925. First, advanced instruction should be given in bibliography and cataloging, as well as "study and practice in some chosen field of Library Science." Rockwell and Pettee also recommended courses in palaeology, diplomatics, and the arrangement of archives. A written thesis should also be required. The final point drew attention to the "necessary character element" to be a successful librarian.

83. Manly to Keogh, 22 Dec. 1925, 1925–45 Presidents' MSS, UC, 112.

84. Ibid.

85. "Memorandum of Conversation between Mason and Keppel," 11 Dec. 1925, GLS Papers, 1923–26, CC.

86. Ibid.

87. "Memorandum of Interview with Milam," 12 Dec. 1925, GLS Papers, 1923–26, CC.

88. Milam "does not regard Burton as a leader in library work and can see no advantage as such in affiliation of library school with Chicago University"; "Excerpt from Conversation with Mr. Milam, Chicago, F. P. Keppel," 6 Sept. 1923, GLS Papers, 1923–26, CC.

89. "*Resolved*, that the University of Chicago be invited . . . ," 24 Dec. 1925, GLS Papers, 1923–26, CC.

90. "Minutes of the Board of Education for Librarianship," pp. 126–36,

31 Dec. 1925, ALAA Series 28/50/1-2. For what it was worth, the BEL at that meeting considered the University of Chicago's proposal, the work of Laing and Burton, the organization of the school under the Graduate School, and the position of the dean or director.

91. Keppel to Mason, 4 Jan. 1926, 1925–45 Presidents' MSS, UC, 112.

92. Laing to Mason, 7 Jan. 1926, 1925–45 Presidents' MSS, UC, 112.

93. "Graduate Library School at the University of Chicago: Suggestion [*sic*] and Recommendations," 7 Jan. 1926, 1925–45, UC, 112.

94. Ibid.

95. Ibid.

96. Mason to Keppel, 12 Jan. 1926, 1925–45 Presidents' MSS, UC, 112.

97. Bogle to Laing, 21 Jan. 1926, ALAA Series 28/50/5-3.

98. Walter A. Payne, university recorder, "University of Chicago Minutes of the University Senate," 20 Feb. 1926, University of Chicago.

99. Ibid.

100. Mason to Keppel, 26 Feb. 1926, GLS Papers, 1923–26, CC.

101. Ibid.; F. P. Keppel, "The Carnegie Corporation and the Graduate Library School: A Historical Outline," *Library Quarterly* 1 (Jan. 1931): 25.

102. C. Edward Carroll, *The Professionalization of Education for Librarianship with Special Reference to the Years 1940–1960* (Metuchen, N.J.: Scarecrow, 1970), p. 63; Charles D. Churchwell, *The Shaping of American Library Education* (Chicago: American Library Association, 1975), p. 53.

103. Keppel, "The Carnegie Corporation," p. 22.

104. Carnegie Corp. to Belden, 20 Mar. 1926, ALAA Series 28/50/6-2.

105. Mason to Keppel, 12 Apr. 1926, GLS Papers, 1923–26, CC.

106. Cartwright to Keppel, 15 Apr. 1926, GLS Papers, 1923–26, CC.

107. Keppel to Mason, 5 May 1926, GLS Papers, 1923–26, CC.

108. Before it could act, however, the Sunday *Chicago Herald Tribune* of 23 May ("Carnegie Fund of $1,385,000 Goes to Chicago U.") carried an article on the advanced graduate library school; so the matter was no longer confidential. Now that it was openly known that the graduate library school was going to Chicago, President Mason received numerous letters of congratulations from individuals such as Harriet Howe of the BEL and Joy E. Morgan, editor of the *Journal of the National Education Association*.

109. J. Spencer Dickerson, secretary, to Keppel, 3 June 1926, GLS Papers, 1923–26, CC.

110. Laing to Mason, 13 Apr. 1926, 1925–45 Presidents' MSS, UC, 112; "Discussion: The Status of Library Schools in Universities," *Journal of Proceedings and Addresses* of the Association of American Universities, 35th Annual Conference (Chicago: University of Chicago Press, 1934), p. 137.

111. Wilson to Milam, 15 May 1926, Wilson MSS, UNC, II–6A.

112. Wilson to Strohm, 14 May 1926, ALAA Series 28/50/5-3.

113. Ibid.

114. "Taped Interview of Dean Louis R. Wilson by Dr. Jesse H. Shera on 15–16 November 1972 in Chapel Hill, North Carolina," School of Library Science, University of North Carolina, Chapel Hill.

115. Louis R. Wilson, "Memorandum Concerning Advanced Graduate Library School," 24 May 1926, 1925–45 Presidents' MSS, 112.

116. Ibid.

117. Ibid.

118. Ibid.

119. Harriet E. Howe, "Possible Special Fields of Theses Subjects," 11 Jan. 1926, ALAA Series 28/50/5-3.

120. Henry to Laing, 22 July 1926, 1925–45 Presidents' MSS, UC, 112.

121. Laing to Wilson, 24 July 1926, Wilson MSS, UNC, II–6A.

122. Wilson to Chase, 31 July 1926, Wilson MSS, UNC, II–6A.

123. Wilson to Raney, 9 Aug. 1926, Wilson MSS, UNC, II–7. Wilson told of asking the committee how it had decided on him, and he reported that "Professor Dodd assured me that any connections I might make with the Schools of Education and Social Science need not be embarrassing connections."

124. Wilson to Knight, 9 Aug. 1926, Wilson MSS, UNC, II–6B. Wilson stated: "I also realize that an opportunity will be afforded for doing a very distinctive thing in the field of American librarianship." As such, the position could not be turned down lightly.

125. Frank P. Graham to Louis R. Wilson, 9 Aug. 1926, Wilson MSS, UNC, II–6B; James K. Hall to Wilson, 10 Aug. 1926; and Raney to Wilson, 12 Aug. 1926, Wilson MSS, UNC, II–7. Frank P. Graham told him: "I do see that the appeal of blazing trails in new forests and on a vaster scale is not to be cast aside. The national scene has great appeal and Chicago is one of the two or three most national and even continental *loci*." Hall, Wilson's medical adviser at the Westbrook Sanatorium in Richmond, Virginia, wrote him that he should go. On the other hand, Raney responded in a characteristically philosophical vein saying: "All real power comes out of contact with the physical earth. Chicago's mode of living is artificial and it will pay for it." Somewhat ironically, Raney eventually decided to go to Chicago.

126. Wilson to Mason, 21 Aug. 1926, 1925–45 Presidents' MSS, UC, 112.

127. Bogle to BEL members, 18 Nov. 1926, ALAA Series 28/50/5-3.

128. Ibid.

129. Milam, "In Re Library School of University of Chicago," [Aug.] 1926, ALAA Series 28/50/5-3.

130. Ibid.

131. Keppel to Laing, 4 Jan. 1927, GLS Papers, 1927–31, CC.

132. Ibid.

133. Milam to Rush, 12 Jan. 1927, ALAA Series 28/50/5-3.

134. Rush to Laing, 17 Jan. 1927, ALAA Series 18/50/5-3.

135. Mason to Learned, 30 Mar. 1927, 1925–45 Presidents' MSS, UC, 112.

136. Learned to Mason, 21 Apr. 1927, 1925–45 Presidents' MSS, UC, 112.

137. Ibid.

138. Keppel to Mason, 27 Apr. 1927, 1925–45 Presidents' MSS, UC, 112.

139. Mason to Keppel, 29 Apr. 1927, GLS Papers, 1927–31, CC.

140. Learned to Mason, 29 Apr. 1927, 1925–45 Presidents' MSS, UC, 112.

141. Ibid.

142. Keppel to Mason, 5 May 1927, 1925–45 Presidents' MSS, UC, 112.

143. Mason to Learned, 9 May 1927, 1925–45 Presidents' MSS, UC, 112.

144. Learned to Mason, 20 May 1927, 1925–45 Presidents' MSS, UC, 112.

145. Laing to Mason, 11 May 1927, 1925–45 Presidents' MSS, UC, 112.

146. Ibid.

147. Ibid.

148. "Prof. Works New Dean of U. of C. Library School," *Chicago Daily News*, 5 July 1927, p. 6; "University of Chicago," *Libraries* 32 (July 1927): 382–83.

Chapter 3

1. "Distribution of State Aid in Texas" (Ed.D. dissertation, Harvard University, 1925).

2. "Necrology," *Cornell Alumni News* (Feb. 1958), p. 377. At Cornell, Works taught "Agriculture in Secondary Schools," "The Rural School," "Methods in Elementary Agriculture," "Methods in Teaching High School Agriculture," and "Teaching"; additional references to Works's tenure at Cornell are in Gould P. Colman's *Education and Agriculture: a History of the New York State College of Agriculture at Cornell University* (Ithaca: Cornell University Press, 1963), pp. 316, 319, 365, 384, 582. For additional biographical material, see John Richardson, "George Works, 1877–1957" (unpublished).

3. George A. Works, *College and University Library Problems: A Study of a Selected Group of Institutions Prepared for the Association of American Universities*, with an Introduction by Samuel P. Capen (Chicago: American Library Association, 1927), pp. vi-vii.

4. Donald G. Davis Jr., *The Association of American Library Schools, 1915–1968: An Analytical History* (Metuchen, N.J.: Scarecrow, 1974), pp. 38, 189.

5. Bishop to Bogle, 6 June 1927, ALAA Series 28/50/5-3.

6. Harold F. Brigham, "ALA Diary, 1926/27" (5 Jan. 1927, pp. 125ff.), Charters MSS, OSU, CA9.

7. "The Graduate Library School, 1928–29," University of Chicago *Announcements* 28 (20 June 1928): 3.

8. George A. Works, "Research and the Graduate Library Schools," *Libraries* 33 (Feb. 1928): 100.

9. Ibid.

10. Ibid, p. 102.

11. Ibid.

12. Ibid., p. 103.

13. "A.L.A. Dinner Meeting," *Library Journal* 52 (15 Dec. 1927): 1171.

14. Works, "Research," p. 102.

15. Ibid., pp. 102–3.

16. General biographical information concerning Dr. Randall has been obtained from C. C. Williamson and Alice L. Jewitt's *Who's Who in Library Service* (New York: H. W. Wilson, 1933); "Dr. William M. Randall," *College and Research Libraries* 8 (Oct. 1947): 451–52; and personal correspondence. Background information about his place of employment, as well as Dr. Butler's alma mater, may be found in Curtis M. Geer, *The Hartford Theological Seminary, 1834–1934* (Hartford: Case, Lockwood, and Brainard, 1934).

17. Randall to Bishop, 30 Nov. 1927, W. W. Bishop Papers, Box 24, Michigan Historical Collections, University of Michigan.

18. In all, Randall taught the principles of thirty-one languages to "budding missionaries," as he put it.

19. Abraham Flexner, *Henry S. Pritchett, a Biography* (New York: Columbia University Press, 1943), p. 150; see also Claud G. Sparks, "William Warner Bishop, a Biography" (Ph.D. dissertation, University of Michigan, 1967), esp. chap. 2.

20. Doane to Works, 15 Dec. 1927, University of Michigan School of Library Science Papers, Box 3, Michigan Historical Collections, University of Michigan.

21. Bishop to Works, 19 Dec. 1927, University of Michigan School of Library Science Papers, Box 3, Michigan Historical Collections, University of Michigan.

22. General biographical information concerning Mr. Hanson has been obtained from Williamson and Jewitt's *Who's Who in Library Service;* Pierce Butler, "James Christian Meinich Hanson," *Library Quarterly* 4 (Apr. 1934): 127–30; J. Christian Bay, "James Christian Meinich Hanson: 1864–1943," *Library Quarterly* 14 (Jan. 1944): 57–59; Edith Scott's "J.C.M. Hanson and His Contribution to Twentieth-Century Cataloging" (Ph.D. dissertation, University of Chicago, 1971); *Encyclopedia of Library and Information Science (ELIS),* s.v. "Hanson, J. C. M.," by Edith Scott; and *Dictionary of American Library Biography (DALB);* s.v. "Hanson, James Christian Meinich," by John P. Immroth.

23. Scott, "J. C. M. Hanson," p. iv.

24. Charters to Gray, 20 Feb. 1925, Charters MSS, OSU, YF9.

25. Charters to Gray, 2 May 1925, Charters MSS, OSU, YF9.

26. For further biographical information concerning Dr. Waples, see John Richardson, "Douglas Waples, 1893–1978," *Journal of Library History* 15 (Winter 1980): 76–83.

27. Waples, *On the March*, p. 2.

28. "An Approach to the Synthetic Study of Interest in Education" (Ph.D. dissertation, University of Pennsylvania, 1920).

29. *On the March*, pp. 4–5.

30. For instance, Waples' *Procedures in High School Teaching* (New York: Macmillan, 1924) and his *Problems in Classroom Method* (New York: Macmillan, 1927).

31. John Moulds, secretary to board of trustees, to Waples, 9 Feb. 1928, Waples' personal papers, Wisconsin Island, Wis.

32. Taped interview of Augustus F. Kuhlman by John Richardson Jr. on 28 Dec. 1977 in Nashville, Tenn.

33. General biographical information concerning Dr. Butler has been obtained from Williamson and Jewitt's *Who's Who in Library Service;* Stanley Pargellis, "Pierce Butler—A Biographical Sketch," *Library Quarterly* 22 (July 1952): 170–73; Bernard I. Bell, "Pierce Butler, Professor and Priest," *Library Quarterly* 22 (July 1952): 174–76; Redmond Burke, "Bibliography of Pierce Butler," *Library Quarterly* 22 (July 1952): 165–69; "Deaths," *Library Journal* 78 (1 May 1953): 795; Lee Ash, "Tribute to Pierce Butler, *Library Journal* 78 (15 May 1953): 826; Leon Carnovsky, "Pierce Butler 1886–1953," *Library Quarterly* 23 (July 1953): 153–54; and "The Pierce Butler Library," *Seabury-Western Bulletin* (Epiphany 1954), pp. 3–4; *Dictionary of American Library Biography (DALB),* s.v. "Butler, Pierce," by Lee Ash; and personal correspondence with Dr. Ruth Butler (Mrs. Pierce).

34. Works, "Research," p. 103.

35. "Studies in the Christology of Irenaeus" (Ph.D. dissertation, Hartford Theological Seminary, 1912).

36. *DALB,* p. 253.

37. Butler to Richardson, 19 Apr. 1978.

38. 1 John 4:1 (NEB).

39. General biographical information concerning Howe has been obtained from Williamson and Jewitt's *Who's Who in Library Service.* Holdings of the Denver Public Library's Western History Department and the University of Denver Library's Department of Special Collections are sparse.

40. Randall to Richardson, 15 Apr. 1978.

41. *DALB,* s.v. "Howe, Harriet Emma," by Martha Boaz, John T. Eastlick, and Laurel A. Grotzinger.

42. American Library Association, *Annual Report of the Board of Education for Librarianship* (Chicago: American Library Association, 1925), p. 9.

43. Charters' students were Susan Akers, Dena Babcock, Nora Beust, Mary Carter, Genevieve Darlington, Gertrude Drury, Edith Erskine, Helen Ganser, Alice I. Hazeltine, Marion Horton, Elizabeth MacB. King, Rena Reece, Edith L. Ruddock, Helen Sharpless, and Margaret Vinton. All of them received a "pass" except Darlington, who received an "incomplete."

44. "A.L.A. Dinner Meeting," pp. 1170–71.

45. He defined library science as "the knowledge and skill by which printed or written records are recognized, selected, organized and utilized. . . . Its purpose is to associate its results with existing needs and demands. Its idea is human enlightenment in a historical continuity" (from his *The Sciences in the Training of the Librarian* [Holstebro, Denmark: N. P. Thomsen, 1928], pp. 7–8); idem, "[Summary of an Address before the] Professional Training Section of A.L.A.," *American Library Association Bulletin* 22 (Sept. 1928): 449.

46. "A.L.A. Dinner Meeting," p. 1171.

47. "Importance of Fellowships for the Graduate Library School," [23 Dec. 1927], GLS Papers, 1927–31, CC.

48. Ibid.

49. Ibid.

50. "Memorandum of Mason and Keppel Interview," 28 Feb. 1928, GLS Papers, 1927–31, CC.

51. Works, "Research," p. 101.

52. Ibid.

53. Ibid.

54. Bogle to Milam, 7 June 1928, ALAA Series 28/50/5-3.

55. Ibid.

56. "The Graduate Library School of the University of Chicago," Mar. 1928, ALAA Series 28/50/5-3.

57. "The Graduate Library School, 1928–29," *Announcements* (20 June 1928).

58. Bogle to Milam, 7 June 1928.

59. "Importance of Fellowships."

60. George A. Works, "The Graduate Library School," *University Record*, n.s., 14 (Jan. 1928): 51.

61. Works, "The Graduate Library School," Mar. 1928.

62. Works, "The Graduate Library School," *University Record*, n.s., 14 (Jan. 1928): 51.

63. Works, "Research," p. 103.

64. "The Graduate Library School, 1928–29," *Announcements* (20 June 1928):12–13.

65. Ibid.

66. Works to Bishop, 13 Dec. 1927, University of Michigan School of Library Science Papers, Box 3, Michigan Historical Collections, University of Michigan.

67. Works, "Research," p. 100.

68. Ibid., p. 101.

69. Ibid.

70. Ibid., pp. 101–2.

71. Laing to Woodward, 10 Apr. 1929, 1925–45 Presidents' MSS, UC, 112.

72. "Library Meetings," *Libraries* 34 (May 1929): 219–20.

73. "Dean Made President," *Detroit Free Press*, 11 Apr. 1929, p. 3.

74. Bogle and Milam to Craver, 19 Dec. 1929, ALAA Series 28/50/5-3.

75. Ibid.

76. George A. Works, "The Graduate Library School of the University of Chicago," *Libraries* 34 (July 1929): 311.

77. Ibid.

78. Works, "Research," p. 102.

79. Works, "The Graduate Library School," p. 311.

80. Ibid.

81. Those of Mary Amy Winslow and Margaret Crompton Taylor, respectively.

82. Works, "The Graduate Library School," p. 312.

83. Ibid.
84. Ibid., p. 313.
85. Ibid.
86. Ibid., p. 312.
87. Ibid.
88. Ibid., p. 313.
89. Laing to David H. Stevens, assistant to president, 21 May 1929, 1925–45 Presidents' MSS, UC, 112.
90. Waples to Charters, 12 Apr. 1929, Charters MSS, OSU, CB5.
91. Thompson to Laing, 15 Apr. 1929, 1925–45 Presidents' MSS, UC, 112.
92. Charters to Works, 19 Apr. 1929, Charters MSS, OSU.
93. Ibid.
94. Works to Charters, 23 Apr. 1929, Charters MSS, OSU.
95. Waples to Charters, 27 Apr. 1929, Charters MSS, OSU, CB5.
96. Charters to Waples, 30 Apr. 1929, Charters MSS, OSU, CB5.
97. Ibid.
98. Waples to Charters, [3 May 1929], Charters MSS, OSU, CB5.
99. Ibid.
100. Bogle to Keppel, 7 May 1929, GLS Papers, 1927–31.
101. Ibid.
102. Milam to Hutchins, 8 May 1929, GLS Papers, 1927–1931, CC.
103. "Memorandum of Interview of Keppel and Hutchins," 14 May 1929, GLS Papers, 1927–1931, CC.
104. Ibid.
105. Ibid.
106. Works to Woodward, 20 May 1929, 1925–45 Presidents' MSS, UC, 112.
107. Waples to Charters, 21 May 1929, Charters MSS, OSU, CB5.
108. Ibid.
109. Laing to Stevens, 21 May 1929, 1925–45 Presidents' MSS, UC, 112.
110. "Memorandum of Meeting with Hutchins by Milam and Bogle re Dr. Works' successor," 27 May 1929, ALAA 28/50/5-3.
111. Ibid.
112. Keppel to Bogle, 28 May 1929, GLS Papers, 1927–1931, CC.
113. Bogle to Keppel, 28 May 1929, GLS Papers, 1927–1931, CC.
114. Keppel to Hutchins, 29 May 1929, 1925–45 Presidents' MSS, UC, 112.
115. Ibid.
116. Ibid.
117. Woodward to Capen, 31 May 1929, 1925–45 Presidents' MSS, UC, 112. The University Archives of the State University of New York at Buffalo "holds an extensive collection of Samuel P. Capen papers, including correspondence, but none for [this] period or with the people" mentioned (Finnegan to Richardson, 10 Apr. 1978).
118. Keppel to Hutchins, 3 June 1929, 1924–45 Presidents' MSS, UC, 112.
119. Capen to Woodward, 3 June 1929, 1925–45 Presidents' MSS, UC, 112.

120. "Dr. Works Resigns from Graduate Library School," *Libraries* 34 (July 1929): 317.
121. Ibid., p. 318.
122. Ibid., pp. 318–19.

Chapter 4

1. Douglas Waples, "First Year Activities of the Graduate Library School, University of Chicago," *American Library Association Bulletin* 23 (Aug. 1929): 336–37.
2. Ibid., p. 336.
3. Douglas Waples, "The Graduate Library School at Chicago," *Library Quarterly* 1 (Jan. 1931): 26–36. Appended is "Some [36] Problems under Investigation at the Graduate Library School, University of Chicago, 1928–30."
4. Ibid., p. 30.
5. Ibid., p. 26.
6. Ibid., p. 30.
7. Ibid., p. 31.
8. Ibid.
9. Ibid., pp. 31–33.
10. "A Detailed Catalog of the Arabic Manuscripts in the Ananikian Collection of the Hartford Seminary Foundation" (Ph.D. dissertation, Hartford Theological Seminary, 1929). In a 20 May 1929 letter to Bishop, Randall stated: "My oral examination consisted largely in a discourse by myself on cataloging theory as applied to Arabic manuscripts. The idea was to justify the admitting of a catalog of manuscripts as a thesis for a Doctorate. Apparently I convinced them that there was sufficient research and pioneer work in such a thing to warrant its acceptance" (W. W. Bishop Papers, Box 24, Michigan Historical Collections [MHP], University of Michigan [UM]).
11. Randall to Bishop, 13 Dec. 1928, W. W. Bishop Papers, Box 24, MHC, UM.
12. Randall to Bishop, 27 Sept. 1929, W. W. Bishop Papers, Box 24, MHC, UM.
13. Randall to Richardson, 15 Apr. 1978.
14. Randall to Bishop, 24 Oct. 1929, University of Michigan School of Library Science Papers, Box 3, MHC, UM.
15. "Some Problems under Investigation at the Graduate Library School, University of Chicago," Dec. 1929, 1925–1945 Presidents' MSS, UC, 112. Specifically, Randall's research included a history of Muhammadan libraries; compilation of a list of subject headings for sociology; codification of cataloging routine; classification system for libraries of chemistry; transliteration and entry of Arabic names; study of actual uses of various types of library catalogs; measurement of vocabulary difficulty in ALA subject headings for representative groups of public library patrons; evaluation of foreign book collections in American public libraries; study of best-seller trends as

indicated by "Bookman" lists to determine the factors involved; comparative study of newsstand literature in the U.S., France, Belgium, and Italy; comparative study of costs of books in various classes of literature in small college libraries; evaluation of librarians' needs for academic training in special fields, with reference to type of library and nature of professional duties; and an analysis of useful techniques in making surveys of catalog departments, with reference to the training of persons to conduct such surveys.

16. Randall to Richardson, 15 Apr. 1978.

17. "Dr. William M. Randall," *College and Research Libraries* 8 (Oct. 1947): 451.

18. Florence Anderson, *Library Program, 1911–1961* (New York: Carnegie, 1963), p. 12.

19. Randall to Richardson, 15 Apr. 1978.

20. *Encyclopedia of Library and Information Science (ELIS)*, s.v. "Denver. University of Denver, Graduate School of Librarianship," by Margaret K. Goggin. Howe's thinking on "The Library School Curriculum" was presented in *Library Quarterly* 1 (July 1931): 283–90, which was revised on the basis of her Denver experience as "The First-Year Library School Curriculum," in *Library Trends*, ed. Louis R. Wilson (Chicago: University of Chicago Press, 1937), pp. 361–74, 384.

21. Edith Scott, "J. C. M. Hanson and His Contribution to Twentieth-Century Cataloging" (Ph.D. dissertation, University of Chicago, 1971), p. 627.

22. "Some Problems under Investigation."

23. Scott, "J. C. M. Hanson," p. 628.

24. J. Christian Bay, "James Christian Meinich Hanson: 1864–1943," *Library Quarterly* 14 (Jan. 1944): 59.

25. Scott, "J. C. M. Hanson," p. 645.

26. Douglas Waples, "Current Activities—Graduate Library School," Dec. 1930, GLS Papers, 1927–31, CC.

27. Waples to Woodward, 1925–45 Presidents' MSS, UC, 112.

28. "Library School Study Finds 'What People Want to Read'—and Why," *University of Chicago Maroon*, 2 Oct. 1931.

29. "Some Problems under Investigation."

30. Waples, "Current Activities."

31. "Among Librarians," *Library Journal* 56 (15 Sept. 1931): 768.

32. Stanley Pargellis, "Pierce Butler—A Biographical Sketch," *Library Quarterly* 22 (July 1952): 173. Thompson's ideal library school is apparent in a letter written to Gordon Laing in Feb. 1927. Citing Harvey W. Cushing's *Life of Sir William Osler* (Oxford: Clarendon, 1925 [2: 573]), Thompson favored Osler's proposal of a "school of the Book," to be established at Oxford in cooperation with the Clarendon Press and the Bodleian and arranged in four departments: (1) library economy, (2) bibliography, (3) school of printing and publication, and (4) the history of books and libraries. Osler's plan, later adopted by University College, London, is more fully developed in an address, "The Library School in the College," given

at the opening of the British Summer School of Library Science, Aberystwyth (see *Library Association Record* 19 [Aug.–Sept. 1917]: 287–308).

33. "Roman Cursive Writing" (Ph.D. dissertation, Princeton University, 1912).

34. Randall to Richardson, 15 Apr. 1978.

35. Ibid.

36. "Proposed Expansion of the Bulletin," *American Library Association Bulletin* 20 (4–9 Oct. 1926): 340.

37. Ibid., p. 341.

38. Ibid.

39. "Journal of Discussion," *American Library Association Bulletin* 23 (Jan. 1929): 12.

40. Carl B. Milam to Williamson, 8 Feb. 1929, Williamson MSS, CU, 1.

41. Hanson to W. W. Bishop, 11 Jan. 1930, University of Michigan School of Library Science Papers, Box 3, MHC, UM.

42. "The Library Quarterly," *American Library Association Bulletin* 24 (Oct. 1930): 600.

43. Bishop to Hanson, 13 Jan. 1930, University of Michigan School of Library Science Papers, Box 3, MHC, UM.

44. Woodward to Keppel, 3 Mar. 1930, Library Quarterly Papers, 1930–40, Carnegie Corp. (hereafter cited as LQ Papers).

45. Learned to Lester, 21 Mar. 1930, LQ Papers, 1930–40, CC.

46. "Memorandum of Keppel and Hanson Interview," 31 Mar. 1930, LQ Papers, 1930–40, CC.

47. Ibid.

48. Hanson to Keppel, 1 Apr. 1930, LQ Papers, 1930–40, CC.

49. Hanson to Keppel, 22 Apr. 1930, LQ Papers, 1930–40, CC.

50. Hanson to Bowker, 21 Apr. 1930, LQ Papers, 1930–40, CC.

51. Keppel to Woodward, 24 Apr. 1930, LQ Papers, 1930–40, CC.

52. Randall to Keppel, 7 June 1930, LQ Papers, 1930–40, CC. His request may have been prompted by Keppel's article, "The Carnegie Tradition and A.L.A." (*American Library Association Bulletin* 22 [Apr. 1928]: 64–66), which suggested that the GLS at Chicago was established "from the very beginning [as] a real part in a real university."

53. Richard Bowker, review of *Library Quarterly* (vol. 1, no. 1), in *Library Journal* 56 (1 Feb. 1931): 124.

54. Williamson to Randall, 13 July 1931, LQ Papers, 1931–45, UC.

55. Gonzalez Lodge, "[Editorial]," *Classical Weekly* 1 (21 Dec. 1907): 1.

56. "Meeting of Editorial Board of the *Library Quarterly*, New Orleans, April 1932," LQ Papers, 1930–40, CC.

57. Ibid.

58. Ibid.

59. Ibid.

60. "The LQ Convention Notebook," 25 Apr. 1932, ALAA.

61. *University of Chicago Maroon*, academic year 1931/32.

62. University of Chicago, *1931 Cap and Gown*.

63. Ibid.

64. "Among Librarians," *Library Journal* 56 (15 Sept. 1931): 768.

65. "Some Problems under Investigation."

66. Stevens to Hanson, 8 Nov. 1929, 1925–45 Presidents' MSS, UC, 112.

67. American Library Association, *Third Annual Report of the Board of Education for Librarianship* (Chicago: American Library Association, 1927), p. 20.

68. Waples to Brown, Aug. 1930, ALAA Series 28/50/5-3.

69. Waples, "The Graduate Library School," p. 27.

70. Waples to Woodward, 28 Feb. 1931, 1925–45 Presidents' MSS, UC, 112.

71. Waples, "Current Activities."

72. Ibid.

73. Ibid.

74. Ibid.

75. Ibid.

76. Waples, "The Graduate Library School," pp. 27–28.

77. Waples, "Current Activities."

78. Ibid.

79. Waples, "The Graduate Library School," p. 28.

80. Ibid.

81. Ibid.

82. Lester to Keppel, "University of Chicago Graduate Library School, Waples Memorandum on Activities, December 1930," 22 Dec. 1930, GLS Papers, 1927–31, CC.

83. Ibid.

84. Ibid.

85. Mary E. Ahern, "American Library Institute Meeting in New Haven, Connecticut, June 23," *Libraries* 36 (Oct. 1931): 348.

86. C. Seymour Thompson, "Do We Want a Library Science?" *Library Journal* 56 (July 1931): 581–87.

87. Carl B. Roden, "[Presidential Address]," *American Library Association Bulletin* 22 (Sept. 1928): 315.

88. Thompson, "Do We Want a Library Science?" p. 582.

89. Ibid.

90. Ibid.

91. Ibid., p. 583.

92. Ibid.

93. Ibid.

94. Ibid., p. 585.

95. Ibid.

96. Ibid., p. 586.

97. Ibid.

98. Ibid.

99. Ibid., p. 587.

100. Raney to Woodward, 1 July 1931, 1925–45 Presidents' MSS, UC, 112.

101. Ahern, "American Library Institute," p. 349; Louis R. Wilson, "Research in the Field of Library Science," Mar. 1931, Wilson MSS, UNC, VI–9.

102. Ibid.

103. Raney to Woodward, 1 July 1931.

104. Ibid.

105. Ibid.

106. Ibid.

107. Abraham Flexner, *Universities: American, English, German* (New York: Oxford University Press, 1930), p. 172, n. 109. For an alternative view, see George A. Works's review of *Universities* in *Library Quarterly* 1 (Apr. 1931): 238–39.

108. Raney to Woodward, 1 July 1931.

109. Ibid.

110. Works to Emery T. Filbey, assistant to the president, 26 Aug. 1931, 1925–45 Presidents' MSS, UC, 112.

111. Douglas Waples, "Do We Want a Library Science? A Reply," *Library Journal* 56 (15 Sept. 1931): 743.

112. Ibid.

113. Ibid.

114. Ibid.

115. Ibid.

116. Ibid.

117. Ibid.

118. Ibid.

119. Ibid., p. 744.

120. Ibid.

121. Ibid., pp. 745–46.

122. Ibid.

123. Ibid., p. 746.

124. Ibid.

125. Ibid.

126. Ibid.

127. C. Seymour Thompson, "Comment on the Reply," *Library Journal* 56 (15 Sept. 1931): 746.

128. Esp. Hutchins to Waples, 21 Sept. 1931, 1925–45 Presidents' MSS, UC, 112; Edward A. Henry, director of libraries at the University of Cincinnati, to Waples, 24 Sept. 1931, 1925–45 Presidents' MSS, UC, 112; Vittorio Camerani, Institut International D'Agriculture, Rome, to Waples, 7 Nov. 1931, 1925–45 Presidents' MSS, UC, 112. Camerani was a University of Michigan Library School graduate who had just written an article on the GLS at Chicago, "Corriere American" (*La Bibliofilia* 33 [Aug.–Sept. 1931]: 350–53).

129. Sarah Bogle, "Memorandum," 25 Sept. 1931, ALAA Series 28/50/5-3.

130. J. Christian Bay, "Every Serious Voice Deserves a Hearing," *Library Journal* 56 (15 Sept. 1931): 748–50.

131. Ibid., p. 748.

132. Ibid.

133. Ibid.

134. William Osler, "The Library School in the College," *Library Association Record* 19 (Aug.–Sept. 1917): 288.

135. Bay, "Every Serious Voice," p. 749.

136. "Editorial Forum," *Library Journal* 56 (15 Sept. 1931): 752.

137. "Williamson Article Free on Request," *Library Journal* 56 (15 Sept. 1931): 756.

138. "Ponderous Attention to Insignificant Detail," *Library Journal* 56 (15 Sept. 1931): 756.

139. C. Seymour Thompson, "On 'Going Scientific,'" *Libraries* 56 (Oct. 1931): 343–44.

140. Mary E. Ahern, "Library Service—A Science? a Philosophy? an Art?" *Libraries* 36 (Oct. 1931): 340.

141. Butler to Ahern, 14 Oct. 1931, Wilson MSS, UNC, II–20.

142. Ibid.

143. Ibid.

144. Ibid.

145. J. H. Shera, "The Place of Library Service in Research: A Suggestion," *Libraries* 36 (Nov. 1931): 387–90.

146. Ibid., p. 387.

147. Ibid., p. 390.

148. Ibid.

149. Randall to Richardson, 15 Apr. 1978. For more background information, see Sister Tressa Piper, "The American Library Institute, 1905–1951: An Historical Study and Analysis of Goals" (M.L.S. paper, University of Wisconsin, 1975).

150. Charles H. Brown, review of *The College Library,* by William M. Randall, in *Library Journal* 57 (July 1932): 625.

151. Randall to Richardson, 15 Apr. 1978.

152. Henry Harap, review of *What People Want to Read About,* by Douglas Waples and Ralph W. Tyler, in *Library Quarterly* 2 (Jan. 1932): 93.

153. Stevens to Works, 23 July 1929, 1925–45 Presidents' MSS, UC, 112.

154. "Memorandum of Frederick Woodward," 20 June 1929, 1925–45 Presidents' MSS, UC, 112.

155. Joseph L. Wheeler to Gordon Laing, 29 July 1929, ALAA Series 28/50/5-3.

156. Bogle to Milam, "Re Van Hoesen Conference," 2 Aug. 1929, ALAA Series 28/50/5-3.

157. Butler, Hanson, Thompson, Randall, and Waples to Stevens, 8 Aug. 1929, 1925–45 Presidents' MSS, UC, 112; Howe to Stevens, 30 July 1929, 1925–45 Presidents' MSS, UC, 112.

158. Works to Stevens, 2 Aug. 1929, 1925–45 Presidents' MSS, UC, 112.

159. Waples to Woodward, 27 Aug. 1929, 1925–45 Presidents' MSS, UC, 112.

160. Bishop to Hutchins, 13 Sept. 1929, 1925–45 Presidents' MSS, UC, 112.

161. Hutchins to Keogh and Gerould, 13 Sept. 1929, 1925–45 Presidents' MSS, UC, 112.

162. Gerould to Hutchins, 13 Sept. 1929, 1925–45 Presidents' MSS, UC, 112.

163. Ibid., manuscript note of Hutchins.

164. Hutchins to Keogh, 17 Sept. 1929, 1925–45 Presidents' MSS, UC, 112.

165. Works to Stevens, 30 Sept. 1929, Presidents' MSS, UC, 112.

166. Stevens to Bishop, 3 Oct. 1929, and Stevens to Keogh, 3 Oct. 1929, 1925–45 Presidents' MSS, UC, 112.

167. E. C. Richardson to Stevens, 21 Oct. 1929, 1925–45 Presidents' MSS, UC, 112.

168. Stevens to Woodward, June 1929, 1925–45 Presidents' MSS, UC, 112.

169. Stevens to Van Hoesen, 10 Dec. 1929, 1925–45 Presidents' MSS, UC, 112.

170. Milam, "Memorandum on the Graduate Library School," 17 Dec. 1929, ALAA Series 28/50/5-3.

171. Bogle and Milam to Craver, 19 Dec. 1929, ALAA Series 28/50/5-3.

172. Keppel to Keogh, 13 Jan. 1930, GLS Papers, 1927–31, CC.

173. Bishop to Keppel, 27 Jan. 1930, GLS Papers, 1927–31, CC.

174. Hutchins to Keogh, 29 Jan. 1930, University of Michigan Library Papers, Box 9, MHC, UM.

175. Keogh to Hutchins, 31 Jan. 1930, 1925–45 Presidents' MSS, UC, 112.

176. Hutchins to Keogh, 6 Feb. 1930, 1925–45 Presidents' MSS, UC, 112.

177. Woodward to Works, 14 Oct. 1930, 1925–45 Presidents' MSS, UC, 112.

178. Works to Woodward, 28 Oct. 1930, 1925–45 Presidents' MSS, UC, 112.

179. Woodward to Works, 10 Nov. 1930, 1925–45 Presidents' MSS, UC, 112.

180. Keppel to Bishop, 30 Jan. 1930, GLS Papers, 1927–31, CC. Readers interested in Keppel's ideas on the role of a foundation might profitably consult his Page-Barbour Lecture of 1930 at the University of Virginia, published as The Foundation: Its Place in American Life (New York: Macmillan, 1930).

181. Quoted in Woodward to Hutchins, 13 Nov. 1930, 1925–45 Presidents' MSS, UC, 112.

182. Ibid.

183. "Memorandum of Lester and Keppel Interview," 15 Dec. 1930, GLS Papers, 1927–31, CC.

184. Waples to Charters, 15 Jan. 1931, Charters MSS, OSU, CB5.

185. "Memorandum of Keppel and Charters Interview, Rochester," 24 Mar. 1931, GLS Papers, 1927–31, CC.

186. Woodward to Hutchins, 29 Aug. 1931, 1925–44 Presidents' MSS, UC, 112-9.

187. Ibid.

188. Woodward to Filbey, 27 July 1931, 1925–45 Presidents' MSS, UC, 112-9.

189. L. R. Wilson to Edwin M. Wilson, 2 Nov. 1931, Wilson MSS, UNC, II–22.

190. Ibid.

191. Mary J. Wing, "A History of the School of Library Science of the University of North Carolina: The First Twenty-five Years" (M.S.L.S. thesis, University of North Carolina, 1958).

192. Wilson to Bishop, 16 Nov. 1931, Wilson MSS, UNC, II–20. Wilson told his biographer, in perhaps more fanciful terms, that Hutchins had said he "would have to give the endowment back to the Indians" if Wilson did not accept the deanship; see Maurice F. Tauber, *Louis Round Wilson: Librarian and Administrator* (New York: Columbia University Press, 1967), p. 145.

193. Wilson to Bishop, 16 Nov. 1931.

194. "Suggestions for Chicago Library School by Mr. Milam," 14 Nov. 1931, Wilson MSS, UNC, II–19.

195. Wilson to M. R. Trabue, 10 Dec. 1931, Wilson MSS, UNC, II–21.

196. Milam to Keppel, 21 Dec. 1931, GLS Papers, 1927–31, CC.

197. Ibid.

198. Keppel to Milam, 28 Dec. 1931, GLS Papers, 1927–31, CC.

199. Louis R. Wilson to Edwin M. Wilson, 23 Dec. 1931, Wilson MSS, UNC, II–22.

200. Wilson to Hutchins, 29 Dec. 1931, Wilson MSS, UNC, II–22.

201. Hutchins to Wilson, 31 Dec. 1931, Wilson MSS, UNC, II–22.

202. Hutchins to Wilson, 13 Jan. 1932, Wilson MSS, UNC, II–23.

203. Wilson to Hutchins, 13 Jan. 1932, Wilson MSS, UNC, II–23.

Chapter 5

1. "Dr. L. R. Wilson to Head U. of C. Library School," *Chicago Tribune*, 16 Jan. 1932, p. 15.

2. Carl Milam to Wilson, 16 Jan. 1932; George Works to Wilson, 16 Jan. 1932; Pierce Butler, 19 Jan. 1932; and Carl Milam, 19 Jan. 1932, Wilson MSS, UNC, II–24.

3. Wilson to Filbey, 8 Feb. 1932, 1925–45 Presidents' MSS, UC, 112-9.

4. Wilson to Waples, 21 Apr. 1932, Wilson MSS, UNC, II–35B.

5. Louis R. Wilson, "Chicago Ideas" (Spring 1932), Wilson MSS, UNC, II–40.

6. Tom Peete Cross, *A List of Books and Articles, Chiefly Bibliographical, Designed to Serve as an Introduction to the Bibliography and Methods of English Literary History* (5th ed.; Chicago: University of Chicago Press, 1930).

7. Waples to Wilson, 19 Apr. 1932, Wilson MSS, UNC, II–35a.

8. Robert M. Lester, memorandum of interview with Wilson, 26 Apr. 1932, GLS Papers, 1932–34, CC.

9. Ibid.

10. Ibid.

11. Lester, memorandum of interview with Waples, 31 Mar. 1932, GLS Papers, 1932–34, CC.

12. Lester, memorandum, 26 Apr. 1932.

13. Randall to Richardson, 15 Apr. 1978.

14. Wilson to W. W. Bishop, 6 Mar. 1933, University of Michigan School of Library Science Papers, Box 3, MHC, UM.

15. Wilson, "Report on the Graduate Library School, 1930–1933," Wilson MSS, UNC, V–96; "Report on the University of Chicago Graduate Library School, July 1, 1932–July 1, 1933," GLS Papers, 1932–34, CC; "Report on the Library Quarterly, 1931–1933," LQ Papers, 1930–40, CC; "Statement Concerning the Plans of the Graduate Library School," 1925–45 Presidents' MSS, UC.

16. Louis R. Wilson, "The Objectives of the Graduate Library School in Extending the Frontiers of Librarianship," in *New Frontiers in Librarianship: Proceedings of the Special Meeting of the Association of American Library Schools and the Board of Education for Librarianship of the American Library Association in Honor of the University of Chicago and the Graduate Library School, December 30, 1940* (Chicago: University of Chicago Press, 1941), pp. 13–26.

17. Bishop to Wilson, 12 Dec. 1932, University of Michigan School of Library Science Papers, Box 3, MHC, UM.

18. "Board of Education for Librarianship," *American Library Association Bulletin* 27 (15 Dec. 1933): 610–13.

19. Ibid., p. 610.

20. Ibid.

21. Ibid.

22. Ibid.

23. American Library Association, Board of Education for Librarianship, "Minutes of the Third Session, 24 March 1934, 8:00 PM," ALAA Series 28/50/1-2.

24. Ibid.

25. Ibid.

26. Ibid.

27. Wilson to Works, 10 Feb. 1932, Wilson MSS, UNC, II–30.

28. Henry to Wilson, 20 Jan. 1932, Wilson MSS, UNC, II–25.

29. Wilson, "Report of the University of Chicago Graduate Library School, July 1, 1932 to July 1, 1933," p. 14, GLS Papers, 1932–34, CC.

30. Robert C. Cook, ed., *Presidents and Professors in American Colleges and Universities* (New York: Robert C. Cook, 1935), p. vii.

31. Keppel to Wilson, 26 Sept. 1933, GLS Papers, 1932–34, CC.

32. Woodward to Wilson, 16 Oct. 1934, Wilson MSS, UNC, II–62.

33. Ralph Munn, *Conditions and Trends in Education for Librarianship* (New York: Carnegie Corp. of New York, 1936), p. 20.

34. Ibid., p. 11.

35. Ibid., p. 18.

36. Leon Carnovsky, "Why Graduate Study in Librarianship?" *Library Quarterly* 7 (Apr. 1937): 250.

37. Ibid.

38. Ibid., p. 253.

39. Ibid., p. 261.

40. Wilhelm Munthe, *American Librarianship from a European Angle: An Attempt at an Evaluation of Policies and Activities* (Chicago: American Library Association, 1939; reprint ed., Hamden, Conn.: Shoe String Press, 1964).

41. Ibid., pp. 144–54.

42. Ibid., p. 148.

43. Ralph Munn, "Fact versus Folklore," *American Library Association Bulletin* 34 (June 1940): 381–82.

44. American Library Association, Committee on Fellowships and Scholarships, *Education for Librarianship: Grants-in-Aid Financed by the Carnegie Corporation of New York, 1929–1942*, with introduction by Paul M. Paine (Chicago: American Library Association, 1943), p. 1.

45. Wilson to Works, 10 Feb. 1932.

46. Milam to Keppel, 26 Nov. 1932, ALAA Series.

47. *Announcements 1932–33*, p. 3, cited by M. Llewellyn Raney in *The University of Chicago Survey* (Chicago: University of Chicago Press, 1933), 7:173.

48. American Library Association, *Education for Librarianship*, p. 12.

49. Ibid.

50. Douglas Waples, "Current Activities—Graduate Library School," Dec. 1930, p. 3, GLS Papers, 1927–31, CC.

51. "Statements Submitted by Students of The Graduate Library School," [25 June 1942], Wilson MSS, UNC, II–30.

52. American Library Association, Board of Education for Librarianship, *Annual Report of the Board of Education for Librarianship* (Chicago: American Library Association, 1925), pp. 9, 25.

53. Wilson to Keppel, 1 Feb. 1933, GLS Papers, 1932–34, CC.

54. Wilson, "Report," p. 7.

55. Wilson to Hostetter, 3 May 1933, ALAA Series 28/50/5-3.

56. Wilson to Keppel, 14 Oct. 1936, Library Schools Studies Papers, 1933–37, Carnegie Corp.

57. Ibid.

58. Filbey to Wilson, 15 Feb. 1937, 1925–45 Presidents' MSS, UC, 112.

59. Ibid.

60. "Memorandum of Interview of Wilson by Keppel," 3 Dec. 1937, GLS Papers, 1937, CC.

61. Wilson to Hutchins, 18 Feb. 1938, 1925–45 Presidents' MSS, UC, 112.

62. Roden to Lester, 28 Feb. 1940, "Survey of the Public Library System Papers," Carnegie Corp.

63. Hopper to Keppel, 8 Mar. 1938, GLS Papers, 1938–42, CC. Additional evidence on this point may be found in Wilson's "Memorandum on the Place of the Graduate Library School of the University of Chicago in Professional Training for Librarianship," submitted to the Association pour Le Dévelopment de la Lecture Publique (Paris), 1 Oct. 1938, Wilson MSS, UNC, V–134.

64. "Columbia Endows Library Teaching; Melvil Dewey Professorship, First of Kind, Founded with Carnegie Gift of $250,000," *New York Times*, 6 Apr. 1938, p. 25, col. 7; "$401,601 in Cash Gifts Listed by Columbia; Largest Donation in March was $250,000 from Carnegie Fund," *New York Times*, 8 Apr. 1938, p. 19, col. 2; "A New Professorship," *New York Times*, 7 Apr. 1938, p. 22, col. 3.

65. "Memorandum of Interview" of Wilson by Keppel, 29 September 1941, One Year Course in Librarianship Papers, Carnegie Corp.

66. Isabel Nichol, "The First-Year Library School Curriculum" (M.A. report, University of Chicago, 1941).

67. She also discussed Chicago's influence on book selection courses, especially attention to reading habits, citing Philip O. and Mary J. Keeney's "Social Content in Library Training," *Wilson Library Bulletin* 14 (Feb. 1940): 429–34.

68. Nichol, "First-Year Library School Curriculum," p. 29.

69. Ibid., p. 31.

70. Wilson to Hutchins, 5 Feb. 1942, 1940–46 Presidents' MSS, UC.

71. Hutchins to Wilson, ca. 9 Feb. 1942, 1940–46 Presidents' MSS, UC.

72. Filbey to Wilson, 13 Feb. 1942, 1940–46 Presidents' MSS, UC.

73. Learned to Walter A. Jessup, 10 Mar. 1942, "One-Year Course in Librarianship Papers," Carnegie Corp.

74. Wilson to Hutchins, 3 Apr. 1942, 1940–46 Presidents' MSS, UC.

75. "University of Chicago Minutes of the University Senate," 9 Apr. 1942, University of Chicago.

76. Wilson to Hutchins, 6 May 1942, Presidents' MSS, UC.

77. Joeckel to Wilson, 23 Sept. 1942, Wilson MSS, UNC, IV–480.

78. Beals to Randall, 9 Oct. 1946, 1940–46 Presidents' MSS, UC.

79. Randall to Richardson, 15 Apr. 1978.

80. Timmerman to Anita Hostetter, 15 Aug. 1932, ALAA Series 28/50/5-3.

81. American Library Association, Board of Education for Librarianship, "Alphabetical List of Library Terms," 21 Jan. 1932.

82. Waples to Hutchins, 8 Jan. 1931, 1925–45 Presidents' MSS, UC.

83. Ibid.

84. *Encyclopedia of the Social Sciences*, s.v. "Research," by Donald Slesinger and Mary Stephenson.

85. Douglas Waples, "The Graduate Library School at Chicago," *Library Quarterly* 1 (Jan. 1931): 26–36.

86. Randall to Richardson, 15 Apr. 1978.
87. Carl Milam, "Suggestion for Chicago Library School," 14 Nov. 1931, Wilson MSS, UNC, II–19.
88. Harriet E. Howe, "Two Decades in Education for Librarianship," *Library Quarterly* 12 (July 1942): 567–68.
89. Douglas Waples, *Investigating Library Problems* (Chicago: University of Chicago Press, 1939). There is no direct evidence, although W. W. Charters is listed in the acknowledgments; however, Waples' book appears to be based, in part, on Harold H. Bixler, *Check Lists for Educational Research*, Standard Research Procedures Series (New York: Columbia University Teachers College, 1928).
90. *Encyclopedia of the Social Sciences*, s.v. "Research," by Donald Slesinger and Mary Stephenson.
91. Pierce Butler, *An Introduction to Library Science*, University of Chicago Library Science Series, no. 1 (Chicago: University of Chicago Press, 1933), p. 11.
92. Wilson to Keppel, 29 Feb. 1936, GLS Papers, 1935–36, CC.
93. Waples to Hutchins, 8 Jan. 1931, 1925–45 Presidents' MSS, UC, 112.
94. Wilson to Keppel, 29 Feb. 1936.
95. Pierce Butler, *The Origin of Printing in Europe*, University of Chicago Studies in Library Science (Chicago: University of Chicago Press, 1940).
96. Ruth Butler to Richardson, 19 Apr. 1978.
97. James W. Thompson, *The Medieval Library*, University of Chicago Studies in Library Science (Chicago: University of Chicago Press, 1939), p. v.
98. *ESS*, s.v. "Research," by Donald Slesinger and Mary Stephenson.
99. Hester Hoffman, "The Graduate Thesis in Library Science" (M.A. thesis, University of Chicago, 1941).
100. Douglas Waples, "Graduate Theses Accepted by Library Schools in the United States from June, 1928 to June, 1932," *Library Quarterly* 3 (July 1933): 273; "Graduate Theses Accepted by Library Schools in the United States from July, 1933 to June, 1935," *Library Quarterly* 6 (Jan. 1936): 76–77.
101. Hoffman, "The Graduate Thesis," p. 9.
102. *ESS*, s.v. "Research," by Donald Slesinger and Mary Stephenson.
103. Waples to Sarah Bogle, 17 Feb. 1931, ALAA Series 28/50/5-3.
104. Wilson to Waples, 30 July 1932, Wilson MSS, UNC, II–43.
105. Rice to Berelson, 23 Feb. 1949, University of Michigan School of Library Science Papers, Box 9, MHC, UM.
106. "Memorandum of Interview of Wilson by Lester," 20 Sept. 1935, GLS Papers, 1935–36, CC.
107. Bishop to Keppel, 19 Oct. 1935, GLS Papers, 1935–36, CC.
108. Ralph E. Ellsworth, "Critique of Library Associations in America," *Library Quarterly* 31 (Oct. 1961): 382–83.
109. Maurice F. Tauber, *Louis Round Wilson: Librarian and Administrator*, foreword by Robert Maynard Hutchins, Columbia University Studies in Library Service (New York: Columbia University Press, 1967), p. 157.

110. "Development of Research in Relation to Library Schools," *Library Journal* 58 (15 Oct. 1933): 817–21; "The Development of a Program of Research in Library Science in the Graduate Library School," *Library Journal* 59 (1 Oct. 1934): 742–46; and "The American Library School Today," *Library Quarterly* 7 (Apr. 1937): 211–45.

111. Louis R. Wilson, "Report on the Library Quarterly, 1931–1933," 17 Aug. 1933, LQ Papers, 1930–40, CC.

112. Wilson to Keppel, 1 June 1934, LQ Papers, 1930–40, CC.

113. Wilson to Keppel, 24 Sept. 1935, LQ Papers, 1930–40, CC.

114. Ibid.

115. Ibid.

116. Ibid.

117. Leon Carnovsky, "Why Graduate Study in Librarianship?" *Library Quarterly* 7 (Apr. 1937): 254.

118. Wilson, "Report," 17 Aug. 1933.

119. Carnovsky to Wilson, 10 Aug. 1951, Wilson MSS, UNC, II–139.

120. Joeckel to Lester, 21 Dec. 1940, LQ Papers, 1930–40, CC.

121. Wilson to Lester, 6 Aug. 1942, LQ Papers, 1930–40, CC.

122. Joeckel to Lester, 25 June 1945, LQ Papers, 1930–40, CC.

123. Waples to Keppel, 20 Oct. 1930, LQ Papers, 1930–40, CC.

124. Lester to Keppel, 6 Nov. 1930, LQ Papers, 1930–40, CC.

125. Keppel to Waples, 10 Nov. 1930, LQ Papers, 1930–40, CC.

126. Randall to Richardson, 15 Apr. 1978.

127. Pierce Butler, *Introduction to Library Science*, foreword by Louis R. Wilson, University of Chicago Library Science Series, no. 1 (Chicago: University of Chicago Press, 1933), p. vi.

128. Ibid.

129. Butler to Wilson, 24 Nov. 1931, Wilson MSS, UNC, II–20.

130. Frank K. Walter, review of *Introduction to Library Science*, by Pierce Butler, in *Library Quarterly* 3 (Oct. 1933): 434.

131. Louis R. Wilson, Foreword to *Introduction to Library Science*, by Pierce Butler (Chicago: University of Chicago Press, 1933), p. vii.

132. Will Durant, *The Story of Philosophy: The Lives and Opinions of the Great Philosophers of the Western World* (New York: Simon and Schuster, 1961), p. 16.

133. Butler, *Introduction*, p. 25.

134. Ibid., p. 26.

135. Ibid., p. 29.

136. Butler used this tripartite scheme in his 14 Oct. 1931 letter, as did George Works in a memorandum entitled "Library School," *terminus ante quem* 29 Aug. 1931: "At least three distinct phases of research are possible. They may be roughly characterized as sociological, psychological, and historical, with their respective centers in the library, the reader and the book" (1925–45 Presidents' MSS, UC, 112).

137. Butler, *Introduction*, p. 51.

138. Ibid., pp. 76–77.

139. Ibid., p. 78.

140. Ibid., p. 79.

141. Ibid., p. 93.

142. Ibid., p. 103.

143. Ibid., p. 104.

144. Ibid., pp. 105–6.

145. Ibid., p. 107.

146. Ibid., p. 110.

147. Ibid., p. 115.

148. Ibid., pp. xiv–xvi.

149. M. E. Walker, review of *Introduction to Library Science*, by Pierce Butler, in *New York Times Book Review*, 30 July 1933, sec. 5, p. 8, col. 2.

150. Ibid.

151. Ibid.

152. Ibid.

153. Ibid.

154. Nathaniel Peffer, review of *Introduction to Library Science*, by Pierce Butler, 9 Aug. 1933, GLS Papers, 1930–40, CC.

155. Walter, review of *Introduction to Library Science*, p. 436.

156. E. J. Reece, review of *Introduction to Library Science*, by Pierce Butler, in *Library Journal* 58 (15 Sept. 1933): 748.

157. Louis R. Wilson, ed., *Library Trends: Papers Presented before the Library Institute at the University of Chicago, August 3–15, 1936*, University of Chicago Studies in Library Science (Chicago: University of Chicago Press, 1937), p. xii.

158. Munthe, *American Librarianship*, p. 153.

159. Wilson, *Library Trends*, p. 1.

160. Randall to Richardson, 15 Apr. 1978.

161. Keppel to Wilson, 15 Aug. 1940, GLS Papers, 1938–42, CC.

162. Wilson to Keppel, 3 Sept. 1940, GLS Papers, 1938–42, CC.

163. Louis R. Wilson, "Frederick P. Keppel: 1875–1943," *Library Quarterly* 14 (Jan. 1944): 55.

164. Ibid., p. 56.

165. Carnovsky to Wilson, 21 Nov. 1942, Wilson MSS, UNC, IV–138.

166. Douglas Waples, *On the March: A Short Autobiography for Friends and Family* (Wisconsin Island, Wis.: Privately printed, 1967), p. 7; Hellmut Lehmann-Haupt to Richardson, 8 Dec. 1980.

167. Ibid.

168. Louis R. Wilson, "Dr. William M. Randall," *College and Research Libraries* 8 (Oct. 1947): 452.

169. Randall to Robert M. Lester, 26 June 1951, William M. Randall Papers, Carnegie Corp.

170. William M. Randall, "Constitution of the Modern Library Building," in *Library Buildings for Library Service: Papers Presented before the Library Institute of the University of Chicago, August 5–10, 1946*, ed. Herman H. Fussler (Chicago: University of Chicago Press, 1947), pp. 182–201. "Just

before entering the service, Randall had completed most of the research for a 'definitive volume' on academic library buildings" (Charles H. Baumann, *The Influence of Angus Snead Macdonald and the Snead Bookstack on Library Architecture* [Methuchen, N.J.: Scarecrow, 1972], p. 157).

171. "Deaths," *Library Journal* 78 (1 May 1953): 795. The July 1953 issue of *Library Quarterly* is a memorial to Pierce Butler.

172. "Memorandum of Interview of William Randall by Robert M. Lester," 12 Dec. 1939, GLS Papers, 1938–42, CC.

173. Beals to Randall, 9 Oct. 1945, 1940–46 Presidents' MSS, UC.

174. Ralph A. Beals, "Education for Librarianship," *Library Quarterly* 17 (Oct. 1947): 296–305.

175. Ibid., p. 300.

176. See, for example, Eugene H. Wilson's "PreProfessional Background of Students in a Library School" (Ph.D. dissertation, University of Illinois, 1937) or I. M. Doyle's "Library School Marks and Success in Library Service" (M.A. thesis, University of Illinois, 1931).

177. Berelson to Wilson, 20 Aug. 1947, Wilson MSS, UNC, IV–84.

178. Berelson to Wilson, 2 Dec. 1948, Wilson MSS, UNC, IV–84.

179. "Memorandum of Interview of Bernard Berelson by C. Dollard," 5 Apr. 1950, GLS Papers, 1946–53, CC.

180. Berelson to Lester, 21 May 1951, GLS Papers, 1946–53, Carnegie Corp. The "Book Courses" included Jesse Shera's *Historians, Books, and Libraries* (1953), Lester Asheim's *The Humanities and the Library* (1957), and Berthold Hoselitz's *A Reader's Guide to the Social Sciences* (1960). The proposed book on the physical sciences was never completed.

181. Wilson to Berelson, 16 July 1951, Wilson MSS, UNC.

182. Bernard Berelson and Gary A. Steiner, *Human Behavior: An Inventory of Scientific Findings* (New York: Harcourt Brace Jovanovich, 1964), p. 370.

183. Wilson was active behind the scenes in the 1925–26 Poole controversy at the University of North Carolina and also in the 1960s; see Frances A. Weaver, *Louis R. Wilson: The Years since 1955* (Chapel Hill, N.C.: Friends of the Library, 1976), p. 3.

184. Joseph L. Wheeler to Gordon Laing, 29 July 1929, ALAA Series 28/50/5-3.

185. See the first section of this chapter and Maurice F. Tauber, *Louis Round Wilson: Librarian and Administrator*, Columbia University Studies in Library Service (New York: Columbia University Press, 1967).

Chapter 6

1. An abbreviated form of this chapter appeared in *Reports of Recent Historical Research on Specific Developments in American Library History* (97th Annual ALA Conference, ALHRT), American Library Association, Chicago, 26 June 1978, 1⅞ ips, 1 audiocassette, 3½ hours.

2. John C. Flanagan, "The Critical Incident Technique in the Study of Individuals," in *Modern Educational Problems*, ed. Arthur E. Traxler (Washington, D.C.: American Council on Education, 1953), p. 61.

3. H. H. B. Meyer, "Librarianship—A Definition," *Library Journal* 50 (15 Feb. 1925): 177.

4. J. Christian Bay, *The Sciences in the Training of The Librarian* (Holstebro, Denmark: N. P. Thomsen, 1928), pp. 7–8.

5. Henry to Burton, 18 Sept. 1924, 1889–1925, Presidents' MSS, UC, 19-17.

6. Douglas Waples, "The Graduate Library School at Chicago," *Library Quarterly* 1 (Jan. 1931): 26.

7. *Encyclopedia of the Social Sciences*, s.v. "Research," by Donald Slesinger and Mary Stephenson.

8. George Works, "The Graduate Library School at the University of Chicago," *Libraries* 34 (July 1929): 313.

9. Pierce Butler, *Introduction to Library Science* (Chicago: University of Chicago Press, 1933), pp. xi, 29; Leon Carnovsky and E. W. McDiarmid Jr., "The Open Round Table," *Library Journal* 59 (9 Jan. 1934): 32–33; James H. Wellard, "A Philosophical Approach to Library Science," *Wilson Library Bulletin* 9 (Dec. 1934): 206–7; LeRoy C. Merritt, "On Uses of the Public Library," *Library Journal* 61 (Jan. 1936): 3; Robert A. Miller, "Search for Fundamentals," *Library Journal* 61 (15 Apr. 1936): 298; Carleton B. Joeckel, ed., *Current Issues in Library Administration* (Chicago: University of Chicago Press, 1939).

10. Apparently the thesis was a barrier to such competent individuals as Ralph A. Beals and Margaret E. Egan; the residence requirement was a barrier to others.

11. American Library Association, *Annual Report of the Board of Education for Librarianship* (Chicago: American Library Association, 1925), p. 15.

12. Robert M. Lester to Frederick P. Keppel, 8 July 1940, GLS Papers, 1938–42, CC.

13. Ralph A. Beals, "Education for Librarianship," *Library Quarterly* 17 (Oct. 1947): 296–305.

14. William M. Randall to Richardson, 15 Apr. 1978.

15. Milam to Keppel, 26 Nov. 1932, ALAA Series.

16. Louis R. Wilson, "Memorandum Concerning Advanced Graduate Library School," 24 May 1926, 1925–45 Presidents' MSS, UC, 112.

17. Frederick P. Keppel, "The Carnegie Corporation and the Graduate Library School: A Historical Outline," *Library Quarterly* 1 (Jan. 1931): 23.

18. George A. Works, "Research and the Graduate Library School," *Libraries* 33 (Feb. 1928): 103.

19. Ibid., p. 102.

20. Nancy D. Lane, "Characteristics Related to Productivity among Doctoral Graduates in Librarianship" (Ph.D. dissertation, University of California, Berkeley, 1975).

21. Ibid., p. 165.

22. Ibid., p. 152.

23. Ibid., p. 197.

24. Ibid., pp. 197, 216.

25. Ibid., pp. 184, 186–87.

26. Ibid., pp. 186–87.

27. Ibid., p. 187.

28. Berelson to Wilson, 28 Feb. 1951, Wilson MSS, UNC.

29. Wilson's assessment of the GLS's impact was that it (1) broadened the concept of librarianship, (2) developed librarianship as a field for scientific study and research, (3) introduced a critical, objective point of view, (4) related librarianship to other disciplines, (5) greatly affected education for librarianship, (6) contributed through publication to the development of a philosophy of librarianship, and (7) furnished leaders in the field of librarianship (from *Addresses by Vice-President R. Wendell Harrison and Dean Emeritus Louis R. Wilson,* On the Occasion of the 25th Anniversary of the Establishment of the Graduate Library School, 12 July 1951 [Chicago: University of Chicago Press, 1951], pp. 5–12). Louis R. Wilson, "Impact of the Graduate Library School upon American Librarianship," in *Education and Libraries: Selected Papers by Louis R. Wilson,* ed. Maurice F. Tauber and Jerrold Orne (Hamden, Conn.: Shoe String Press, 1966), pp. 268–77. Letters to Wilson can be found in Louis R. Wilson Papers (Series II, Folders 139–42), Southern Historical Collection, University of North Carolina, Chapel Hill.

Bibliography

Books

Akers, Susan. *Simple Library Cataloging*. Chicago: American Library Association, 1927.

American Library Association. *Annual Report of the Board of Education for Librarianship*. Chicago: American Library Association, 1925.

_____. *Reports of Recent Historical Research on Specific Developments in American Library History* (97th Annual Conference, ALHRT). Chicago: American Library Association, 26 June 1978. 1⅞ ips, 1 audiocassette, 3½ hrs.

_____. *Second Annual Report of the Board of Education for Librarianship*. Chicago: American Library Association, 1926.

_____. *Third Annual Report of the Board of Education for Librarianship*. Chicago: American Library Association, 1927.

_____. Committee on Fellowships and Scholarships. *Education for Librarianship: Grants-in-Aid Financed by the Carnegie Corporation of New York, 1929–1942*. Introduction by Paul M. Paine. Chicago: American Library Association, 1943.

Anderson, Florence. *Library Program 1911–1961*. New York: Carnegie Corporation, 1963.

Asheim, Lester. *The Humanities and the Library*. Chicago: American Library Association, 1957.

Baumann, Charles H. *The Influence of Angus Snead Macdonald and the Snead Bookstack on Library Architecture*. Metuchen, N.J.: Scarecrow, 1972.

Bay, J. Christian. *The Sciences in the Training of the Librarian*. Holstebro, Denmark: N. P. Thomsen, 1928.

Beer, Thomas. *Mark Hanna.* New York: Knopf, 1929.

Berelson, Bernard, and Steiner, Gary A. *Human Behavior: An Inventory of Scientific Findings.* New York: Harcourt Brace and World, 1964.

Bixler, Harold H. *Check Lists for Educational Research.* Standard Research Procedure Series. New York: Columbia University Teachers College Press, 1928.

Bobinski, George S. *Carnegie Libraries: Their History and Impact on American Public Library Development.* Chicago: American Library Association, 1969.

Brown, Karl, comp. *American Library Directory.* New York: Bowker, 1930.

Butler, Pierce. *An Introduction to Library Science [A New Approach to Librarianship].* Foreword by Louis R. Wilson. University of Chicago Library Science Series, no. 1. Chicago: University of Chicago Press, 1933.

————. *The Origin of Printing in Europe.* University of Chicago Studies in Library Science. Chicago: University of Chicago Press, 1940.

Carman, Harry J., et al. *Appreciations of Frederick P. Keppel.* New York: Columbia University Press, 1951.

Carroll, C. Edward. *The Professionalization of Education for Librarianship with Special Reference to the Years 1940–1960.* Metuchen, N.J.: Scarecrow, 1970.

Charters, Werrett W. *Curriculum Construction.* New York: Macmillan, 1924.

Churchwell, Charles D. *The Shaping of American Library Education.* ACRL Publications in Librarianship, no. 36. Chicago: American Library Association, 1975.

Colman, Gould P. *Education and Agriculture: a History of the New York State College of Agriculture at Cornell University.* Ithaca: Cornell University Press, 1963.

Cook, Robert C., ed. *Presidents and Professors in American Colleges and Universities.* New York: Robert C. Cook Co., 1935.

Cordasco, Francesco. *Shaping of American Graduate Education: Daniel Coit Gilman and Protean Ph.D.* Totowa, N.J.: Rowman and Littlefield, 1972.

Cross, Tom Peete. *A List of Books and Articles, Chiefly Bibliographical, Designed to Serve as an Introduction to the Bibliography and Methods of English Literary History.* 5th ed. Chicago: University of Chicago Press, 1930.

Cushing, Harvey W. *Life of Sir William Osler.* Oxford: Clarendon, 1925.

Davis, Donald G., Jr. *The Association of American Library Schools, 1915–1968: An Analytical History.* Metuchen, N.J.: Scarecrow, 1974.

Dewey, John. *The Sources of a Science of Education.* New York: Liveright, 1929.

District of Columbia Public Library. *26th Annual Report for the Fiscal Year Ending June 30, 1923.* Washington, D.C.: Public Library, 1923.

————. *29th Annual Report for the Fiscal Year Ending June 30, 1926.* Washington, D.C.: Public Library, 1926.

————. *30th Annual Report for the Fiscal Year Ending June 30, 1927.* Washington, D. C.: Public Library, 1927.

Durant, Will. *The Story of Philosophy: The Lives and Opinions of the Great Philosophers of the Western World.* New York: Simon and Schuster, 1961.

Ellsworth, Ralph E. *Ellsworth on Ellsworth: An Unchronological, Mostly True Account of Some Moments of Contact between "Library Science" and Me, since Our Confluence in 1931, with Appropriate Sidelights.* Metuchen, N.J.: Scarecrow, 1980.

Flanagan, John C. "The Critical Incident Technique in the Study of Individuals." In *Modern Educational Problems,* pp. 61–70. Ed. Arthur E. Traxler. Washington, D.C.: American Council on Education, 1953.

Flexner, Abraham. *Henry S. Pritchett, a Biography.* New York: Columbia University Press, 1943.

—————. *Universities: American, English, German.* New York: Oxford University Press, 1930.

Friedel, H. J. *Training for Librarianship: Library Work as a Career.* Philadelphia: Lippincott, 1921.

Geer, Curtis M. *The Hartford Theological Seminary, 1834–1934.* Hartford, Conn.: Case, Lockwood, and Brainard, 1934.

Gilman, Daniel C. *The Launching of a University and Other Papers: A Study of Remembrance.* New York: Dodd, Mead, 1906.

Gottschalk, Louis R. *Understanding History.* New York: Macmillan, 1961.

Grotzinger, Laurel Ann. *The Power and the Dignity: Librarianship and Katharine Sharp.* New York: Scarecrow, 1966.

Hockett, Homer C. *The Critical Method in Historical Research and Writing.* New York: Macmillan, 1955.

Hofstadter, Richard, and Metzger, Walter P. *The Development of Academic Freedom in the United States.* New York: Columbia University Press, 1955.

Hoselitz, Berthold F., ed. *A Reader's Guide to the Social Sciences.* New York: Free Press, 1960.

Houser, Lloyd, and Schrader, Alvin M. *The Search for a Scientific Profession: Library Science Education in the U.S. and Canada.* Metuchen, N.J.: Scarecrow, 1978.

Howe, Harriet E. "The First-Year Library School Curriculum." In *Library Trends,* pp. 361–74. Ed. Louis R. Wilson. Chicago: University of Chicago Press, 1937.

Hyman, Herman H. *Interviewing in Social Research.* Chicago: University of Chicago Press, 1954.

Joeckel, Carleton B. *The Government of the American Public Library.* University of Chicago Studies in Library Science Series. Chicago: University of Chicago Press, 1935.

—————, ed. *Current Issues in Library Administration.* University of Chicago Studies in Library Science Series. Chicago: University of Chicago Press, 1939.

Johnson, Alvin S. *A Report to the Carnegie Corporation of New York on the Policy of Donations to Free Public Libraries.* New York: Carnegie, 1917.

Kelly, Robert L. *Tendencies in a College Administration.* Lancaster, Pa.: Science Press, 1925.

Keppel, Frederick P. *Columbia.* New York: Oxford University Press, 1914.

_____. *The Foundation: Its Place in American Life.* Page-Barbour Lecture Series. New York: Macmillan, 1930.

Kerr, Chester. *A Report on American University Presses.* Washington, D.C.: Association of American University Presses, 1949.

Learned, William S. *The American Public Library and the Diffusion of Knowledge.* New York: Harcourt Brace, 1924.

Munn, Ralph. *Conditions and Trends in Education for Librarianship.* New York: Carnegie, 1936.

Munthe, Wilhelm. *American Librarianship from a European Angle: An Attempt at an Evaluation of Policies and Activities.* Chicago: American Library Association, 1939; reprint, Hamden, Conn.: Shoe String Press, 1964.

Murphy, William M., and Bruckner, D. J. R. *The Idea of the University of Chicago: Selections from the Papers of the First Eight Chief Executives of the University of Chicago, 1891 to 1975.* Chicago: University of Chicago Press, 1976.

New York. State Library School. *The First Quarter Century of the New York State Library School, 1887–1912.* Albany: Education Dept., 1912.

_____. *New York State Library School Register, 1887–1926.* New York: New York State Library School Association, 1928.

New York. State University. *106th (1891–92) Annual Report of the University of the State of New York.* Albany: James B. Lyon, State Printer, 1893.

Ogg, Frederic A. *Research in the Humanistic and Social Sciences: Report of a Study Conducted for the American Council of Learned Societies.* New York: Century, 1928.

Randall, William M. *The College Library: A Descriptive Study of the Libraries in Four-Year Liberal Arts Colleges in the United States.* Chicago: American Library Association and University of Chicago Press, 1932.

_____. "Constitution of the Modern Library Building." In *Library Buildings for Library Service: Papers Presented before the Library Institute of the University of Chicago, August 5–10, 1946,* pp. 182–201. Ed. Herman H. Fussler. University of Chicago Studies in Library Science series. Chicago: University of Chicago Press, 1947.

_____ and Goodrich, Francis L. D. *Principles of College Library Administration.* University of Chicago Studies in Library Science. Chicago: American Library Association and University of Chicago Press, 1936.

Raney, M. Llewellyn. *The University Libraries.* University of Chicago Survey, vol. 7. Chicago: University of Chicago Press, 1933.

Rush, Charles E., and Winslow, Amy. *Modern Aladdins and Their Magic: The Science of Things around Us.* Boston: Little, Brown, 1926.

Sharp, Katharine L. *Local Public Libraries and Their Relation to University Extension.* Home Education Department Bulletin, no. 4. Albany: University of the State of New York, 1892.

Shera, Jesse H. *Historians, Books, and Libraries: a Survey of Historical Scholarship in Relation to Library Resources, Organization and Services.* Cleveland: Press of Western Reserve University, 1953.

————. *The Foundations of Education for Librarianship.* Information Science Series. New York: Becker and Hayes, 1972.

Stearns, Raymond P. *Science in the British Colonies of America.* Urbana: University of Illinois Press, 1970.

Sullivan, Peggy. *Carl H. Milam and the American Library Association.* New York: H. W. Wilson, 1976.

Tai, Tse-Chien. *Professional Education for Librarianship.* Introduction by John B. Kaiser. New York: H. W. Wilson, 1925.

Tauber, Maurice F. *Louis Round Wilson: Librarian and Administrator.* Foreword by Robert Maynard Hutchins. Columbia University Studies in Library Service. New York: Columbia University Press, 1967.

Thompson, James W. *The Medieval Library.* University of Chicago Studies in Library Science Series. Chicago: University of Chicago Press, 1939.

Trautman, Ray. *A History of the School of Library Service.* New York: Columbia University Press, 1954.

University of Chicago. *1930 Cap and Gown.* [Chicago: University of Chicago Press, 1930.]

————. *1931 Cap and Gown.* [Chicago: University of Chicago Press, 1931.]

Van Hoesen, Henry B. *Roman Cursive Writing.* Princeton: Princeton University Press, 1915.

———— and Walter, Frank K. *Bibliography: Practical, Enumerative, and Historical.* New York: Scribner, 1928.

Vann, Sarah K. *Training for Librarianship before 1923: Education for Librarianship prior to the Publication of Williamson's Report, "Training for Library Service."* Chicago: American Library Association, 1961.

————. *The Williamson Reports: A Study.* Metuchen, N.J.: Scarecrow, 1971.

Waples, Douglas. *Investigating Library Problems.* University of Chicago Studies in Library Science Series. Chicago: University of Chicago Press, 1939.

————. *On the March: A Short Autobiography for Friends and Family.* Washington Island, Wis.: Privately printed, 1967.

————. *Problems in Classroom Method.* New York: Macmillan, 1927.

————. *Procedures in High School Teaching.* New York: Macmillan, 1924.

———— and Tyler, Ralph. *What People Want to Read About.* Chicago: American Library Association and University of Chicago Press, 1931.

Weaver, Frances A. *Louis R. Wilson: The Years since 1955.* Chapel Hill, N.C.: Friends of the Library, 1976.

Wheeler, Joseph. *Progress and Problems in Education for Librarianship.* New York: Carnegie, 1946.

White, Carl M. *A Historical Introduction to Library Education: Problems and Progress to 1951.* Metuchen, N.J.: Scarecrow, 1976.

Williamson, Charles C. *Training for Library Service.* New York: Carnegie, 1923.

_____. *Training for Library Work: A Report Prepared for the Carnegie Corporation of New York.* Reprint ed., Metuchen, N.J.: Scarecrow, 1971.

_____ and Jewitt, Alice L. *Who's Who in Library Service.* New York: H. W. Wilson, 1933.

Wilson, Louis R. "Historical Development of Education for Librarianship in the United States." In *Education for Librarianship: Papers Presented at the Library Conference, University of Chicago, August 16–21, 1948,* pp. 44–59. Ed. Bernard Berelson. University of Chicago Studies in Library Science Series. Chicago: University of Chicago Press, 1949.

_____. "Impact of the Graduate Library School upon American Librarianship." In *Education and Libraries: Selected Papers by Louis R. Wilson,* pp. 268–77. Ed. Maurice F. Tauber and Jerrold Orne. Hamden, Conn.: Shoe String Press, 1966.

_____, ed. *Library Trends: Papers Presented before the Library Institute at the University of Chicago, August 3–15, 1936.* University of Chicago Studies in Library Science Series. Chicago: University of Chicago Press, 1937.

_____. "The Objectives of the Graduate Library School in Extending the Frontiers of Librarianship." In *New Frontiers in Librarianship: Proceedings of the Special Meeting of the Association of American Library Schools and the Board of Education for Librarianship of the American Library Association in Honor of the University of Chicago and the Graduate Library School, December 30, 1940,* pp. 13–26. Chicago: University of Chicago Press, 1941.

Works, George A. *College and University Library Problems: A Study of a Selected Group of Institutions Prepared for the Association of American Universities.* Introduction by Samuel P. Capen. Chicago: American Library Association, 1927.

Wyer, James I. *Reference Work.* Chicago: American Library Association, 1930.

_____. *U.S. Government Documents.* Chicago: American Library Association, 1922.

Theses and Dissertations

Butler, Pierce. "Studies in the Christology of Iraenaeus." Ph.D. dissertation, Hartford Theological Seminary, 1912.

Doyle, I. M. "Library School Marks and Success in Library Service." M.A. thesis, University of Illinois, 1931.

Fenster, Valmai R. "The University of Wisconsin Library School, a History, 1895–1921." Ph.D. dissertation, University of Wisconsin, 1977.

Flood, Francis J. "History of the Bibliographical Movement Called the 'New Bibliography' and an Evaluation of Its Contributions to Literary and Historical Research." Ph.D. dissertation proposal, University of Michigan, Feb. 1972.

Hoffman, Hester. "The Graduate Thesis in Library Science." M.A. thesis, University of Chicago, 1941.

Lane, Nancy D. "Characteristics Related to Productivity among Doctoral Graduates in Librarianship." Ph.D. dissertation, University of California, Berkeley, 1975.

Mickey, Melissa B. "The Role of the Carnegie Corporation in the Development of Education for Librarianship." Ph.D. dissertation proposal, University of Chicago, 11 Apr. 1974.

Nichol, Isabel. "The First-Year Library School Curriculum." M.A. report, University of Chicago, 1941.

Piper, Sister Tressa. "The American Library Institute, 1905–1951: An Historical Study and Analysis of Goals." M.L.S. paper, University of Wisconsin, 1975.

Randall, William M. "A Detailed Catalog of the Arabic Manuscripts in the Ananikian Collection of the Hartford Theological Seminary Foundation." Ph.D. dissertation, Hartford Theological Seminary, 1929.

Rehfus, Ruth O., and Stearns, Eugene I. "The Library Quarterly, 1931–1966: An Index with Commentary." M.A. thesis, Kent State University, 1967.

Rosenstock, Sheldon A. "[W. W. Charters]." Ph.D. dissertation proposal, Ohio State University, 1977.

Scott, Edith. "J. C. M. Hanson and His Contribution to Twentieth-Century Cataloging." Ph.D. dissertation, University of Chicago, 1971.

Sparks, Claud G. "William Warner Bishop, a Biography." Ph.D. dissertation, University of Michigan, 1967.

Van Hoesen, Henry B. "Roman Cursive Writing." Ph.D. dissertation, Princeton University, 1912.

Waples, Douglas. "An Approach to the Synthetic Study of Interest in Education." Ph.D. dissertation, University of Pennsylvania, 1920.

Weaver, Frances A. "An Analytical Description of the Papers of Louis Round Wilson which Relate to the History of Professional Librarianship in the United States." M.S.L.S. thesis, University of North Carolina, Chapel Hill, 1977.

Wilson, Eugene H. "Pre-Professional Background of Students in a Library School." Ph.D. dissertation, University of Illinois, 1937.

Wilson, Louis R. Chaucer's Relative Constructions. Studies in Philology, no. 1. Chapel Hill: University of North Carolina Press, 1906.

Winckler, Paul A. "Charles Clarence Williamson (1877–1965): His Professional Life and Work in Librarianship and Library Education in the United States." Ph.D. dissertation, New York University, 1968.

Wing, Mary J. "A History of the School of Library Science of the University of North Carolina: The First Twenty-five Years." M.S.L.S. thesis, University of North Carolina, Chapel Hill, 1958.

George A. Works. "Distribution of State Aid in Texas." Ed.D. dissertation, Harvard University, 1925.

Dictionaries and Encyclopedias

Dictionary of American Library Biography (DALB),
S.v. "Butler, Pierce," by Lee Ash.
S.v. "Hanson, James Christian Meinich," by John P. Immroth.
S.v. "Howe, Harriet Emma," by Martha Boaz, John T. Eastlick, and Laurel A. Grotzinger.
Dictionary of Education, 3d ed.
S.v. "Objective."
Dictionary of the History of Ideas,
S.v. "The Idea of Progress in the Professions," by E. R. Dodds.
Encyclopedia of Library and Information Science (ELIS),
S.v. "Denver. University of Denver, Graduate School of Librarianship," by Margaret K. Goggin.
S.v. "Hanson, J. C. M.," by Edith Scott.
Encyclopedia of the Social Sciences (ESS),
S.v. "Research," by Donald Slesinger and Mary Stephenson.

Periodical Articles

"A.L.A. Dinner Meeting." *Library Journal* 52 (15 Dec. 1927): 1171.
"An Advanced School of Librarianship." *Library Journal* 50 (15 Feb. 1925): 171.
Ahern, Mary E. "American Library Institute Meeting in New Haven, Connecticut, June 23." *Libraries* 36 (Oct. 1931): 348.
————. "Library Service—A Science? a Philosophy? an Art?" *Libraries* 36 (Oct. 1931): 340.
American Library Association. Temporary Library Training Board. "Report." *American Library Association Bulletin* 18 (Aug. 1924): 264.
"Among Librarians." *Library Journal* 56 (15 Sept. 1931): 768.
Angell, James R. "Report of Committee O on Requirements for the Ph.D. Degree." *American Association of University Professors Bulletin* 5 (Jan.–Feb. 1919): 12–18.
Ash, Lee. "Tribute to Pierce Butler." *Library Journal* 78 (15 May 1953): 826.
Association of American Universities. "Report of the Committee on Academic and Professional Higher Degrees." *Journal of Proceedings and Addresses* 26 (31 Oct.–1 Nov. 1924): 25–26.
Baker, Hy. "University Teaching and Research." *Journal of Education* 55 (Jan. 1923): 13.
Bay, J. Christian. "Every Serious Voice Deserves a Hearing." *Library Journal* 56 (15 Sept. 1931): 748–50.
————. "James Christian Meinich Hanson: 1864–1943." *Library Quarterly* 14 (Jan. 1944): 57–59.

————. "[Summary of an Address before the] Professional Training Section of A.L.A." *American Library Association Bulletin* 22 (Sept. 1928): 449.

Beals, Ralph A. "Education for Librarianship." *Library Quarterly* 17 (Oct. 1947): 296–305.

Bell, Bernard I. "Pierce Butler, Professor and Priest." *Library Quarterly* 22 (July 1952): 174–76.

"Board of Education for Librarianship." *American Library Association Bulletin* 19 (May 1925): 83.

"Board of Education for Librarianship." *American Library Association Bulletin* 27 (15 Dec. 1933): 610–13.

Bowker, Richard. Review of *Library Quarterly* (vol. 1, no. 1). *Library Journal* 56 (1 Feb. 1931): 124.

Brown, Charles H. Review of *The College Library*, by William M. Randall. *Library Journal* 57 (July 1932): 625.

Burke, Redmond. "Bibliography of Pierce Butler." *Library Quarterly* 22 (July 1952): 165–69.

"[Dr. Burton's Funeral.]" *New York Times* 27 May 1925, p. 23; 29 May 1925, p. 17.

Butler, Pierce. "James Christian Meinich Hanson." *Library Quarterly* 4 (Apr. 1934): 127–30.

Camerani, Vittorio. "Corriere Americano." *La Bibliofilia* 33 (Aug.–Sept. 1931): 350–53.

"Carnegie Fund of $1,385,000 Goes to Chicago U." *Chicago Herald Tribune*, 23 May 1926, pt. 1, p. 6.

Carnovsky, Leon. "Pierce Butler, 1886–1953." *Library Quarterly* 23 (July 1953): 153–54.

————. "Why Graduate Study in Librarianship?" *Library Quarterly* 7 (Apr. 1931): 250–54.

———— and McDiarmid, E. W., Jr. "The Open Round Table." *Library Journal* 59 (9 Jan. 1934): 32–33.

"Chicago." *Public Libraries* 28 (May 1923): 250–51.

"Columbia Endows Library Teaching; Melvil Dewey Professorship, First of Kind, Founded with Carnegie Gift of $250,000." *New York Times*, 6 Apr. 1938, p. 25, col. 7.

Cutler, Mary S. "Library School." *Library Journal* 16 (Oct. 1890): 308.

Cutter, W. P. "Library Schools and Training Classes: Columbian University." *Library Journal* 22 (Nov. 1897): 708.

Danton, J. Periam. "Corrigendum and Addendum to a Footnote on the History of Library Education." *Journal of Education for Librarianship* 18 (Fall 1977): 93–98.

Davis, Donald G., Jr. "Education for Librarianship." *Library Trends* 25 (July 1976): 113–14.

"Dean Made President." *Detroit Free Press* 11 Apr. 1929, p. 3.

"Deaths." *Library Journal* 78 (1 May 1953): 795.

Dewey, Melvil. "Editorial." *Library Notes* 1 (June 1886): 10.

"Discussion: The Status of Library Schools in Universities." *Journal of Proceedings and Addresses* of the Association of American Universities, the Thirty-fifth Annual Conference (1934), p. 137.

"Dr. L. R. Wilson to Head U. of C. Library School." *Chicago Tribune*, 16 Jan. 1932, p. 15.

"Dr. Works Resigns from Graduate Library School" *Libraries* 34 (July 1929): 317.

"Editorial Forum." *Library Journal* 56 (15 Sept. 1931): 752.

Ellsworth, Ralph E. "Critique of Library Associations in America." *Library Quarterly* 31 (Oct. 1961): 382–83.

"$401,601 in Cash Gifts Listed by Columbia; Largest Donation in March was $250,000 from Carnegie Fund." *New York Times*, 8 Apr. 1938, p. 19, col. 2.

Hadley, Arthur T. "To What Extent Should Professors Engaged in Research Be Relieved from Teaching?" *Educational Review* 31 (Apr. 1906): 325.

Hall, G. Stanley. "Editorial." *Pedagogical Seminary* 1 (Dec. 1891): 311–26.

————. "How Can Universities Be So Organized as to Stimulate More Work for the Advancement of Science?" *Journal of the Proceedings of the Association of American Universities* (1916), pp. 25–38.

————. "Research the Vital Spirit of Teaching." *Forum* 17 (July 1894): 558–70.

————. "What Is Research in a University Sense, and How May It Best Be Promoted?" *Pedagogical Seminary* 9 (Mar. 1902): 74–80.

Harap, Henry. Review of *What People Want to Read About*, by Douglas Waples and Ralph W. Tyler. *Library Quarterly* 2 (Jan. 1932): 93.

Howe, Harriet E. "The Library School Curriculum." *Library Quarterly* 1 (July 1931): 283–90.

————. "Two Decades in Education for Librarianship." *Library Quarterly* 12 (July 1942): 567–68.

Irvine, J. C. "Development of Research in Universities." *Nature* 110 (22 July 1922): 131–33.

James, William. "The Ph.D. Octopus." *Harvard Monthly* 36 (Mar. 1903): 1–9.

Josephson, Askel G. S. "A Post-Graduate School of Bibliography." *Library Journal* 26 (Aug. 1901): 197–99.

"Journal of Discussion." *American Library Association Bulletin* 23 (Jan. 1929): 12.

Keeney, Philip O., and Keeney, Mary J. "Social Content in Library Training." *Wilson Library Bulletin* 14 (Feb. 1940): 429–34.

Keogh, Andrew. "Advanced Training for Research Workers." *American Library Association Bulletin* 13 (Sept. 1919): 165–67; *Library Journal* 44 (Sept. 1919): 581–82.

Keppel, Frederick P. "The Carnegie Corporation and the Graduate Library School: A Historical Outline." *Library Quarterly* 1 (Jan. 1931): 23–25.

————. "The Carnegie Tradition and A.L.A." *American Library Association Bulletin* 22 (Apr. 1928): 64–66.

"Librarians' Advanced School Project Gains at Convention." *Christian Science Monitor*, 2 July 1924, p. 7.

"Library Meetings." *Libraries* 34 (May 1929): 219–20.

"The Library Quarterly." *American Library Association Bulletin* 24 (Oct. 1930): 600.

"Library School Study Finds 'What People Want to Read'—and Why." *University of Chicago Maroon*, 2 Oct. 1931.

Lichtenstein, Walter. "The Question of a Graduate Library School." *Library Journal* 42 (Apr. 1918): 233.

Lodge, Gonzalez. "Editorial." *The Classical Weekly* 1 (21 Dec. 1907): 1.

Merritt, LeRoy C. "On Uses of the Public Library." *Library Journal* 61 (Jan. 1936): 3.

Meyer, Herman H. B. "Librarianship—A Definition." *Library Journal* 50 (15 Feb. 1925): 177.

Miller, Robert A. "Search for Fundamentals." *Library Journal* 61 (15 Apr. 1936): 298.

Munn, Ralph. "Fact versus Folklore." *American Library Association Bulletin* 34 (June 1940): 381–82.

"Necrology." *Cornell Alumni News* (Feb. 1958), p. 377.

"A New Professorship." *New York Times* 7 Apr. 1938, p. 22, col. 3.

Noé, Adolf C. "Our University Libraries." *School and Society* 10 (19 July 1919): 70–72.

Osler, William. "The Library School in the College." *Library Association Record* 19 (Aug.–Sept. 1917): 287–308.

Pargellis, Stanley. "Pierce Butler—A Biographical Sketch." *Library Quarterly* 22 (July 1952): 170–73.

"The Pierce Butler Library." *Seabury-Western Bulletin* (Epiphany 1954), pp. 3–4.

"Ponderous Attention to Insignificant Detail." *Library Journal* 56 (15 Sept. 1931): 756.

Pratt, Allan D. "The Information of the Image: A Model of the Communications Process." *Libri* 27 (Sept. 1977): 217.

"Prof. Works New Dean of U. of C. Library School." *Chicago Daily News* 5 July 1927, p. 6.

"Proposed Expansion of the Bulletin." *American Library Association Bulletin* 20 (4–9 Oct. 1926): 340.

Reece, Ernest J. Review of *Introduction to Library Science*, by Pierce Butler. *Library Journal* 58 (15 Sept. 1933): 748.

Richardson, John V., Jr. "Douglas Waples, 1893–1978." *Journal of Library History* 15 (Winter 1980): 76–83.

————. "George Alan Works: A Biographical Sketch." Unpublished.

————. "Louis Round Wilson and American University Librarianship" (Los Angeles). Prepared for Council on Library Resources, 1980.

Roden, Carl B. "[Presidential Address]." *American Library Association Bulletin* 22 (Sept. 1928): 315.

Roscoe, H. E. "Original Research as a Means of Education." *Nature* 8 (23 Oct. 1873): 538.

Shera, Jesse H. "The Place of Library Service in Research: A Suggestion." *Libraries* 36 (Nov. 1931): 387–90.

Sisler, Della J., and Coulter, Edith M. "Suggested Programs for the Second, Third and Fourth Years of a Graduate Library School." *Libraries* 31 (Apr. 1926): 164–66.

Small, Albion W. "Some Research into Research." *Journal of Applied Sociology* 9 (Sept.–Dec. 1924): 3–11, 98–107.

Strohm, Adam. "Board of Education for Librarianship." *American Library Association Bulletin* 19 (Jan. 1925): 15.

Thompson, C. Seymour. "Comment on the Reply." *Library Journal* 56 (15 Sept. 1931): 746.

_____. "Do We Want a Library Science?" *Library Journal* 56 (July 1931): 581–87.

_____. "On 'Going Scientific.'" *Library Journal* 56 (Oct. 1931): 343–44.

University of Chicago. "The Graduate Library School, 1928–27." *Announcements* 28 (20 June 1928): 3.

Walker, M. E. Review of *Introduction to Library Science*, by Pierce Butler. *New York Times Book Review*, 30 July 1933, sec. 5, p. 8, col. 2.

Walter, Frank K. Review of *Introduction to Library Science*, by Pierce Butler. *Library Quarterly* 3 (Oct. 1933): 434.

Waples, Douglas. "Do We Want a Library Science? A Reply." *Library Journal* 56 (15 Sept. 1931): 743.

_____. "First Year Activities of the Graduate Library School, University of Chicago." *American Library Association Bulletin* 23 (Aug. 1929): 336–37.

_____. "The Graduate Library School at Chicago." *Library Quarterly* 1 (Jan. 1931): 26–36.

_____. "Graduate Theses Accepted by Library Schools in the United States from June, 1928 to June, 1932." *Library Quarterly* 3 (July 1933): 273.

_____. "Graduate Theses Accepted by Library Schools in the United States from July, 1933 to June, 1935." *Library Quarterly* 6 (Jan. 1936): 76–77.

Wellard, James H. "A Philosophical Approach to Library Science." *Wilson Library Bulletin* 9 (Dec. 1934): 206–7.

"Williamson Article Free on Request." *Library Journal* 56 (15 Sept. 1931): 756.

Williamson, Charles C. "The Place of Research in Library Service." *Library Quarterly* 1 (Jan. 1931): 1–17.

_____. "Some Present-Day Aspects of Library Training." *American Library Association Bulletin* 13 (July 1919): 120–26.

_____. "[Summary of Findings and Recommendations in] Training for Library Service." *Library Journal* 48 (1 Sept. 1923): 711–14.

Wilson, Louis R. "The American Library School Today." *Library Quarterly* 7 (Apr. 1937): 211–45.

_____. "The Development of a Program of Research in Library Science in the Graduate Library School." *Library Journal* 59 (1 Oct. 1934): 742–46.

_____. "Development of Research in Relation to Library Schools." *Library Journal* 58 (15 Oct. 1933): 817–21.

_____. "Dr. William M. Randall." *College and Research Libraries* 8 (Oct. 1947): 451–52.

_____. "Frederick P. Keppel: 1875–1943." *Library Quarterly* 14 (Jan. 1944): 55.

Works, George A. "The Graduate Library School." *University Record*, n.s., 14 (Jan. 1928): 51.

_____. "The Graduate Library School at the University of Chicago." *Libraries* 34 (July 1929): 311–13.

_____. "Research and the Graduate Library School." *Libraries* 33 (Feb. 1928): 100–103.

_____. Review of *Universities*, by Abraham Flexner. *Library Quarterly* 1 (Apr. 1931): 238–39.

"University of Chicago." *Libraries* 32 (July 1927): 382–83.

Young, Arthur P. "Daniel Coit Gilman in the Formative Period of American Librarianship." *Library Quarterly* 45 (Apr. 1975): 117–40.

Index

All references are to page numbers; n. stands for note. Subentries under personal names are chronological rather than alphabetical.

invites Wilson to 25th anniversary, 156
Bertram, James, 179n.6
Beust, Nora, 188n.43
"Bibliographical and Literary Study of the First Appearance of the *Arabian Nights* in Europe, A" (MacDonald), 131
Bibliography, 6, 7, 14, 35, 47, 62, 71, 72, 76, 77, 82, 85, 92, 94, 103, 105, 119, 124, 125, 145, 182n.74, 183n.79, 183n.82, 192n.32
"Bibliography of Sources and More Important Secondary Material Relating to Early American Libraries" (Butler), 156
Bibliography: Practical, Enumerative, and Historical (Van Hoesen and Walter), 77
Bishop, William Warner
  develops library school at Michigan, 14
  first choice at Columbia, 18
  advises Laing, 33
  on-site consultant, 38, 146
  mentioned for GLS directorship, 40
  Columbia's offer, 41
  advisor on Works's book, 45
  reaction to Works's appointment, 47
  role in selection of Randall, 51-52
  opinion of Doane's allegation, 52
  Vatican Library, 52
  George Works, 62
  ALA Bulletin, 80
  Randall as editor, 81
  Randall and college libraries, 98
  and Van Hoesen, 99
  and J. I. Wyer, 99
  sees Stevens about deanship, 100
  advisor to Hutchins, 100
  disappointed by GLS, 101
  Hutchins' plans for GLS, 102-3
  supports GLS accreditation, 108
  BEL inspection team member, 108
  avoid pseudo-statistical studies, 128
  frequent *LQ* contributor, 132
  research and library schools, 177n.56
  Randall's doctoral defense, 191n.10
Bixler, Harold H., 202n.89
Bogle, Sarah C. N.
  secretary of BEL, 11

and C. C. Williamson, 12
  views on library schools, 23
  University of Chicago's plans, 28
  incites BEL members, 41-42
  lacks appreciation of Chicago, 43
  overshadows Howe, 57
  disappointing quality of GLS applicants, 60
  lack of GLS recruitment publicity, 61
  critical of GLS, 63-64
  attempts to influence Hutchins, 68
  recommends Learned and Ferguson, 68
  opinion of Capen, 68
  paucity of men, 89
  North Shore Librarians meeting, 95
  GLS not functioning, 100
  understands GLS better, 102
  signs CLC memorandum, 179n.6
  lacks biography, 179n.18
  distribution of schools, 180n.21
Book arts. *See* History of books and printing
Book courses, 142, 205n.180
Book selection, 71, 94, 110, 119, 125, 183n.79, 201n.67
Bowerman, George F., 15, 153
Bowker, Richard, 82, 83
Brandt, Margrethe D., 75, 85, 86, 113
Branscomb, Lewis, 151
Brigham, Harold F., 47, 68, 108
British Summer School of Library Science, Aberystwyth, 193n.32
Brockelmann, Carl, 73
Brown, Charles H., 48, 98
Brown, Jack Ernest, 113
Brown, Karl, 87
Brown University, 61, 77
Brownlow, Louis, 123
Buffalo, University of, 67. *See also* State University of New York
Burgess, Ernest W., 123
Burgess, Robert, 127, 154
Burlington Railroad, 54
Burton, Ernest DeWitt
  benefits from Michigan memoranda, 14
  addresses CLC, 20
  and C. C. Williamson, 25
  Chicago's interest in library school, 25
  appointed acting president, 26

sends Stevens, 100
exasperated by new search, 101
and J. I. Wyer, 101
confers with Woodward, 101
and Waples' work, 102
librarian as dean, 102
to interview Wilson, 102
plans for the GLS, 103, 149
offers Wilson deanship, 103-4
salary offer to Wilson, 103
approached about first-year program, 118
threatens to give endowment back, 198n.192
H. W. Wilson Company, 82

Illinois, University of
Library, 29, 45
Library School, 12, 17, 23, 28, 40, 57, 118, 126, 142, 143, 151, 177n.56
Indianapolis Public Library, 42, 60
Information science, 35, 142, 145
Inquiry, spirit of, 63, 87, 117, 148, 177n.56
Institute for Instructors of Library Science, 45, 46, 57, 58, 60, 136, 188n.43
Institute for Librarians and Teachers of Library Science, 110, 136-37, 139, 150, 154, 157, 173
Institute on Bibliographic Organization, 142, 173
Internship, 141
Introduction to Library Science, An (Butler), 97, 121, 124, 133, 152, 153, 154-55
Investigating Library Problems (Waples) 123, 152, 202n.89
Investigation of problems, 48, 62, 66, 88, 90, 108, 110, 115, 117, 121, 122, 123, 133, 147, 152-53, 175n.12. *See also* Research
Iowa State College, 61
Iowa State Library Commission, 17
Iowa, University of, 16, 65
Irvine, J. C., 2

James, Mary E., 113
James Terry White Award, 115
James, William, 3, 72
Jessup, Walter A., 16, 17
Job analysis, 16, 119

Joeckel, Carleton B.
considered for deanship, 68
LQ editorial board, 81
Government of the American Public Library, 110, 115, 125, 149, 155
Carnegie fellow, 112, 113
appointed to GLS, 116, 129, 152
influence on students, 117
first-year program, 120
dean, 120, 140-41, 171
professorship at California, 141, 149
role in GLS degradation, 121
theory of library science, 147
Chicago Public Library, 154
John Carter Brown Library, 61
John Crerar Library, 6, 28, 58, 95, 179n.6
"John Crerar Library as a Regional Center, The" (Harding), 125
Johns Hopkins University, 1, 6, 174n.2
Librarian, 41, 52
Medical School, 12
Johnson, Alvin S., 8
Johnson Report, 8
Josephson, Askel G. S., 6
Journal of Library Science. See Library Quarterly
Journal of the National Education Association, 184n.108
Judd, Charles H., 24, 54, 67, 123, 182n.71
Judson, Harry P., 25-26

Kaiser, Walter H., 113
Keeney, Mary J., 201n.67
Keeney, Philip O., 201n.67
Kennedy School of Missions, 52
Keogh, Andrew
member of BEL, 11
Christian Science Monitor interview, 11
plans for library school, 14-15
adviser to Keppel, 15
adviser to Hutchins, 15
favors New York, 18
report on advanced school, 28
present at BEL meeting, 30
replaced on BEL, 38
Wilson as successor, 40
advisor on Works's book, 45
assessment of his role, 47

DATE DUE
